MAPS

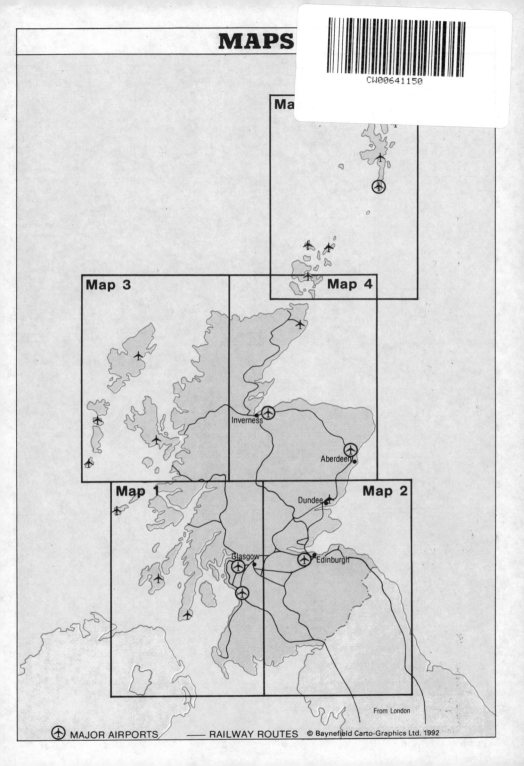

Map 3

Map 4

Map 1

Map 2

Inverness

Aberdeen

Dundee

Glasgow

Edinburgh

From London

⊕ MAJOR AIRPORTS — RAILWAY ROUTES © Bayenfield Carto-Graphics Ltd. 1992

CW00641150

MAP 1

Reproduced with kind permission of the Scottish Tourist Board.

© Baynefield Carto-Graphics Ltd. 1992

Car Ferries and Terminals

SCALE 1:1 300 000

10   0   10   20miles

COLL
Arinagour
Coll
Isle of Tiree
Scarinish
TIREE

IONA
Iona
Fionnphort
Bunessan

MULL
Tobermory
Calgary
Dervaig
Salen
Fishnish
Craignure
Tiroran
Pennyghael

Glencripesdale
Strontian
Lochaline
Benderloch
North Connel
Connel
Oban
Taynuilt
Kilmore
Lerags
Kilniver
Clachan
Seil
Cuan
South Cuan
Arduaine
Ardfern
Craobh Haven
Crinan
Ardrishaig

Onich
Kentallen
Duror
Appin
Port Appin
Ledaig
Lismore
Lochnell

Ballachulish
Glencoe

Kinlochleven

Rannoch Station
Loch Rannoch

Bridge of Orchy
Tyndrum
Crianlarich
Dalmally
Lochawe
Kilchrenan
St. Catherine's
Inveraray
Strachur
Cairndow
Ardlui
Cairnbaan
Lochgilphead
Cairnbaan

Killin
Lochearnhead
Balquhidder
Strathyre
Trossachs
Port of Menteith
Aberfoyle
Rowardennan
Kinlochard

Arrochar
Lochgoilhead
Carrick Castle
Ardentinny
Rhu
Luss
Helensburgh
Sandbank
Gourock
Greenock
Cardross
Balloch
Strathblane
Alexandria
Milngavie
Dumbarton
Bearsden
Clydebank
GLASGOW
Renfrew
Paisley
Barrhead
Johnstone
Howwood
Uplawmoor
Burnhouse
Dunlop
Stewarton
Fenwick
Newmilns

Drymen
Killearn

JURA
Craighouse

COLONSAY
Colonsay
Scalasaig

ISLAY
Port Askaig
Feolin
Ballygrant
Bridgend
Bowmore
Bruichladdich
Port Charlotte
Port Ellen

Gigha
Ardminish
Tayinloan
Tarbert
Kennacraig

BUTE
Clanoaig
Kingarth
Kilchatt
Bay
Rothesay
Colintraive
Rhubadoch
Innellan
Dunoon
Tighnabruaich
Kilfinan

CUMBRAE
Millport
Cumbrae
Largs
Skelmorlie
Wemyss Bay
Langbank
Houston
Seamill

ARRAN
Lochranza
Sannox
Corrie
Brodick
Lamlash
Whiting Bay
Lagg
Blackwaterfoot
Catacol

Carradale
Machrihanish
Campbeltown

ATLANTIC OCEAN

Firth of Clyde
Ardrossan
Irvine
Troon
Prestwick
Ayr
Alloway
Mauchline
Stair
Catrine
Cumnock
Coylton
Kilmarnock

Maidens
Kirkoswald
Girvan
Barr
Ballantrae
Barrhill
Newton Stewart
Cairnryan
Stranraer
Glenluce
Portpatrick
Sandhead
Luce Bay
Port William
Whithorn
Isle of Whithorn

NORTHERN IRELAND
LARNE

MAP 2

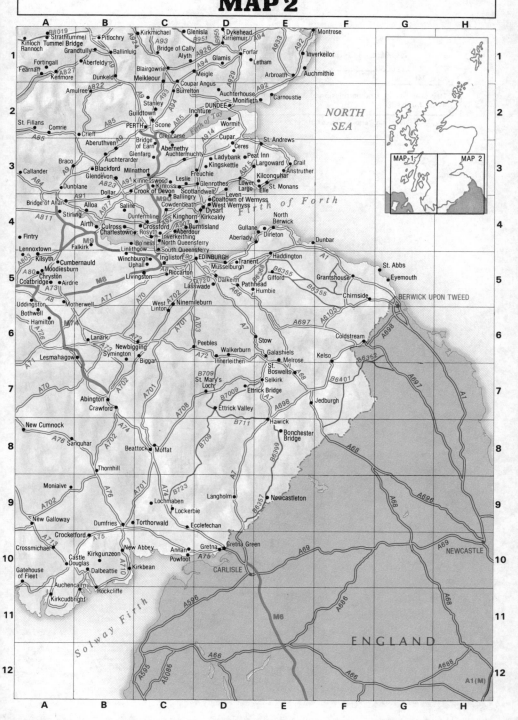

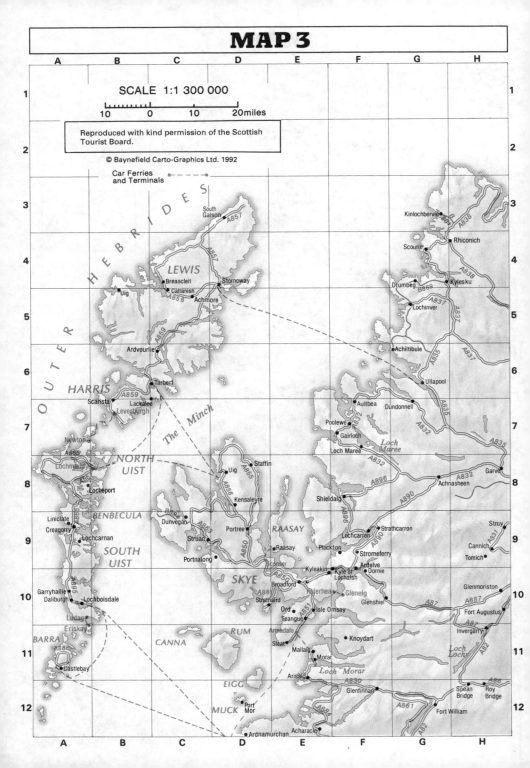

MAP 4

	A	B	C	D	E	F	G	H

ORKNEY

To Faroes (Summer Only)

Stromness
B9047
Lyness
Longhope
A967
Pentland Firth

1

To Stromness

MAP 3 MAP 4

2

Scrabster
Mey
John o' Groats
Forss
A836
Thurso
Castletown
Melvich
Keiss
Halkirk
A882
A9
A836
Bettyhill
Watten
A83
Tongue
Wick

3

Forsinard
A897
A895
Lybster
A9
Dunbeath

4

A836
Helmsdale
A9

5

Lairg
A839
Rogart
Brora
A837
Golspie
A836
Bonar
Bridge
Dornoch Firth
A9
Ardgay
Spinningdale
Dornoch
A836
A9
Tain
B9165
Portmahomack

6

Moray Firth
Lossiemouth
A941
Rosehearty
Fraserburgh
Alness
Invergordon
Burghead
Garmouth
Buckie
Cullen
Banff
Macduff
St. Combs
A98
A952
Evanton
Cromarty
Forres
A96
Elgin
Fochabers
Portsoy
A98
A981
A92
Strathpeffer
Rosemarkie
A832
Nairn
A940
A941
Keith
A95
A97
Mintlaw
Contin
Fortrose
Auldearn
Dallas
Rothes
A96
B9170
Peterhead
Boddam
A950
Beauly
Muir of Ord
North Kessock
A96
Craigellachie
A98
A948
A862
Kirkhill
INVERNESS
Cro
A939
Aberlour
Huntly
A941
B9170
Cruden
Bay
Ballindalloch
Carron
Dufftown
A95
B9005
Farr
Moy
A9
Glenlivet
A941
Old
Rayne
A96
Udny
Newburgh
Drumnadrochit
Grantown
on Spey
Rhynie
Insch
A941
B9170
B999
Tomatin
A938
Inverurie
Foyers
Carrbridge
A95
Dulnain Bridge
Kildrummy
Alford
A944
To Lerwick
A82
Nethy Bridge
Tomintoul
A9
Invermoriston
Boat of Garten
A939
Strathdon
Lumphanan
A980
ABERDEEN
Whitebridge
Kincraig
A944
B9119
Kincardine
O'Neil
Aviemore
Dinnet
Aboyne
Blairs
A92
Kingussie
B970
Crathie
A93
Banchory
A93
Newtonmore
Braemar
Ballater
A957
Laggan
A9
Stonehaven
A86
A93
Dalwhinnie
Glen Clova
Laurencekirk
Glenshee
B966
Edzell
A92
Blair Atholl
A924
B957
B955
Brechin
A94
Killiecrankie

7 **8** **9** **10** **11** **12**

MAP 5

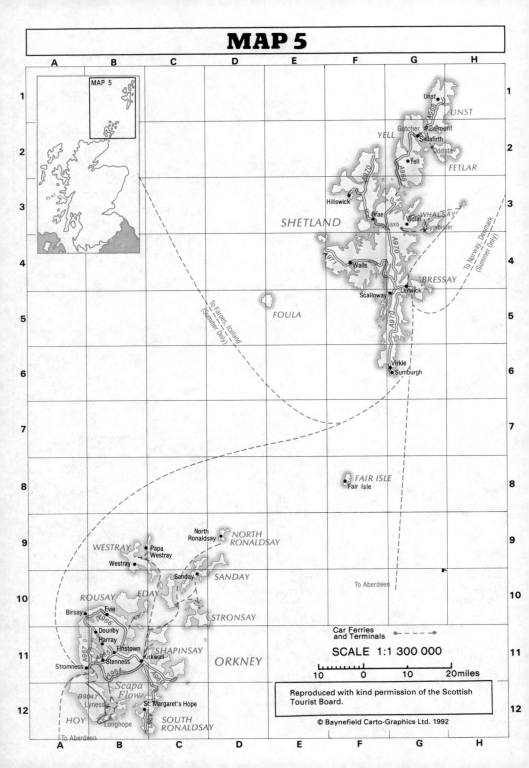

MAP 5

UNST
Unst
A968
Gutcher • Belmont
Sellafirth
Oddsta
YELL
Yell •
FETLAR

Hillswick •
SHETLAND
Brae
Voe
Vidlin • WHALSAY
Symbister
A970
To Norway, Denmark
(Summer Only)

Walls •
A971
BRESSAY
Scalloway •
Lerwick
A970

To Faroes, Iceland
(Summer Only)
FOULA

Virkie •
Sumburgh

FAIR ISLE
Fair Isle

North
Ronaldsay • NORTH
RONALDSAY
WESTRAY
Papa
Westray
Westray • SANDAY
Sanday •
ROUSAY EDAY
Birsay • Evie STRONSAY
A966
Dounby SHAPINSAY
Harray
Finstown
Stenness Kirkwall
Stromness A965 ORKNEY
A964 A960
B9047 Scapa
Flow To Aberdeen
Lyness St. Margaret's Hope
HOY SOUTH
Longhope RONALDSAY
To Aberdeen

Car Ferries
and Terminals

SCALE 1:1 300 000

10   0   10   20miles

Reproduced with kind permission of the Scottish
Tourist Board.

© Baynefield Carto-Graphics Ltd. 1992

NAIRN

THE PLACE TO BE FOR FAMILY FUN

THE PLACE FOR A PERFECT HOLIDAY

The historic Seaside Resort in the Highlands where there's always something to interest you and your family; a busy harbour, and safe sandy beaches; Historic Fishertown; Museums; An attractive shopping centre; and superb golf courses. Nairn Leisure Park – one of the North's foremost leisure facilities, with indoor swimming pool and steamroom; Summer activities centre for children; and a host of other sports and leisure facilities.

For further information or for a free copy of the Nairn Leisure Guide.
Tel: Hugh Allison 0667 56144
We've planned lots of events too!
HIGHLAND GAMES, THEME WEEKS AND FESTIVALS,
MAJOR EVENTS OF NATIONAL IMPORTANCE,
DAILY ENTERTAINMENTS FOR ALL THE FAMILY

NAIRN – AWARD WINNING BEACHES AND AWARD WINNING AMENITIES

Nairn – one of the late Charlie Chaplin's favourite holiday haunts – has gone through a remarkable process of redevelopment in the past 10 years that would have met with the approval of the lovable little man.

The improvements, which will be capped by the completion of the massive facelift under way in the harbour area, will, in the opinion of tourist entertainments officer, Mr. Hugh Allison, see the town forge ahead of many competitors as it moves into a higher grade of holiday resort.

Nairn has been a popular holiday destination since 1885 and prides itself on the fact that it can offer the inherited experience of a Victorian resort combined with an understanding of what visitors require in the 1990's.

Set on the pleasant coastal plain of the Moray Firth, it is easily accessible by road, rail and air through some of Scotland's most picturesque and historic country.

It enjoys more hours of sunshine and more dry days than many other parts of Scotland.

Thanks to the fine weather, miles of gently-shelving sandy beaches provide safe sea-bathing, which received a major boost recently when the resort gained a prestigious Golden Sand Castle Award from the consumer magazine "Which?"

Nairn came top of the poll in Scotland in the best popular-beach category. It was described as being a very good family resort – high praise from such a prestigious source.

The town has plenty to offer in the way of entertainment and leisure facilities, with two well-established golf courses, an attractive harbour, used mostly by pleasure craft, plenty of shopping variety, children's entertainment, riverside walks and a leisure park, which has also been upgraded and extended recently.

Nairn Entertainments and Tourism Committee, a voluntary body, take a leading role in promoting week-long festivals throughout the summer.

They organise such events as the Gala Week, Victorian Week, Children's Week and Competitions Week throughout the season.

CONTENTS

Cover design by Jennifer Thomson

Pastime Publications Ltd gratefully acknowledge the assistance of The Scottish Tourist Board, Area Tourist Boards, Historic Buildings and Monuments, and others in compiling this guide.

First published by The Scottish Tourist Board 1970

U.K. distribution by A.A. Developments Ltd.

Typesetting by Imagesenter & Typewise.
Printed and Bound in the U.K.

Worldwide distribution by The British Tourist Authority

ADVERTISERS' INDEX

ALSO SEE COLOUR ADVERTS
AND TASTE OF SCOTLAND SECTION

CARLISLE

INTRODUCTION
By JACKIE STEWART O.B.E.

The charm of Scotland's roads for me, despite my background as a racing driver, has always been the variety of minor roads and byways. It always seems a shame to drive from A to B by the fast route when I know there is so much to enjoy on the lesser roads to either side.

On most of Scotland's roads, speed is a positive disadvantage as it distracts you from the splendour of the scenery. Even with years of experience of driving around Scotland, I always find something new and glorious about the countryside - and I don't just mean new parks and buildings.

The light and the seasons change the look of the land almost beyond belief, so that what might appear a bleak windswept moor one day will be a magnificent swathe of muted greens and browns the next.

Even in the central belt of Scotland, where so many people live and work, there are many excellent alternatives to the motorways, and often just a short distance will take you away from all signs of civilisation.

The real wonder of all this beauty, however, is the accessibility of remote places by roads that are kept in good repair and are often devoid of other traffic. Compared to many other countries, Scotland's roads are paid a great deal of attention by local authorities, even in the remote areas.

When I passed my driving test, at the age of 17, I drove my heart out all over Scotland. It was wonderful, a voyage of discovery that instilled in me a pride in my own country that I hold to this day.

I hope you, too, will discover the magic of Scotland by car.

SCOTLAND FOR THE MOTORIST
A Pastime Publication

I/We have seen your advertisement and wish to know if you have the following vacancy:

Name...

Address ....

....

Dates from pm..

Please give date and day of week in each case ....

To am ....

Number in Party ....

Details of Children ....

(Please remember to include a stamped addressed envelope with your enquiry.)

SCOTLAND FOR THE MOTORIST
A Pastime Publication

I/We have seen your advertisement and wish to know if you have the following vacancy:

Name...

Address ....

....

Dates from pm..

Please give date and day of week in each case ....

To am ....

Number in Party ....

Details of Children ....

(Please remember to include a stamped addressed envelope with your enquiry.)

CAITHNESS

DUMFRIESSHIRE

DUNBARTONSHIRE

THE SCOTTISH DEER CENTRE

The Scottish Deer Centre is "The Total Deer Experience".

Learning and entertainment combine in an ideal, all-weather setting.

Here, pride of place goes to the majestic red deer. Let our expert rangers take you to meet them, and other species, on a 'nose-to-nose' guided tour.

There is so much else besides. Exhibition, film theatre and Antler-Room tell the story of deer and their special place in Scotland.

Stroll around the nature-trail (suitable for the disabled)...photograph from viewing platforms...enjoy the spectacular aerial-walkway. Picnic areas are plentiful.

Our famous Adventureland and indoor Playbarn will entrance the young (and not so young!)

The shop is imaginatively stocked with Scottish crafts, whilst 'Staggies' licensed restaurant offers quality Scottish fare and home-baking. A unique Scottish Winery is a special feature.

A brief visit...a whole day out...The Scottish Deer Centre provides a memorable visit for all the family.

Find us on the A91, three miles west of Cupar between the M90 Motorway and St. Andrews. From the Forth Bridge the upgraded A92 allows easy access but do NOT follow it all the way to Cupar.

Coaches welcome: ample parking, discount prices for advance booking and facilities for drivers.

OPENING TIMES March to October: 7 days a week. 10.00am 5.00pm and later during the summer months.

The Centre offers:

- STAGGIES RESTAURANT excellent but inexpensive local fare in elegant Georgian Courtyard surroundings.
- THE GIFT SHOP a wide range of quality giftware, crafts and books.
- FILM THEATRE short, specially produced films in a relaxed and comfortable atmosphere.
- IMAGINATIVE INTERPRETATION the history of deer and their Scottish environment.
- CENTRE FOR SCOTTISH WINES oak-leaf, tayberry and more.
- INDOOR PLAYBARN AND PICNIC AREA aerial slides and scramble nets.
- SHOW PADDOCKS 30 minute Ranger-led tours take you to meet our tame but majestic stags.
- ADVENTURELAND one of the biggest and best in Scotland.

**The Scottish Deer Centre,
Bow-of-Fife, by Cupar KY15 4NQ.
Tel: Letham (033 781) 391.**

22

LOTHIAN

COLL EARN HOTEL
Auchterarder PH3 1DF

Situated in the heart of the beautiful Perthshire countryside, this delightful hotel is a marvellous tribute to the extravagance and eccentricities of Victorian architecture, with beautiful wood panelling and fascinating stained glass. Bedrooms are spacious and luxurious and all have private facilities. In the intimate diningroom the constantly changing menu offers the finest traditional Scottish and European cuisine, all beautifully prepared. Set in its own grounds, yet easily accessible from the M90 Edinburgh/Perth motorway, this is an ideal place to find true peace and quiet.

£47–£63 per day for dinner, bed and breakfast, based on stays of 3 days or more. Open all year.

Tel: 0764 63553 Fax: 0764 63059

ROYAL HOTEL
Allan Street, Blairgowrie, Perthshire

54 bedrooms, 25 with private facilities and TV. A Georgian-fronted hotel privately owned and situated in the town centre. Licensed. Large comfortable cocktail lounge (serving bar lunches), snooker table, television lounge. Games: table-tennis available. All rooms have tea/coffee making facilities and central heating. Car and coach park. Children welcome.

Telephone: Blairgowrie (STD 0250) 872226

Bridgend House Hotel
Bridgend, Callander FK17 8AH
Tel: Callander (0877) 30130

Family run 17th century house hotel which prides itself in providing personal, friendly service in a warm and relaxed atmosphere. En suite rooms with tea makers and televisions. Two bars and restaurant, offering bar lunches, bar suppers and a la carte dinners, special childrens menu. S.T.B. 3 Crowns Commended, Taste of Scotland Specialities, AA 2 Star.

Your Hosts: **Sandy and Maria Park. Tel: 0877 30130 or FAX: 0877 31512**

WOLSELEY PARK HOTEL
Stirling Road, CALLANDER, Perthshire
Telephone (0877) 30261.

Callander is the ideal base for the "Day Touring" holiday as it is centrally situated, in an area steeped in history and surrounded by countless places of current and historical interest, as well as many famous beauty spots. The Hotel is fully licensed and has rooms with or without private facilities, all to STB 3 Crown standard. Ample private parking. B&B from £20.50 per person Dinner "a la carte"

ROXBURGHSHIRE

STIRLINGSHIRE SUTHERLAND

SCOTLAND FOR THE MOTORIST
A Pastime Publication

I/We have seen your advertisement and wish to know if you have the following vacancy:

Name..

Address ....

....

Dates from pm..

Please give date and day of week in each case ....

To am ....

Number in Party ....

Details of Children ....

(Please remember to include a stamped addressed envelope with your enquiry.)

SCOTLAND FOR THE MOTORIST
A Pastime Publication

I/We have seen your advertisement and wish to know if you have the following vacancy:

Name..

Address ....

....

Dates from pm..

Please give date and day of week in each case ....

To am ....

Number in Party ....

Details of Children ....

(Please remember to include a stamped addressed envelope with your enquiry.)

HOLIDAY NOTES

SCOTLAND FOR THE MOTORIST
A Pastime Publication

I/We have seen your advertisement and wish to know if you have the following vacancy:

Name..

Address ....

....

Dates from pm...

Please give date and day of week in each case ....

To am ....

Number in Party ....

Details of Children ....

(Please remember to include a stamped addressed envelope with your enquiry.)

SCOTLAND FOR THE MOTORIST
A Pastime Publication

I/We have seen your advertisement and wish to know if you have the following vacancy:

Name..

Address ....

....

Dates from pm...

Please give date and day of week in each case ....

To am ....

Number in Party ....

Details of Children ....

(Please remember to include a stamped addressed envelope with your enquiry.)

MOTORING NOTES

APPLICATION FORMS TO ASSIST IN ENQUIRIES FOR VACANCIES
Please give as much information as you can

SCOTLAND FOR THE MOTORIST
A Pastime Publication

I/We have seen your advertisement and wish to know if you have the following vacancy:

Name...

Address ....

....

Dates from pm...

Please give date and day of week in each case ....

To am ....

Number in Party ....

Details of Children ....

(Please remember to include a stamped addressed envelope with your enquiry.)

SCOTLAND FOR THE MOTORIST
A Pastime Publication

I/We have seen your advertisement and wish to know if you have the following vacancy:

Name...

Address ....

....

Dates from pm...

Please give date and day of week in each case ....

To am ....

Number in Party ....

Details of Children ....

(Please remember to include a stamped addressed envelope with your enquiry.)

MOTORING NOTES

EDITORIAL CONTENT

This information is divided into the following geographical sections:-

Borders
Edinburgh
Lothian
Fife
Perth
Angus
Aberdeen
North East
The Northern Highlands
Western & Central Highlands
Central & South West Scotland
Glasgow
Scotland's Islands

Within these sections the places of interest are listed alphabetically.

READERS ARE ADVISED TO CHECK ADMISSION TIMES AND OTHER DATA.

PLACES OF INTEREST

BORDERS

Abbey St. Bathans
Turn off A1 at Grantshouse (A6112 to Duns), take 1st or 2nd unclassified road to right. Signposted Abbey St. Bathans thereafter. Easter-Sept 11.00–17.00 or by arrangement. Parking available. Tel: (036 14) 249 or 242.
Gallery with display of selected work by Scottish craftsmen and artists. Colourful range of domestic pottery by Abbey Ceramics. Tearoom for light lunches and afternoon tea. Walks along riverside through natural oak woodlands and up to open moorland. Pictish Broch. Site of Cistercian Priory.

Abbotsford House
A7, 2¹/₂m SSE of Galashiels. Late Mar-end Oct. Mon-Sat 10.00–17.00, Sun 14.00–17.00. (Mrs. P Maxwell-Scott, OBE). Tel: Galashiels (0896) 2043.
Sir Walter Scott's romantic mansion built 1817–1822. Much as in his day, it contains the many remarkable historical relics he collected, armouries, the library with some 9,000 volumes and his study. He died here in 1832. Free car park, with private entrance for disabled drivers. Teashop and gift shop.

Ayton Castle
At Ayton, by Eyemouth, on A1, 8m N of Berwick. Sun 14.00–17.00, or by appointment. Parking available. Tel: Ayton (08907) 81212.
Scottish Baronial style castle built in 1846 in red sandstone. Now fully lived in as a family home.

Bedrule Church
Bedrule, nr. Denholm, off A698, Bedrule/Chesters Road. Tel: Hawick (0450) 506.
Bedrule Church, with its remarkable stained glass and armorial bearings and picturesque location high above the river, is the focus of the area from which 'fighting Turnbulls' came, numbers amongst them William Turnbull, born 1400, Bishop of Glasgow and founder of Glasgow University (1451). Although nothing remains of Bedrule Castle, the mound of Fulton Tower still dominates this reach of the Rule.

Biggar Gasworks Museum
Gasworks Road, near the War Memorial, Biggar. 28 May-30 Sept. Mon-Thurs 14.00–17.00. Closed
Fridays. Working exhibits and live steam on special occasions. For details phone. (National Museums of Scotland). Free. Tel: 031–225 7534.
Biggar Gasworks was built in 1839 and closed in 1973 on the arrival of natural gas. It is now the only surviving coal gasworks in Scotland. The buildings, plant and associated displays give a concise picture of the coal-gas industry. Working machinery and gas lights, guided tours, display of gas appliances, video show. Limited car parking.

Biggar Puppet Theatre
On the B7016 E of Biggar. All year, Mon-Sat 11.00–17.00; closed Wed; Sun 14.00–17.00. Parking available. Tel: (0899) 20631.
Complete Victorian theatre in miniature seating 100. Attractive grounds with tearoom, shop, games, picnic area and car park. Licensed. Disabled visitors welcome but prior notice required. Induction loop.

Bowhill
Off A708, 3m W of Selkirk. Grounds and playground open 28 Apr-28 Aug (not Fri). House open 1–31 Jul. Daily (incl Fri) 12.00–17.00, Sun 14.00–18.00. (House 13.00–16.30). Dates subject to slight alteration each year. Please telephone for precise information. Tel: Selkirk (0750) 20732.
For many generations Bowhill has been the Border home of the Scotts of Buccleuch. Inside the house, begun in 1812, there is an outstanding collection of pictures, including works of Van Dyck, Reynolds, Gainsborough, Canaletto, Guardi, Claude Lorraine, Raeburn, etc. Also porcelain and furniture, much of which was made in the famous workshop of Andre Boulle in Paris. In the grounds are an adventure woodland play area, a riding centre, garden, nature trails, tearoom and gift shop.

Broughton Gallery
On the A701 just N of Broughton Village. End Mar-end Sept, daily 10.30–18.00 (incl Sun); closed Wed. Free. Parking available. Tel: Broughton (08994) 234.
An imposing building designed by Basil Spence in 1938 in the style of a 16th-century Scottish fortified tower house. Contains continuous exhibitions of paintings and crafts by living British artists for sale. The walled garden contains dovecote and knot garden with fine views of the Tweeddale Hills.

Nearby in Broughton Village at the corner of Biggar road is a garden which contains no less than 14,000 bedding plants.

John Buchan Centre
S end of Broughton, 5m E of Biggar. Easter-mid Oct, daily 14.00–17.00. Parking available. (Biggar Museum Trust). Tel: Biggar (0899) 21050.
The Centre tells the story of John Buchan, 1st Lord Tweedsmuir, author of "The 39 Steps" and also lawyer, politician, soldier, historian and Governor-General of Canada. Broughton village was his mother's birthplace, and a much-loved holiday home.

Castle Jail
Castlegate, Jedburgh. Weekdays 10.00–17.00, Sun 13.00–17.00. Parking available. (Roxburgh District Council). Tel: Jedburgh (0835) 63254/(0450) 73457.
On the site of Jedburgh Castle, a 'modern' reform jail was built in 1825. Rooms have been interestingly reconstructed to re-create the 'reformed' system of the early 19th century. The jail is set in a grassy area, suitable for picnics and also forms part of the Jedburgh Town Trail.

Clapperton Daylight Photographic Studio
Scott's Place, E of Selkirk town centre on right near Police Station. Apr-Oct, Sat and Sun 14.00–16.30; other times by arrangement. Tel: (0750) 20523.
One of the oldest original daylight photographic studios in existence, still in family hands. With changing displays of photographs dating back to the 1860s.

Jim Clark Memorial Trophy Room
44 Newtown Street, Duns. Easter-end Oct, Mon-Sat 10.00–13.00, 14.00–17.00, Sun 14.00–17.00. Parking available. (Berwickshire District Council). Tel: Duns (0361) 82600, ext 36/37.
A memorial to the late Jim Clark, twice world motor racing champion, with a large number of his trophies.

Coldstream Museum
Market Square. Easter-Oct, Mon-Fri 10.00–13.00, 14.00–17.00; Sat 10.00–13.00, 14.00–17.30; Sun 14.00–17.30. Parking available. Tel: Coldstream (0890) 2486/2630.
Small museum rebuilt in 1863 in the original headquarters of the Coldstream Guards (founded 1659).

The Cornice Museum of Ornamental Plasterwork
Down close next to electricity showroom on Peebles High Street. Apr ,June and Sept, Sat 10.30–12.30, Fri-Mon 14.00–16.00; May, Sat-Mon 14.00–16.00; Jul and Aug, Mon-Fri 14.00–17.00, Sat 10.30–12.30; Oct, Sat and Sun 14.00–16.00; other times by arrangement. Tel: (0721) 20212.
Re-creation of a plasterer's casting shop illustrating methods of creating ornamental plasterwork. Car park nearby.

Craigcleuch Collection
2m NW of Langholm on B709. Easter, 1 May-30 Sept, daily 10.00–17.00, or by arrangement. Woodlands Walks. Parking available. (Mr. David Young). Tel: Langholm (03873) 80137.
Baronial Scottish stone mansion exhibiting the Craigcleuch collection, hundreds of superb selected curiosities. Fine rare tribal ethnographic carvings, sculptures, masks, painting on silk. Prehistoric American Indian carved stone animals and birds. Exquisite red coral carving. Chinese Jade animals, Japanese Ivories. Unspoiled panoramic views overlooking "Gates of Eden", woodlands.

Dawyck Botanic Gardens
B712, 8m SW of Peebles. 15 Mar-22 Oct inc., daily 10.00–18.00. No animals (except guide dogs). (Royal Botanic Garden, Edinburgh). Tel: Peebles (07216) 254.
All year round colour from spring bulbs to autumn tints. Rare trees, including many very fine conifers, shrubs, rhododendrons and narcissi, among woodland walks. In the woods is Dawyck Chapel, designed by William Burn.

Devil's Beef Tub
A701, 6m N of Moffat. Free. Parking available. Tel: Moffat (0683) 20620.
A huge, spectacular hollow among the hills, at the head of Annandale. In the swirling mists of this out-of-the-way retreat Border reivers hid cattle 'lifted' in their raids. Can be seen from the road.

Dryburgh Abbey
Off A68, 6m SE of Melrose. Opening standard. (HS). Tel:031–244 3101.
Peacefully situated on the banks of the Tweed, Dryburgh Abbey is one of the four famous Border abbeys founded in the reign of David I by Hugh de Morville, Constable of Scotland. Though little save the transepts has been spared of the church itself, the cloister buildings have survived in a more complete state than in any other Scottish monastery, except Iona and Inchcolm. Much of the

existing remains are 12/13th century. Sir Walter Scott is buried in the church.

The Edinburgh Woollen Mill
Jedburgh. Open daily 10.00–18.00.
Plenty of free parking. Seating capacity for over 100 within the Spinning Wheel coffee shop. Disabled facilities. On the outskirts of one of the most beautiful towns in the Scottish Borders. Buy the best from the Borders in the Woollen Mill Shop. You will find the full range of Edinburgh Woollen Mill goods including the famous Clan Royal Collection. Browse in the gift gallery, which has a wide range of gift ideas for all the family.

Eyemouth Museum
Market Place, Eyemouth. Easter-Oct, Mon-Fri 10.00 to various closing times. Sun 14.00. (Eyemouth Museum Trust). Tel: Eyemouth (08907) 50678.
Opened in 1981 to commemorate the Great East Coast Fishing Disaster in which 189 fishermen were lost, 129 of them from Eyemouth. Displays include Eyemouth tapestry, and the wheelhouse of a modern fishing boat. Museum reflects the fishing and farming history of East Berwickshire.

Ferniehirst Castle
1½m S of Jedburgh. Open May-Oct, Wed 13.30–16.30. Parking available. Tel: (0835) 62201.
Scotland's frontier fortress. 16th century Border Castle, ancestral home of the Kerr family, recently restored by the Marquis of Lothian, Chief of the Kerrs. A 17th century stable has been adapted to incorporate an information centre giving details on Border families and Border history.

Flodden Monument
Town Centre, Selkirk. All times. Free. Tel: (0750) 20096.
The monument was erected in 1913 on the 400th anniversary of the battle and is inscribed 'O Flodden Field'. The memorial is the work of sculptor Thomas Clapperton.

Floors Castle
B6089, 2m NW of Kelso. (Castle and grounds) Open Easter Sun and Mon, from early May-late Sep, 10.30–17.50. (Garden centre) all year, daily 09.30–17.00. (Duke of Roxburghe). Tel: Kelso (0573) 23333.
A large and impressive mansion, built by William Adam in 1721, with additions in the 1840s by William Playfair. A holly tree in the grounds is said to mark the spot where James II was killed by the bursting of a cannon in 1460. Location of the film 'Greystoke'.

Gladstone Court Street Museum
A702 North Back Road, Biggar, 26m from Edinburgh, 12m from A74 (South). Easter-Oct, daily 10.00–12.30, 14.00–17.00; Sun 14.00–17.00; other times by arrangement. Parking available. (Biggar Museum Trust). Tel: Biggar (0899) 21050.
An indoor street museum of shops and windows. Grocers, photographers, dressmakers, bank, school, library, ironmonger, chemist, china merchant, telephone exchange, etc.

Grey Mare's Tail
Off A708, 10m NE of Moffat. (NTS). Tel: 041-552 8391.
A spectacular 200-feet waterfall formed by the Tail Burn dropping from Loch Skene. The area is rich in wild flowers and there is a herd of wild goats.
NB. Visitors should keep to the path to the foot of the falls: there have been serious accidents to people scrambling up and care should be exercised.

Halliwell's House Museum and Gallery
Off main square, town centre, Selkirk. Apr-Oct, Mon-Sat 10.00–17.00, Sun 14.00–16.00. Jul & Aug open daily until 18.00. Nov-Dec, daily 14.00–16.00. (Ettrick and Lauderdale District Council). Tel: Selkirk (0750) 20096/20054.
This row of 18th-century dwelling houses has recently been extensively renovated and now houses an attractive and lively museum dealing with Selkirk's long and rich history. The building's history and its long link with the ironmongery trade are thoughtfully re-created. The Robson Gallery has constantly changing exhibitions. Listening post in ironmongers shop, and video in upstairs gallery.

Hawick Museum
In Wilton Lodge Park, on western outskirts of Hawick. Apr-Sep, Mon-Sat 10.00–12.00 and 13.00–17.00, Sun 14.00–17.00; Oct-Mar, Mon-Fri 13.00–16.00, closed Sat, Sun 14.00–16.00. (Roxburgh District Council). Tel: Hawick (0450) 73457.
In the ancestral home of the Langlands of that Ilk, an unrivalled collection of local and Scottish Border relics, natural history, art gallery, etc. Situated in 107-acre Wilton Lodge Park, open at all times: riverside walks, gardens, greenhouses, recreations and playing fields. Small cafe.

Hermitage Castle
In Liddesdale, 5½m NE of Newcastleton. Opening standard; weekends only in winter. (HS). Tel: 031-244 3101.
This strikingly dramatic 13th-century castle was a stronghold of the de Soulis family and, after 1341, of the Douglases. It has had a vivid, sometimes

cruel history; to here Mary, Queen of Scots made her exhausting ride from Jedburgh in 1566 to meet Bothwell, a journey which almost cost her her life. The building consists of four towers and connecting walls, outwardly almost perfect.

The Hirsel, Homestead Museum, Craft Centre and Grounds
On A697, immediately W of Coldstream. All reasonable daylight hours every day of the year. (Lord Home of the Hirsel, KT). Tel: Coldstream (0890) 2834.
Museum housed in old farmstead buildings (with integrated Craft Centre) with history of estate, old tools, natural history. Walks in Leet Valley, round the grounds of Hirsel House (not open to the public). Famous rhododendron wood. Tearoom open Sun and bank holiday afternoons, and for groups by arrangement.

James Hogg Monument
By Ettrick 1m W of B7009. All times. Free. Parking available.
A monument on the site of the birthplace of James Hogg (1770–1835), known as 'The Ettrick Shepherd', friend of Scott. His grave is in the nearby church.

Jedburgh Abbey and Visitor Centre
High Street, Jedburgh. Opening standard, except Oct-Mar closed Thurs afternoon and Fri. (HS). Tel: 031–244 3101.
This Augustinian abbey is perhaps the most impressive of the four great border abbeys, founded by David I in 1138. The noble remains are extensive, the west front has a fine rose window, known as St. Catherine's Wheel, and there is a richly carved Norman doorway. Remains of other domestic buildings have been recovered recently.

Kailzie Gardens
2m E of Peebles on B7062. Daily 11.00–17.30. Parking available. (Mrs. M.A. Richard). Tel: Peebles (0721) 20007.
17 acres of garden surrounded by mature timber. Walled garden dated 1812 with greenhouses, laburnum alley, shrub borders and collection of shrub roses. Woodland and burnside walks. Also collection of waterfowl. Gift shop, art gallery and licensed tearoom.

Kelso Abbey
Bridge Street, Kelso. Opening standard. Free. (HS). Tel: 031–244 3101.
This 12th-century Tironensian abbey, was one of the earliest completed by David I and was built on

a plan unique to Scotland. It was one of the largest of the Border abbeys. When the Earl of Hertford entered Kelso in 1545 the abbey was garrisoned as a fortress and was taken only at the point of the sword; the garrison of 100 men, including 12 monks, was slaughtered, and the building was almost entirely razed. The tower is part of the original building.

Kelso Museum
Turret House, Abbey Court, off Bridge Street. Apr-Oct. Parking available. (Roxburgh District Council). Tel: Kelso (0573) 23464/(0450) 73457.
Located in one of Kelso's oldest and most attractive buildings, owned by the National Trust for Scotland, the Museum interprets Kelso's history as a market town, concentrating on the skinning and tanning industry. Nearby car parking. Access to ground floor only for wheelchair visitors.

Leyden Obelisk and Tablet
Denholm on A698 NE of Hawick. All times. Free. Tel: Denholm (045 087) 506.
The village was the birthplace of John Leyden (1776–1811), poet, orientalist and friend of Sir Walter Scott. An obelisk was set up in 1861 and a tablet on a thatched cottage records his birth there. Another famous son of Denholm was Sir James Murray, editor of the Oxford English Dictionary whose birth is commemorated on a tablet on a house in Main Street.

Hugh MacDiarmid Memorial Sculpture
At Whita Hill Yett, approx. 2m NE of Langholm on the Langholm to Newcastleton road. At any time. Tel: (0835) 22650.
Steel and bronze sculpture by Jake Harvey to commemorate the literary achievements of the Langholm-born poet and Scots Revivalist. Nearby is Malcolm Monument.

Manderston
Off A6105, 2m E of Duns. Mid May-Sep, Thu & Sun 14.00–17.30. Groups by arrangement. (Mr A Palmer). Tel: Duns (0361) 83450.
This Edwardian country house is one of the last great classical houses to be built in Scotland. The house contains a silver staircase, thought to be unique. It also gives an insight into life 'below stairs'. It has extensive estate buildings and gardens particularly noted for their rhododendrons. Tearoom, shop, gardens, stables and marble dairy.

Mary, Queen of Scots House
Queen Street, Jedburgh. Easter-mid Nov, daily 10.00–17.00. (Roxburgh District Council). Tel:

Jedburgh (0835) 63331/(0450) 73457.
A 16th century bastel house in which Mary, Queen of Scots is reputed to have stayed in 1566 when attending the Court of Justice. Now a museum containing several relics associated with the Queen. Delightful gardens surround the house which also forms part of the Jedburgh Town Trail.

Mellerstain House
Off A6089, 7m NW of Kelso. Easter; 1 May-30 Sept, Sun-Fri 12.30–16.30. Admission charge. Tel: Gordon (057 381) 225.
This is one of the most attractive mansions open to the public in Scotland, with exceptionally beautiful interior decoration and plaster work. Begun about 1725 by William Adam, it was completed between 1770 and 1778 by William's son Robert. There are attractive terraced gardens and pleasant grounds with fine views. Self-service tearoom, gift shop, lake, thatched cottage and garden.

Melrose Abbey
Main Square, Melrose. Opening standard. (HS). Tel: 031-244 3101.
This Cistercian Abbey is the finest and largest of the Border abbeys, founded in 1136 by David I. It is notable for its fine traceried stonework. It suffered the usual attacks of all the Border abbeys during English invasions, but parts of the nave and choir dating from a rebuilding of 1385 include some of the best and most elaborate work of the period in Scotland. In addition to the flamboyant stonework, note on the roof the figure of a pig playing bagpipes. There is an interesting museum in the Commendator's House, at the entrance.

Melrose Motor Museum
200 yards from Melrose Abbey, towards Newstead. Mid May-mid Oct, daily 10.30–17.30 or by arrangement. Part-time from Easter to mid May. Parking available. Tel: Melrose (089 682) 2624/(0835) 22356.
Private collection with vehicles on loan, mainly vintage from 1909 to the late 1960s. Excellent motorcycles and bicycles with a quantity of old signs and items of memorabilia. Display cases of toy cars, cigarette cards, etc. Shop.

Melrose Station
Situated just off the market square in the centre of Melrose. All year (except 25/26 Dec and 1/2 Jan). Daily 1 Apr-31 Oct 10.00–18.00; 1 Nov-31 Mar 10.00–17.00. Restaurant also open Thurs, Fri and Sat evenings. Voluntary donation. Parking available. Tel: (089 682) 2546.
Described upon its opening in 1849 as "The handsomest provincial Station in Scotland".

Melrose Station is a major relic of the bygone railway age, and the only town station to remain from the Edinburgh to Carlisle "Waverley Route", which was closed in 1969. Waverley Route Heritage Centre, licensed restaurant, craft shop, craft workshops, Roman Heritage Exhibition.

Mertoun Gardens
St. Boswells. Apr-Sept, Sat, Sun & Mon Public Holidays 14.00–18.00 (last entry 17.30). Parking available. Tel: St. Boswells (0835) 23236.
20 acres of beatiful grounds with delightful walks and river views. Fine trees, herbaceous borders and flowering shrubs. Walled garden and well preserved circular dovecote thought to be the oldest in the county. No dogs. No guide dogs.

The Millshop
Tweedvale Mills, Walkerburn. On the A72, 8 miles south of Peebles, 3/4 hr. drive from Edinburgh. Open Mon.-Sat. 09.00–17.30; Sun. (during Summer) 11.00–17.00.
Plenty of free parking. Situated in the heart of the Borders, it offers a wide range of attractions. Home of the famous "Scottish Museum of Woollen Textiles" which attracts as many visitors as the Millshop with its fantastic bargains. Visitors can also relax in the mill's Coffee House.

Moat Park Heritage Centre
Biggar town centre. 1 Apr-31 Oct, daily 10.00–17.00, Sun 14.00–17.00. Tel: Biggar (0899) 21050 (Biggar Museum Trust).
This former church has been adapted to display the history of the Upper Clyde and Tweed Valleys, from the days of the volcano and the glacier right up to yesterday's newspapers. Fine collection of embroidery including the largest known patchwork cover, containing over eighty figures from the 1850's.

Moffat Museum
Moffat. Easter Week. Whit.-Sept 10.30–13.00, 14.30–17.00, Sun 14.30–17.00. (Moffat Museum Trust). Tel: Moffat (0683) 20868.
Situated in an old bakehouse in the oldest part of the town. The Scotch oven is a feature of the ground floor. No guide dogs.

Museum of Border Arms and Armour
9m S of Hawick on A7 at Teviothead. All year, daily 09.00–19.00. Parking available. Tel: (045 085) 237.
Former smithy with craft gallery. The museum houses a display of weapons and equipment from the 16th century.

Neidpath Castle

A72, 1m W of Peebles. Thurs before Easter until Sept 30. Other times by appointment, parties only. Mon-Sat 11.00–17.00, Sun 13.00–17.00. (Lord Wemyss' Trust). Tel: Aberlady (087 57) 201/(0721) 20333.

In a beautiful valley among wooded hills, Neidpath Castle is dramatically situated high above the River Tweed. This mediaeval castle, with walls nearly 12 feet thick, contains a rock-hewn well and pit prison, and two of the three original vaults. It is also an interesting example of how such a fortress could be adapted to the more civilised living conditions of the 17th century. There are fine views from several levels, right up to the parapet. The castle was once besieged by Cromwell and cannon damage is still visible.

Newark Castle, near Selkirk

Off A708, 4m W of Selkirk. Entry on application to Buccleuch Estates, Bowhill, Selkirk. Free. (Buccleuch Estates). Tel: Selkirk (0750) 20753.

First mentioned in 1423, Newark or New Wark was so called to distinguish it from the older Auldwark Castle which stood nearby. This 5-storeyed oblong tower house, standing within a barmkin, was a royal hunting seat for the Forest of Ettrick; and Royal Arms of James I are on the west gable. In the courtyard 100 prisoners from the Battle of Philiphaugh (1645) were shot by Leslie. Care should be taken in the building.

Old Gala House and Christopher Boyd Gallery

On A7 northbound; fork left at St. Peter's Church School. Southbound: follows signs from War Memorial. Easter-early Nov. Easter-Sept 10.00–16.00 (Sun 14.00–16.00); Oct 12.00–16.00 (Sun 14.00–16.00). Parking available.

Dating from 1583, Old Gala House is the former home of the Lairds of Gala. Reopened in 1988 as an interpretation centre. Especially interesting painted ceiling (1635). Gardens, coffee room (seating 16–20), small sales point. Temporary Art Galleries.

Peter Anderson Woollen Mill

Nether Mill, Galashiels. All year, Mon-Sat 09.00–17.00; also Jun-Sept, Sun 12.00–17.00. (Conducted tours) Apr-Sept, Mon-Fri 10.30, 11.30, 13.30, 14.30. Tel: Galashiels (0896) 2091.

Museum and exhibition of the past of Galashiels, showing all aspects of the growth of the town, including health, education, labour and textiles. Also tours of the manufacturing of tartans, tweeds, etc. Museum, mill tours and mill shop.

Priorwood Gardens

In Melrose, by Abbey, on B6361. Open 2–30 Apr and 1 May-24 Dec, Mon-Sat 10.00–17.30; 1 May-31 Oct, Mon-Sat 10.00–17.30, Sun 13.30–17.30. Admission by donation. (NTS). Tel: Melrose (089 682) 2555.

A garden which specialises in flowers suitable for drying, also apple trees in variety. There is an NTS Visitor Centre. Picnic tables, orchard walk, dry flower garden, NTS shop.

Rennie's Bridge

Kelso. All times. Free. (Borders Regional Council).

A fine 5-arched bridge built over the River Tweed in 1803 by Rennie to replace one destroyed by the floods of 1797. On the bridge are two lamp posts from the demolished Old Waterloo Bridge in London, which Rennie built in 1811. There is also a fine view to Floors Castle.

Roxburgh Castle

Off A699, 1m SW of Kelso. All times. Free. Tel: Kelso (0573) 23333.

The earthworks are all that remain of the once mighty castle, destroyed by the Scots in the 15th century, and the walled Royal Burgh which gave its name to the county. The present village of Roxburgh dates from a later period.

St. Abb's Head Nature Reserve

1m N of St. Abbs. Best season Apr-July. Free (donations). Groups by prior arrangement. Parking available. Tel: Coldingham (08907) 71443.

Rocky cliffs, home to a wide variety of seabirds. Coldingham Bay nearby is particularly noted for its coloured pebbles. National Nature Reserve managed jointly by National Trust for Scotland and Scottish Wildlife Trust. Cliff paths totally unsuitable for disabled people.

St. Mary's Loch

Off A708, 14m ESE of Selkirk. Parking available.

Beautifully set among smooth green hills, this three-mile-long loch is used for sailing and fishing. On the neck of land separating it from Loch of the Lowes at the south end stands Tibbie Shiel's Inn, long kept by Tibbie Shiel (Elizabeth Richardson, 1783–1878) from 1823, and a meeting place for many 19th-century literati. Beside the road towards the north end of the loch is a seated statue of James Hogg, the 'Ettrick Shepherd', author of the Confessions of a Justified Sinner and a friend of Scott, who farmed in this district. Tearoom and two hotels nearby.

Scottish Museum of Woollen Textiles

On main road (A72) at Walkerburn, 9m ESE of Peebles. All year, Mon-Sat 10.00–17.30. Easter-Christmas, Sun 12.00–16.30. Free. (Scottish Worsted and Woollens Ltd). Tel: Walkerburn (089 687) 619/281/283 (0900–1500).

This display features the development of the woollen industry from a cottage industry to a major occupation of the Borders. Many interesting exhibits. Group bookings by arrangement. Coffee and tea shop.

Scott's View

B6356, 7m ESE of Galashiels.

A view over the Tweed to the Eildon Hills, beloved by Scott; here the horses taking his remains to Dryburgh for burial stopped as they had so often before for Sir Walter to enjoy this panorama.

Scotus Statue, Duns

At Duns, in public park. All times. Free.

Duns was the birthplace of John Duns Scotus (1266–1308), a Franciscan who became a leading divine and one of the greatest medieval philosophers. It is said the word 'dunce' came into the English language as a result of criticism of his work after his death.

Selkirk Glass

Off A7 N of Selkirk. All year, Mon-Fri 09.00–17.00, Sat 10.00–16.30, Sun 12.00–16.00. Glass making: Mon-Fri 09.00–16.30. Free. Tel: Selkirk (0750) 20954.

Visitors are welcome at factory and showroom to see a range of paperweights and watch craftsmen at work. Coffee shop.

Sir Walter Scott's Courtroom

Market Place, Selkirk. Jul-Aug, Mon-Fri 14.00–16.00, other times by appointment. By application to: Ettrick and Lauderdale District Council, Municipal Buildings, High Street, Selkirk. Free. Parking available. Tel: Selkirk (0750) 20096.

The bench and chair from which Sir Walter Scott, as Sheriff of Selkirk, administered justice here for 30 years, are on display, with portraits of Scott, James Hogg, Mungo Park and Robert Burns, with ancient charters. Also displayed are watercolours by Tom Scott, RSA.

Smailholm Tower

Off B6404, 6m NW of Kelso. Opening standard, closed in winter. (HS). Tel: 031–244 3101.

An outstanding example of a 16th-century Border peel tower built to give surveillance over a wide expanse of country. It is 57 feet high, in a good state of preservation and houses an exhibition of costumed dolls and tapestries on the theme of Sir Walter Scott's 'Minstrelsy of the Scottish Border'. At nearby Sandyknowe Farm, Scott spent some childhood years.

Robert Smail's Printing Works

7/9 High Street, Innerleithen, 30m S of Edinburgh. Shop only: 1 May-midsummer daily, except Tues & Sun. Restored Printing Works and Shop: daily midsummer-31 Oct, Mon-Sat 10.00–13.00 and 14.00–17.00, Sun 14.00–17.00. Parking available (NTS) Tel: (0896) 830206.

These buildings contain an office, a paper store with reconstructed water wheel, composing and press rooms. Visitors may view the printer at work. Victorian office contains many historic items. Trust Shop.

Stichill Smithy Gallery

2m N of Kelso on the B6364 to Greenlaw. Apr-Nov, daily (except Wed) 11.00–17.00. Free. Parking available. Tel: Stichill (05737) 346.

The shoeing end of an old smithy. Temporary exhibitions space and collection of prints.

Thirlestane Castle and Border Country Life Museum

Lauder, 28m S of Edinburgh on A68. Easter week, May, Jun, & Sep, Wed, Thu & Sun only; Jul & Aug, every day except Sat. (grounds) 12.00–18.00, (castle) 14.00–17.00. Tel: Lauder (05782) 430.

Fine castle steeped in Scottish history, still the home of the Maitland family after four centuries. Magnificent 17th-century state rooms. Tea room, gift shop, gardens, museum and castle. The Border Country Life Museum Trust was established in 1981 to set up a museum to depict country life in the Scottish Borders from prehistoric times to the present day. Displays reflect the traditions, folklore and land use of the Borders. Demonstrations of vintage tractors and traditional farming methods are organised periodically by the Border Vintage Agricultural Association.

Torwoodlee House

2m NW of Galashiels off A72. 1 Jun-31 Aug, by appointment. Tel: Galashiels (0896) 2151.

A small Georgian mansion with Victorian alterations, which was built in 1783 by the 9th Laird, James Pringle. The Pringle family has lived at Torwoodlee since 1501.

Traquair House

B709, off A72, 8m ESE of Peebles. Easter Sat, Sun and following week. Daily 26 May-30 Sept

13.30–17.30; Sun and Mon in May, 13.30–17.30.
Last admission 17.00. July and Aug 10.30–17.30.
Grounds open from Easter 10.30–17.40. Bus
parties must book in advance. (C. Maxwell Stuart).
Tel: Innerleithen (0896) 830323.

Dating back to the 10th century, this is said to be
the oldest continuously inhabited house in
Scotland. 27 Scottish and English monarchs have
visited it, including Mary, Queen of Scots, of
whom there are relics. It was once the home of
William the Lion who held court here in 1209. The
well-known Bear Gates were closed in 1745, not to
be reopened until the Stuarts should ascend the
throne. Ale is regularly produced at the 18th-
century brewhouse, and there are woodland walks
and four craft workshops. Exhibitions are held
during the summer months and the annual Traquair
Fair is held the first weekend in August. Material
available on cassette by arrangement.
Restaurant/tearoom, gift shop, gallery, brewery,
woodland and River Tweed walks and newly
planted maze.

Tweed Bridge
A698 at Coldstream, 9m ENE of Kelso. Tel: St.
Boswells (0835) 23301.

The 300 feet long bridge was built in 1766 by
Smeaton and in the past was a crossing into
Scotland for eloping couples taking advantage of
Scotland's then-easier marriage laws.

Tweeddale Museum
High Street, Peebles. All year. Apr-Oct, Sat & Sun
14.00–17.00. Free. Parking available. (Tweeddale
District Council). Tel: Peebles (0721) 20123, ext.
15.

Housed in the Chambers Institution, which was
given to Peebles in 1859 by William Chambers the
publisher, the museum presents regularly changing
displays on various themes of Tweeddale's heritage
and culture.

Union Suspension Bridge
Across River Tweed, 2m S of Paxton on
unclassified road. (Borders Regional Council). Tel:
St. Boswells (0835) 22301.

This suspension bridge, the first of its type in
Britain, was built by Samuel Brown in 1820 and
links England and Scotland.

Waterloo Monument
Off B6400, 5m N of Jedburgh. All times. Free. No
access to interior. Tel: Ancrum (08353) 306.

This prominent landmark on the summit of
Penielheugh Hill (741 feet) was built in 1815 by
the Marquess of Lothian and his tenants. Can be
seen from a walk from the Woodland Centre.

The John Wood Collection
Fishers Brae, Coldingham. 1 Apr-31 Oct.
09.00–18.00, Mon-Sat. Free. Parking available.
Tel: (08907) 71259.

Photographic exhibition of Border life in the early
1900s. Printed from the original glass plates which
were discovered in a potting shed.

The Woodland Visitor Centre
At Monteviot, 3m N of Jedburgh at junction of A68
and B6400. Easter-end Oct. Open daily
10.30–17.30, or by prior arrangement for parties.
(Marquis of Lothian). Tel: Ancrum (08353) 306.

An interpretation centre, based on the old home
farm of a large country estate. The major theme is
the use of woodlands and timber. Exhibitions,
woodland walks, pinery, games and puzzles, shop,
slide show, adventure play area, tea room, parking.

Yarrow Kirk
A708, W from Selkirk. Parking available.

A lovely valley praised by many writers including
Scott, Wordsworth and Hogg, who lived in this
area. Little Yarrow Kirk dates back from 1640.
Scott's great-great-grandfather was minister there.
The nearby Deuchar Bridge (not now in use) was
built in the 17th-century. On the hills around
Yarrow are the remains of ancient Border keeps.

EDINBURGH

Acheson House
Canongate, Royal Mile. All year, Mon-Sat
10.00–17.30. Free. Tel: 031–556 8136/7370.

A mansion of 1633–34 entered through a small
courtyard, now the Scottish Craft Centre. It
displays and sells the work of Scotland's
contemporary craft workers, including pottery,
weaving, silver, woodwork, textiles, glass and
jewellery.

Ainslie Park Leisure Centre
Off Ferry Road, $$1/4m E of Crewe Toll
roundabout. Centre is on left after Northern
General Hospital into Pilton Drive. All year, Mon-
Fri 10.00–22.00, Sat & Sun 10.00–18.00. Charges
variable according to activity. Parking available.
Tel: 031–551 2400.

Opened in 1989; superbly equipped, brightly
designed building on leisure theme with swimming
pools, flumes and a leisure complex. Function
room for 150. Bar, cafe and audio visual library.

Brass Rubbing Centre.
Trinity Apse, Chalmers Close, Royal Mile. Jun-Sep,
weekdays 10.00–18.00; Oct-May, weekdays

10.00–17.00; Suns during Festival 14.00–17.00. Free. A charge is made for every rubbing, which includes cost of materials and a royalty to the churches where applicable. Tel: 031–225 2424, ext 6638/6678.

Rubbings of the brass commemorating Robert the Bruce and the Burghead Bull, a Pictish incised stone c AD 700 are among the selection available. Instruction and materials supplied.

Butterfly and Insect World
5m S of Edinburgh on A7 towards Dalkeith. 25 Mar-31 Oct, daily 10.00–17.30. (Dobbies Gardening World) Tel: 031–663 4932.

The farm, housed in a large greenhouse with lush tropical plants, cascading waterfalls and lily ponds, provides the setting for butterflies from all over the world to fly freely around. Exotic insects, photographic displays, tearoom, garden centre, tropical fish shop, children's playground and picnic area. Free car parking.

Calton Hill
Off Regent Road at E end of city centre. All times. Free. Monument: Apr-Sep, Tues, Sat 10.00–18.00, Mon 13.00–18.00; Oct-Mar 10.00–15.00. (Edinburgh District Council) Tel: 031–225 2424, ext. 6689.

A city centre hill, 350 feet above sea level, with magnificent views over Edinburgh and the Firth of Forth. The monumental collection on top includes a part reproduction of the Parthenon, intended to commemorate the Scottish dead in the Napoleonic Wars; it was begun in 1824 but ran out of funds and was never completed. The 102 feet high Nelson Monument (completed 1815) improves the view from its high parapets. The buildings of the Royal Observatory (1744 and 1818) are open on application to: The Custodian, City Observatory, Calton Hill, Edinburgh.

Canongate Kirk.
On the Canongate, Royal Mile. If closed apply the Manse, Reid's Court, near the church. Tel: 031–556 3515.

The church, built by order of James VII in 1688, is the Parish Church of the Canongate and also the Kirk of Holyroodhouse and Edinburgh Castle. The church silver dates from 1611. Restored in 1951, the church contains much heraldry. The burial ground contains the graves of Adam Smith, the economist, 'Clarinda', friend of Robert Burns, and Robert Fergusson, the poet.

City Art Centre
Market Street. Open Jun-Sep, Mon-Sat,

10.00–18.00, Sun during Festival, 14.00–17.00. Oct-May, Mon-Sat 10.00–17.00, usually free, occasionally charges for special exhibitions. Tel: 031–225 2424, ext. 6650.

The City of Edinburgh's Art Gallery. A converted warehouse on four floors with a programme of changing exhibitions and displays from the City's collection of paintings.

Craigmillar Castle
A68, 3$\frac{1}{2}$m SE of city centre. Opening standard (closed Thu (pm) and Fri) in winter. (HS). Tel: 031–244 3101.

Imposing ruins of massive 14th-century keep enclosed in the early 15th century by an embattled curtain wall; within are the remains of the stately ranges of apartments dating from the 16th and 17th centuries. The castle was burnt by Hertford in 1544. There are strong connections with Mary, Queen of Scots, who frequently stayed here. While she was in residence in 1566 the plot to murder Darnley was forged.

Cramond
5m NW of city centre, on the shores of the Firth of Forth. Parking available. Tel: 031–336 2163.

This picturesque 18th century village is situated at the mouth of the River Almond. See particularly the Roman fort and medieval tower, the kirk, kirkyard and manse, the old schoolhouse and the iron mills. Conducted walks around the village start from The Maltings, June-Sep, Sun 15.00, free. Exhibition at The Maltings, Cramond Village, Jun-Sep, Sat & Sun 14.00–17.00, free.

Crystal Visitor Centre
Eastfield, Penicuik, 10m S of Edinburgh. All year. Tours Mon-Fri 09.00–15.30. Shop, Restaurant and Audio-Visual, 09.00–17.00 Mon-Sat and Sun 11.00–17.00. Tour charge (except for disabled). Children under 10 years not admitted to factory tour. Tel: (0968) 75128.

Conducted tours are available, unveiling every aspect of the glassmaker's craft. Children under 10 years not admitted on factory tours. No photography. Audio-visual presentations Mon-Sat, 0900–1630. Licensed cafeteria, children's play area and picnic facilities.

Dean Village
Bell's Brae, off Queensferry Street, on Water of Leith.

There was grain milling in this notable village of Edinburgh for over 800 years. The view downstream through the high arches of Dean Bridge is among the most picturesque in the city. A walk along the waterside leads to St. Bernard's Well, an old mineral source (open by arrangement).

Richard Demarco Gallery
17–21 Blackfriars Street (off Royal Mile). All year, Mon-Sat 10.00–18.00. Free except during Edinburgh Festival. (Richard Demarco). Tel: 031-557 0707.
An international communications centre for artists and those interested in contemporary visual arts, as well as theatre, performance, music and art education. It is concerned with Scotland's celtic and prehistoric cultures in relation to Europe and contemporary art and explores this relationship in the form of "Edinburgh Arts" journey. The Gallery opened in 1966 and has presented over 900 exhibitions and 300 related events.

Edinburgh Castle
Castle Rock, top of the Royal Mile. Apr-Sep, Mon-Sat 09.30–17.05, Sun 11.00–17.05; Oct-Mar Mon-Sat 09.30–16.20, Sun 12.30–15.35. (HS). Tel: 031-244 3101.
One of the most famous castles in the world, whose battlements overlook the Esplanade where the floodlit Military Tattoo is staged each year, late August to early September. The castle stands on a rock which has been a fortress from time immemorial. The oldest part of the buildings which make up the castle is the 12th-century chapel dedicated to St. Margaret. In addition to the Great Hall built by James IV, with fine timbered roof, and the Old Palace, which houses the Regalia of Scotland and the Military Museum, the castle also holds the Scottish National War Memorial, opened in 1927.

Fountain Brewery
Scottish & Newcastle Breweries plc, Gilmore Park. By arrangement. Free. Parking available. Tel: 031-229 9377 (ext. 3015 between 10.00–16.00).
A tour of the complete brewing process and high-speed canning line, in the most fully automated brewery in Europe.

The Fruitmarket Gallery
29 Market Street. All year. Tues-Sat 10.00–19.00, Sun 12.00–17.00. Cafe, bookshop. Admission free. Tel: 031-225 2383.
An independent gallery hosting varied exhibitions of contemporary painting, sculpture, architecture & photography from Scotland and the international art world.

Georgian House
No 7 Charlotte Square. 1 Apr-31 Oct, Mon-Sat 10.00–17.00, Sun 14.00–17.00. Last admission ¹/₂ hour before closing. (NTS). Tel: 031-225 2160.
The lower floors have been furnished as they might have been by their first owners, showing the domestic surroundings and reflecting the social conditions of that age. Charlotte Square itself was built at the end of the 18th century and is one of the most outstanding examples of its period in Europe. Bute House is the official residence of the Secretary of State for Scotland. The West side of the square is dominated by the green dome of St. George's Church, now West Register House.

Gladstone's Land
477B Lawnmarket, Royal Mile. 1 Apr-31 Oct, Mon-Sat 10.00–17.00, Sun 14.00–17.00. Last admission ¹/₂ hour before closing. (NTS). Tel: 031-226 5856.
Completed in 1620, the six-storey tenement contains remarkable painted ceilings, and has been refurbished as a typical home of the period.

Gorgie City Farm Project
51 Gorgie Road. All year 09.00–16.30 daily including public holidays. Free. Tel: 031-337 4202.
2¹/₂ acres of land adjacent to Gorgie Road, Edinburgh. This city farm has a variety of animals, animal pens, a farm kitchen with workshop/craft facilities. Picnic and play area.

Greyfriar's Bobby
Corner of George IV Bridge and Candlemaker Row. All time. Free.
Statue of Greyfriar's Bobby, the Skye terrier who, after his master's death in 1858, watched over his grave in the nearby Greyfriars Churchyard for 14 years.

George Heriot's School
Lauriston Place. May be viewed from the grounds. Gates close 16.30. Tel: 031-229 7263 (Trust Office).
Now a school, the splendid building was begun in 1628, endowed by George Heriot, goldsmith and jeweller to James VI and I, the 'Jingling Geordie' of Scott's novel Fortunes of Nigel.

Hillend
Biggar Road, S outskirts of Edinburgh. Apr-Sept, Mon-Fri 09.30–21.00. Oct-Mar 09.30–22.00 each day. (Lothian Regional Council). Tel: 031-445 4433.
The largest artificial ski slope in Britain. Facilities include chairlift, drag lift, ski-hire, tuition, showers and changing rooms. Grass ski-ing available May to September. Fine views from top of chairlift

(available to non-skiers) of the Pentland Hills, over Edinburgh and beyond. Refreshments and picnic area.

Huntly House
Canongate, Royal Mile. Jun-Sep, Mon-Sat 10.00–18.00; Oct-May, Mon-Sat 10.00–17.00; Sun during Festival 14.00–17.00. Free. Tel: 031–225 2424, ext 6689.
Built in 1570, this fine house was later associated with members of the Huntly Family. It is now a city museum illustrating Edinburgh Life down the ages, and contains important collections of Edinburgh silver and glass and Scottish pottery.

King's Theatre
2 Leven Street. Box Office: 10.00–12.00. Tel: 031–229 1201.
Opened in 1906. 4 licensed bars and coffee bars. Completely restored 1985. Seating 1350. Producing ballet, opera, comedy, farce, variety, drama, dance etc. Productions normally change weekly. Details and advance booking from Box Office.

Kirk of the Greyfriars
Greyfriars Place, S end of George IV Bridge. Easter-Sep, Mon-Fri 10.00–16.00, Sat 10.00–12.00. Free. Tel: 031–225 1900.
The Kirk, dedicated on Christmas Day, 1620, was the scene of the adoption and Signing of the National Covenant on 28 February 1638. The Kirkyard, inaugurated in 1562, is on the site of a 15th century Franciscan Friary. In 1679, 1,400 Covenanters were imprisoned in the Kirkyard. Various literature available.

John Knox House
45 High Street, Royal Mile. All year, Mon-Sat 10.00–17.00. Tel: 031–556 9579/2647.
A picturesque house, said to be the only 15th century house in Scotland, having traditional connections with John Knox, the famous Scottish reformer. The recent restoration programme has revealed the original walls, fireplaces and painted ceiling. There is also a 10-minute video film of John Knox's life in Geneva and Scotland.

Lady Stair's House
Off Lawnmarket, Royal Mile. Jun-Sept, weekdays 10.00–18.00; Oct-May, weekdays 10.00–17.00; Sun during Festival 14.00–17.00. Free. Tel: 031–225 2424, ext. 6593.
Built in 1622, this is now a museum of Burns, Scott and Stevenson.

Lamb's House
Burgess Street, Leith. All year, daily 09.00–17.00.
Free (NTS). Tel: 031–554 3131.
The restored residence and warehouse of Andrew Lamb, a prosperous merchant of the 17th century. Now an old people's day centre.

Lauriston Castle
N of A90 at Cramond Road South, 4m WNW of city centre. Apr-Oct, daily except Fri 11.00–13.00, 14.00–17.00; Nov-Mar, Sat and Sun only, 14.00–16.00. Tel: 031–336 2060/225 2424, ext. 6678.
The original tower house built by Sir Archibald Napier, father of the inventor of logarithms was much extended by William Burn in the 1820's. The last occupant, W.R. Reid, owner of the prestigious Edinburgh furnishing firm of Morison & Co., completely refurbished the Castle in 1903 and his Edwardian interior has been carefully preserved. It includes a fine collection of eighteenth century Italian furniture, oriental rugs etc. Now administered by the City of Edinburgh. Car park.

Magdalen Chapel
Cowgate, off the Grassmarket. By arrangement. Free. (Scottish Reformation Society). Tel: 031–220 1450.
This 16th-century chapel, is notable for its stained-glass windows.

Museum of Childhood
High Street, Royal Mile. Jun-Sep weekdays 10.00–18.00; Oct-May weekdays 10.00–17.00; Sun during Festival 14.00–17.00. Free. Tel: 031–225 2424, ext. 6645/6647.
This unique museum has a fine collection of toys, dolls, dolls' houses, costumes and nursery equipment. It has recently been extended into a former Georgian theatre and completely refurbished.

Museum of Communication
James Clerk Maxwell Building, Kings Building, Mayfield Road. Open Jan-Dec 09.00–19.00, except Xmas-New Year. Refreshments & Parking available. Tel: 0506 824507.
A display of electrical communication equipment. It also houses the dept of computer science, geophysics, mathematics, meteorology, physics, statistics and the regional computing centre.

Museum of Fire
Lauriston Place. Visits by arrangement with Fire Brigade Headquarters. Free. (Lothians & Borders Fire Brigade). No Parking. Tel: 031–228 2401.
Guided tours round the museum, with its collection of old uniforms, equipment and engines, subject to the availability of a Fireman Guide.

National Gallery of Scotland

The Mound. Mon-Sat 10.00–17.00 (extended hours during Festival); Sun 14.00–17.00. Free. Tel: 031–556 8921.

One of the most distinguished of the smaller gallleries of Europe, the National Gallery of Scotland contains a comprehensive collection of old masters, impressionist and Scottish paintings. This includes masterpieces by Raphael, El Greco, Rembrandt, Constable, Titian, Velasquez, Raeburn, Van Gogh and Gauguin. Drawings, watercolours and original prints (Turner, Goya, Blake etc.) are shown on request (Mon-Fri 10.00–12.30, 14.00–16.30).

National Library of Scotland

George IV Bridge. All year (Reading Room) Mon, Tues, Thurs, Fri 09.30–20.30, Wed 10.00–20.30, Sat 09.30–13.00. (Exhibition) Mon-Fri 09.30–17.00 (09.30–20.30 during Festival), Sat 09.30–17.00, Sun 14.00–17.00. Free. Publications counter. Tel: 031–226 4531.

Founded in 1689, this is one of the four largest libraries in Great Britain. Its unparalled collection on Scottish history and culture is available to researchers, and its frequently changing exhibitions are open to the general public.

Netherbow Arts Centre

43 High Street. All year, Mon-Sat 10.00–16.30 (also in evenings for theatre). Free. Cafe/refreshments. Tel: 031–556 9579/2647.

A modern arts centre in Edinburgh's Old Town offering a range of exhibitions and performances with an emphasis on the Scottish arts. Open-air courtyard. Restaurant.

New Town Conservation Centre

13A Dundas Street. All year. Mon-Fri 09.00–13.00, 14.00–17.00. Free. Tel: 031–557 5222.

Headquarters of committee which administers grants for the conservation of the Georgian 'New Town'. There is a display of work in progresss and a conservation reference library. Publications are on sale. There are guided walks from June to September and at other times by arrangement. Particulars from Conservation Centre.

Outlook Tower and Camera Obscura

Castle Hill, between the Castle and Lawnmarket. All year daily, Apr-Oct, Mon-Fri 09.30–17.30, Sat & Sun 10.00–18.00; Nov-Mar, Mon-Fri 09.30–17.00, Sat & Sun 10.30–16.30. Last admission 45 minutes before closing. (Landmark). Tel: 031–226 3709.

This unique Victorian optical device projects a spectacular live image of the surrounding city onto a viewing table high in the Outlook Tower. Also rooftop terrace, and related optical displays including 'Holography', a permanent public collection of 3D laser images; pin-hole photography; space photography.

Palace of Holyroodhouse

Foot of the Royal Mile. Apr-Oct 09.30–17.15, Sun 10.30–16.30; Nov-Mar 09.30–15.45 (not Sun). The Palace is also closed during Royal and State Visits and for periods before and after visits; check dates in May to July. Tel: 031–556 7371.

The Palace of Holyroodhouse is the official residence of the Queen in Scotland. The oldest part is built against the monastic nave of Holyrood Abbey, little of which remains. The rest of the palace was reconstructed by the architect Sir William Bruce for Charles II. Here Mary, Queen of Scots lived for six years; here she met John Knox; here Rizzio was murdered, and here Prince Charles Edward Stuart held court in 1745. State apartments, house tapestries and paintings; the picture gallery has portraits of over 70 Scottish kings, painted by De Wet in 1684–86.

Parliament House

Parliament Square, behind the High Kirk of St. Giles, Royal Mile. All year, Tue-Fri 10.00–16.00. Free. Tel: 031–225 2595.

Built 1632–39 this was the seat of Scottish government until 1707, when the governments of Scotland and England were united. Now the Supreme Law Courts of Scotland. See the Parliament Hall with fine hammer beam roof and portraits by Raeburn and other major Scottish artists. Access (free) to the splendid Signet Library on an upper floor is by prior written request only, to: The Librarian, Signet Library, Parliament House, Edinburgh. Outside is the mediaeval Mercat Cross, which was restored in 1885 by W E Gladstone. Royal proclamations are still read from its platform. Restaurant.

Register House

E end of Princes Street. All year, Mon-Fri. Legal: 09.30–16.30; Historical: 09.00–16.45 (last admission time 16.25). Exhibitions 10.00–16.00. Free. Tel: 031–556 6585.

This fine Robert Adam building, founded 1774, is the headquarters of the Scottish Record Office and the home of the national archives of Scotland. There is a branch repository at West Register House in Charlotte Square. In front is a notable statue of the Duke of Wellington (1852). Alternative wheelchair entrance. No guide dogs inside.

Royal Botanic Garden

Inverleith Row, Arboretum Road (car parking). Daily 09.00 (Sun 11.00) to one hour before sunset, summer; 09.00-dusk, winter. Free. Plant houses 10.00 (Sun 11.00) to 17.00, summer; 10.00 (Sun 11.00) to dusk, winter. Free. Tel: 031-552 7171.

The Royal Botanic Garden has a world famous rock garden and probably the biggest collection of rhododendrons in the world. The unique exhibition plant houses show a great range of exotic plants displayed as indoor landscapes and a plant exhibition hall displays many aspects of botany and horticulture. Tearoom and publications counter.

Royal Commonwealth Pool & Nautilus Flume Complex

From Princes Street turn onto North Bridge, follow road for about 1m, turn left onto Salisbury Place, then right into Salisbury Road; pool is on left. Swimming pools – Summer (Jun-Sept), Mon-Fri 09.00–21.00; Sat and Sun 08.00–19.00. Winter (Oct-May), Mon-Fri 09.00–21.00; Sat and Sun 10.00–16.00. Flumes – Summer, Mon-Fri 10.00–20.00; Sat and Sun 10.00–15.00. Winter, Mon-Fri 14.30–20.00; Sat and Sun 10.00–15.00. Parking available. Tel: 031–667 7211.

50m swimming pool, diving pool, teaching pool, Nautilus Flume Complex (Europe's largest indoor flume). Cafeteria. Fitness centre.

Royal Lyceum Theatre Company

Grindlay Street. All year. Group rates. Tel: 031–229 9697.

Resident company in fine Victorian theatre. Up to 12 plays a year. 3 bars, restaurant. Facilities: easy booking; disabled access; concessions; tours and more.

Royal Museum of Scotland, Chambers Street

(National Museums of Scotland)

Mon-Sat 10.00–17.00, Sun 14.00–17.00. Free. Tel: 031–225 7534.

Part of the National Museums of Scotland in a fine Victorian building. Houses the national collections of decorative arts of the world, ethnography, natural history, geology, technology and science. Special exhibitions, lectures, gallery talks, films and other activities for adults and children. Tearoom.

Royal Museum of Scotland, Queen Street.

(National Museums of Scotland)

All year, Mon-Sat 10.00–17.00; Sun 14.00–17.00. Tel: 031–225 7534.

An intriguing and comprehensive collection of the history and everyday life of Scotland from the Stone Age to modern times. Also 'Dynasty' – the Royal House of Stewart exhibition traces 300 years of Stewart rule in Scotland through portraits and objects from the Scottish National Collection.

Royal Observatory

Blackford Hill. (Visitor Centre) all year, daily, Mon-Fri 10.00–16.00, Sat, Sun & public hols 12.00–17.00. Tel: 031–668 8405.

Situated at the home of the Royal Observatory and University Department of Astronomy, the Visitor Centre demonstrates the work of astronomers, especially with telescopes in Australia and Hawaii. Also on show is the largest telescope in Scotland. Wide ranging bookshop, fine views of Edinburgh from hill. Alternative entrance for wheelchairs.

Royal Scottish Academy

At the foot of the Mound, on Princes Street. Mon-Sat 10.00–19.00, Sun 14.00–17.00. Tel: 031–225 6671. Open for its Annual Exhibition late Apr-Jul, and for Festival exhibitions.

The Academy has annual exhibitions and special Festival exhibitions. Ramped wheelchair entrance at side.

Royal Scots Dragoon Guards Display Room

The Castle. All year, daily, Mon-Fri 09.30–16.00. Free.

Display of pictures, badges, brassware and other historical relics of the regiment. Souvenir Shop.

St. Cecilia's Hall

The Cowgate, off the Grassmarket. Wed 14.00–17.00, Sat 14.00–17.00. (University of Edinburgh). Tel: 031–667 1011, ext. 4577/4415.

This elegant concert hall was built for the Edinburgh Musical Society in 1762. Restored by the University of Edinburgh in 1968, it houses the Russell Collection of Early Keyboard Instruments.

St. Cuthbert's Church

Lothian Road. Open with guides Jun-Sep, Mon-Fri 11.00–16.00; other times by arrangement. Free. Parking available. Tel: 031–229 1142.

An ancient church, the 'West Kirk', rebuilt by Hippolyte Blanc in 1894. The tower is 18th century, and there is a monument to Napier of Merchiston, inventor of logarithms. Thomas de Quincey is buried in the churchyard. Coffee served Tuesday mornings.

St. Giles Cathedral

(The High Kirk of Edinburgh)

On the Royal Mile. Mon-Sat 09.00–17.00 (19.00 in summer), Sun (pm). Free. Tel: 031–225 4363.

There has been a church here since the 9th century. Of the present building, the tower is late 15th century. At one time, there were four churches here, and yet another served as a prison. See also the exquisite Thistle Chapel. In the street outside the west door is the Heart of Midlothian, a heart-shaped design in the cobblestones. It marks the site of the Old Tolbooth, built 1466, which was stormed in the 1736 Porteous Riots and demolished in 1817. Restaurant.

St. John's Church
W end of Princes Street. All reasonable times. Free. Tel: 031–229 7565.
An impressive 19th-century church, the nave of which was built in 1817 by William Burn. There is a fine collection of Victorian stained glass. SPCK bookshop, Peace and Justice Resource Centre, One World Shop, Corner Stone Restaurant and the International Voluntary Service.

St. Mary's Cathedral
In Palmerston Place, West End. Tel: 031–225 6293.
Built 1879, with the western towers added in 1917. The central spire is 276 feet high and the interior is impressive. Nearby is the charming Easter Coates House, built in the late 17th century with some stones filched from the old town; it is now St. Mary's Music School. Gardens with seats.

St. Triduana's Chapel
At Restalrig Church, in Restalrig district, $1\frac{1}{2}$m E of city centre. Opening standard. Free. (HS). Tel: 031–244 3101.
From the late 15th century the shrine of St. Triduana was situated in the lower chamber of the King's Chapel built by James III, adjacent to Restalrig Church. The design, a two storey vaulted hexagon, is unique. The lower chapel of St. Triduana survives intact but the upper chamber was demolished in 1560.

The Scotch Whisky Heritage Centre
358 Castlehill, The Royal Mile. 1 June-30 Sept 09.00–18.30. 1 Oct-31 May 10.00–17.00. Tel: 031–220 0441.
A visit brings the story of Scotch Whisky to life. Find out how and where whisky is made from a guided tour and audio-visual show. Travel in a whisky barrel through the history of Scotch Whisky with sound effects, aromas and commentary (choice of 7 languages). Whisky and gift shop.

Scotland's Clan Tartan Centre
70–74 Bangor Road, Leith, Edinburgh. Daily 09.00–17.30. Free. Tel: 031–553 5100/5161.

Exhibition, reference library and audio-visual display. Computerised tracing of clan links, extensive range of tartan accessories and clan crests. Full Highland dress. Restaurant, large free car park and free courtesy bus (phone for details).

Scott Monument
In Princes Street. Apr-Sep, Mon-Fri 09.00–18.00; Oct-Mar, Mon-Fri 09.00–15.00. Tel: 031–225 2424, ext. 6596/6689.
Completed in 1844, a statue of Sir Walter Scott and his dog Maida, under a canopy and spire 200 feet high, with 64 statuettes of Scott characters. Fine view of the city from the top.
(Closed for refurbishment)

Scottish Agricultural Museum
Ingliston, nr. Edinburgh Airport. 16 Apr-28 Sep, Mon-Fri, 3 Jun-2 Sep, Sun also. All year in school term – Wed 10.00–16.30. Free. Open to groups outside normal hours/season. (National Museums of Scotland). Tel: 031–333 2674 or 031–225 7534, ext 313.
Scotland's national museum of country life. Farming, old trades and skills, social and home life. Fascinating displays, old photographs, audio visual presentation. Teas, shop, parking, disabled facilities and access.

Scottish National Gallery of Modern Art
Belford Road. All year, Mon-Sat 10.00–17.00, Sun 14.00–17.00 (extended hours during Festival). Free. Tel: 031–556 8921.
Scotland's collection of 20th-century painting, sculpture and graphic art, with masterpieces by Derain, Matisse, Braque, Hepworth, Picasso and Giacometti; and work by Hockney, Caulfield and Sol Le Witt. Also Scottish School. Cafe.

Scottish National Portrait Gallery
E end of Queen Street. Mon-Sat 10.00–17.00 (extended hours during Festival), Sun 14.00–17.00. Free. Tel: 031–556 8921.
Illustrates the history of Scotland through portraits of the famous men and women who contributed to it in all fields of activity from the 16th century to the present day, such as Mary, Queen of Scots, James VI and I, Flora MacDonald, Robert Burns, Sir Walter Scott, David Hume and Ramsay MacDonald. The artists include Raeburn, Ramsay, Reynolds and Gainsborough. Reference section of engravings and photographs including calotypes by Hill and Adamson.

Scottish Rugby Union Museum
At Murrayfield, off Roseburn Street, Edinburgh, on main bus routes west from Edinburgh City Centre.

Museum: Sun, Mon, Wed 14.00–16.30, other times by arrangement. Free. Parking available. Tel: 031–337 9551.
Visit the stadium which houses the Scottish Rugby Museum with the history of the game from its beginning to the present. There is also a library for reference purposes and a shop with a large selection of rugby souvenirs and leisurewear.

Talbot Rice Gallery
University of Edinburgh, Old College, South Bridge. Tues-Sat 10.00–17.00. Free. Closed certain Sats if no special exhibition, check press or Tel: 031–667 1011, ext. 4308.
Edinburgh University's Torrie Collection and changing exhibitions are on public display in this fine building, part of the University of Edinburgh, begun by Robert Adam in 1789 and completed by William Playfair around 1830. Visitors are invited to view the fine architecture of Robert Adam and William Playfair in the Old College building.

Traverse Theatre
112 West Bow, Grassmarket. All year. Tel: 031–226 2633 for details of events.
One of Britain's most successful theatres for new plays. Theatre, cabaret, bar, restaurant in historic 200 year old Grassmarket building.

University Collection of Historic Musical Instruments
Reid Concert Hall, Bristo Square. All year, Wed 15.00–17.00, Sat 10.00–13.00. Free. Tel: 031–447 4791 or 031–667 1011, ext 2573.
The collection now consists of over 1,000 instruments and is maintained by the University for the purposes of research, performance and support for teaching. Some 350 are woodwind, over 150 are brass, about 250 stringed and the rest percussion, bagpipes, ethnographic and acoustical instruments. Study room by arrangement.

Usher Hall
From West End of Princes Street, turn onto Lothian Road; Usher Hall is on left. Please contact the Usher Hall for further details. Tel: 031–228 1155.
Edinburgh's premier concert hall which offers a wide and exciting range of concerts and dance performances.

West Register House
W side of Charlotte Square. Mon-Fri. Exhibitions: 10.00–16.00. Search Room: 09.00–16.45. Free. Tel: 031–556 6585.
Formerly St. George's Church, 1811, this now holds the more modern documents of the Scottish Record Office. Permanent exhibition on many aspects of Scottish history, including the Declaration of Arbroath, 1320. No guide dogs.

White Horse Close
Off Canongate, Royal Mile.
A restored group of 17th-century buildings off the High Street. The coaches to London left from White Horse Inn (named after Queen Mary's Palfrey), and there are Jacobite links.

Zoo
Entrance from Corstorphine Road (A8), 4m W of city centre. All year, daily, summer 09.00–18.00, winter 09.00–17.00 (or dusk if earlier). Sun opening 09.30. Tel: 031–334 9171.
Established in 1913 by the Royal Zoological Society of Scotland, this is one of Britain's leading zoos, with a large and varied collection of mammals, birds and reptiles in extensive grounds on Corstorphine Hill. Edinburgh Zoo is world famous for its large breeding colony of Antarctic Penguins. Restaurants, bars, adventure playground and shops.

LOTHIAN

Abercorn Church
Off unclassified road 2m N of A904, by Hopetoun, South Queensferry. All year, daily. Free. Tel: 031–331 1869.
Ancient church dedicated to St. Serf, founded in 5th century. Abercorn was the first bishopric in Scotland dating from AD 681. Present building, on site of 7th century monastery, dates from 12th century (see Norman Arch in S wall), reconstructed in 1579 and 1893. Display of 8th century Anglian crosses and hogback monuments; Duddingston aisle 1603; Binns aisle 1618. Also Hopetoun gallery and retiring rooms: 1704.

Almondell and Calderwood Country Park
On B7015 (A71) at East Calder or off A89 at Broxburn. 12m SSW of Edinburgh. Visitor Centre opening hours. Apr-Sept Mon-Wed 09.00–17.00, Thur 09.00–16.00, Sun 10.30–18.00. Oct-Mar Mon-Thur 09.00–17.00, Sun 10.00–16.30 closed for lunch 12.00–13.00. Free except for barbecues (small booking charge). Parking available. Tel: Mid Calder (0506) 882 254.
Extensive riverside and woodland walks in former estate, with large picnic and grassy areas. Visitor Centre housed in old stable block has large freshwater aquaria, displays on natural and local history, and short slide show. Ranger Service, guided walks programme in summer.

Antonine Wall
From Bo'ness to Old Kilpatrick, best seen off A803 E of Bonnybridge, 12m S of Stirling. All reasonable times. Free. (HS). Tel: 031-244 3101.
This Roman fortification stretched from Bo'ness on the Forth to Old Kilpatrick on the Clyde. Built about AD 142–143, it consisted of a turf rampart behind a ditch, with forts about every two miles. It was probably abandoned about AD 163. Remains are probably best preserved in the Falkirk/Bonnybridge area, notably Rough Castle, and at Bearsden.

Arniston House
Take A7 for 11m S out of Edinburgh, turn right onto B6372. Arniston House is 2nd on right about 1m from A7. June-Mid Sept, Tues afternoons; also first Sun afternoons (June-Sept). Guided tours leave on the $1/2$ hour. Pre-booked parties for 10–50 visitors on other days throughout the year. Applications in writing to Mrs. A. Dundas-Bekker, Arniston House, Gorebridge EH23 4RY. Parking available. Tel: Temple (087530) 238.
William Adam designed Palladian style mansion house. Fine examples of portraiture, stucco work and furniture. Garden and policy ground with fine trees and landscaping. Clay pigeon shooting. Home baked teas.

Athelstaneford Church
Off B1343, 4m N of Haddington. All reasonable times. Free; donations. Tel: Athelstaneford (062088) 249 or (062088) 378.
The plaque by the church tells the story of the origins of St Andrews Cross (the Saltire), which was first adopted as the Scottish flag at this place. A floodlit flag flies permanently on the site.

Bass Rock
Off North Berwick. Boat trips from North Berwick go round the Bass Rock. Tel: North Berwick (0620) 2197 (Tourist Information Centre).
A massive 350-feet-high rock, 1 mile in circumference, 3.25 miles ENE of North Berwick whose many thousands of raucous seabirds include the third largest gannetry in the world. Once a Covenanters' prison. Accessible on SW side only.

Beecraigs Country Park, Linlithgow
From Linlithgow take Preston Road S for 2m, signposted on left. Country Park open all year; Visitor Centre all year, 08.30–17.00. Free. Tel: (0506) 844516.
700 acre country park with nature trails, trout farm, deer farm, country crafts, trim course and plenty of opportunities for a variety of sporting pursuits.

Birkhill Clay Mine
From Bo'ness take A706 towards Linlithgow, right at crossroads at top of hill, 2m to Upper Kinneil Farm, turn right down unclassified signposted road. Weekends: Sat and Sun Easter (14 April)-16 Oct 12.30–16.00 (11.30–16.00 Jul and Aug). Weekdays: Daily Mon-Sun 16 Jul-31 Aug 11.30–16.00. Parking available.
Fireclay mine. Discover the secrets of fireclay deep in the underground tunnels at the heart of the mine. See 300-million-year-old fossils, learn how miners worked the clay. Meadow walk, ancient woodlands. Small shop selling confectionary/refreshments. Mine tour not accessible to disabled visitors.

Blackness Castle
B903, 4m NE of Linlithgow. Opening standard, except Oct-Mar closed Thur afternoon and Fri. (HS). Tel: 031-244 3101.
Interesting 15th century castle built out of the shore of the Forth, suggesting a fortified ship in appearance. Once it was one of the most important fortresses in Scotland and was one of the four castles which by the Articles of Union were to be left fortified. Since then it has been a state prison in Covenanting time, a powder magazine in the 1870's, and more recently, for a period, a youth hostel.

Bo'ness & Kinneil Railway
Off Union Street, Bo'ness. All year, Sat and Sun. Tel: Bo'ness (0506) 822298
Working steam railway system, with historic locomotive and rolling stock. Live steam and authentic station buildings. Refreshments and sales stand. Buffer Stop Cafe (snacks), picnic area, visitor trail and visitor centre. Free car parking. Steam trains run summer weekends from 12.00–17.00.

Crichton Castle
B6367, 7m SE of Dalkeith, nr. Pathead, Midlothian. Opening standard, except Oct-Mar, Sat and Sun only. (HS). Tel: 031-244 3101.
The keep dates from the 14th century, although today's ruins are mostly 15th/17th century. This castle, elaborate in style, has an arcaded range and impressive Italianate facade, including piazza. The upper frontage of which is wrought with faceted stonework and was erected by the Earl of Bothwell in the 16th century. The little Collegiate Church, $1/2$m north, dating from 1499 and still in use, is notable for its tower and barrel vaulting. Signposted walk to Borthwick.

Dalkeith Park
At E end of Dalkeith High Street, 7m S of Edinburgh on A68. Easter-end Oct, daily 11.00–18.00. (Duke of Buccleuch). Tel: 031–663 5684 (11.00–18.00) or 031–665 3277 outwith these hours.
Woodland walks beside the river in the extensive grounds of Dalkeith Palace. Tunnel walk, adventure woodland play area, nature trails, 18th century bridge and orangery.

Dalmeny House
By South Queensferry, 7m W of Edinburgh, take A90 then B924. May to Sep, daily 14.00–17.30. Closed Fri and Sat. (Earl of Rosebery). Tel: 031–331 1888.
The Primrose family, Earls of Rosebery, have lived here for over 300 years. The present house dates from 1815, in Tudor Gothic style, built by William Wilkins. Interior Gothic splendour of hammerbeamed hall, vaulted corridors and classical main rooms. Magnificent collection of 18th-century British portraits, French furniture, tapestries, porcelain from the Rothschild Mentmore collection, the Napoleon collection and other works of art. Lovely grounds and $4^1/_2$-mile shore walk from Crammond to South Queensferry.

Dirleton Castle
A198, 8m W of North Berwick. Opening standard. (HS). Tel: 031–244 3101.
Near the wide village green of Dirleton, these beautiful ruins date back to 1225 with 15th/17th century additions. The castle had an eventful history from its first siege by Edward I in 1298 until its destruction in 1650. The 'clustered' donjon dates from the 13th century and the garden encloses a 17th century bowling green surrounded by yews.

Forth Bridges
Queensferry, 10m W of Edinburgh. Tel: 031–331 1699.
For over 800 years travellers were ferried across the Firth of Forth. Queensferry was named from Queen Margaret who regularly used this passage between Dunfermline and Edinburgh in the 11th century. The ferry ceased in 1964 when the Queen opened the Forth Road Bridge, a suspension bridge then the longest of its kind in Europe (1,993 yards). Also here is the rail bridge of 1883–90, one of the greatest engineering feats of its time. It is 2,765 yards long.

Gosford House
Longniddry. Jun & Jul, Wed, Sat & Sun 14.00–17.00. Parking available. (Lord Wemyss'

Trust). Tel: Aberlady (087 57) 201.
In fine setting on the Firth of Forth. Central part of the house by Robert Adam, 1800. North and south wings by William Young, 1890. South wing contains celebrated marble hall. Ornamental waters with wildlife including (since 1983) nesting wild geese. Prior notice preferred for disabled visitors.

Hailes Castle
Off A1, 5m E of Haddington. Keykeeper monument. (HS). Tel: 031–244 3101.
13th/15th century stronghold in oddly low-lying situation. Here Bothwell brought Mary, Queen of Scots on their flight from Borthwick Castle in 1567. There is a fine 16th-century chapel.

The Heritage of Golf
West Links Road, Gullane, 14m ENE of Edinburgh. Open by appointment. Free. Tel: Aberlady (087 57) 277.
The exhibition shows how the game of golf developed after it arrived in Scotland from Holland in the 15th century. The visitor can see the simple origins, the natural materials and the skill of the early makers; and the development of golf from early days to the present.

Hopetoun House
W of South Queensferry, Easter-Sept, daily 10.00–17.00 (last admission 16.45). (Hopetoun House Preservation Trust). Tel: 031–331 2451 (09.00–17.00).
This great Adam mansion is the home of the Hope family, Earls of Hopetoun and later Marquesses of Linlithgow. Started in 1699 to the designs of Sir William Bruce, it was enlarged between 1721–54 by William Adam and his son, Robert. The mansion still contains much of the original furniture from the 1760's and many portraits, which include, Rubens, Rembrandt and Canaletto. The extensive grounds include deer parks with fallow and red deer and St Kilda sheep. Also sea walk, formal rose gardens, educational day centre and stables museum featuring 'Horse and Man in Lowland Scotland'. Nature trail, licensed restaurant. Family museum, rooftop viewing platform. Free parking.

The House of the Binns
Off A904, 4m E of Linlithgow. Easter and 1 May-Sep, daily (except Fri) 14.00–17.00 (last tour 16.30). Parties to book beforehand. (Park) 10.00–19.00. (NTS). Tel: Linlithgow (050683) 4255.
Occupied for more than 350 years, The Binns dates largely from the time of General Tam Dalyell,

1615–1685, and his father. It reflects the early 17th-century transition in Scottish architecture from fortified stronghold to gracious mansion. There are magnificent plaster ceilings, fine views across the Forth and a visitor trail.

Inchcolm Abbey
On Inchcolm Island in the Firth of Forth; check at Aberdour or South Queensferry for boat trips or hire. Opening standard, except closed Wed afternoon and Thurs in winter. Parking available. (HS). Tel: 031–244 3101.
The monastic buildings, which include a fine 13th century octagonal chapter house, are the best preserved in Scotland.

Inveresk Lodge Garden
S of Musselburgh, A6124, 7m E of Edinburgh. All year, Mon-Fri 10.00–16.30, Sun 14.00–17.00. (NTS). Tel: 031–226 5922.
This garden of a 17th-century house (not open to the public) displays a range of plants suitable for the small garden. Good shrub rose border and selection of climbing roses.

Kinneil House
Off A904, 4m NW of Linlithgow to the W of Bo'ness. Opening standard, except closed Tue afternoon and Fri in Winter. Free. (HS). Tel: 031–244 3101.
In the grounds of this 16th/17th-century seat of the Dukes of Hamilton (which contains some of the finest contemporary wall paintings and decorated ceilings in Scotland) is the outhouse where James Watt developed his invention of the steam engine, the first being erected at a nearby colliery in 1765.

Kinneil Museum and Roman Fortlet
In Bo'ness, 16m WNW of Edinburgh on A904 (adjacent to Kinneil House). Apr-Sept, Mon-Fri 10.00–13.30, 14.30–17.00, Sat 10.00–17.00, Sun (Jun, Jul, Aug only) 10.00–17.00. Oct-Apr, Sat only 10.00–17.00. Free. (Falkirk District Council). Tel: Falkirk (0324) 24911, ext. 2472.
Converted 17th century stables, with displays of Bo'ness Pottery and cast iron work. An exhibition entitled '2000 years of history' provides an insight into the estate's colourful history and provides guidance for viewing the remaining monuments, including a consolidated Roman fortlet, medieval house, church & village remains,and James Watt's cottage. History tours of the estate by costumed interpreters is available by calling (0506) 824318.

Lady Gifford's Well
At West Linton, 17m SSW of Edinburgh. Information and Exhibition Centre open weekends,
Sat and Sun 14.00–17.00. Tel: West Linton (0968) 60346.
The village of West Linton was well-known in former days for its stonemasons. The figure on 'Lady Gifford's Well' was carved in 1666. There are other carvings, probably by the same hand, on a house across the road, dated 1660 and 1678. There is a village information and exhibition centre in the Raemartin Square.

Lady Victoria Colliery
Newtongrange. On A7 past Dalkeith. Open all year (closed Mondays) Tues-Fri 10.00–16.30, Sat-Sun 12.00–17.00. Tearoom. Tel: 031–663 7519.
Recently renovated Victorian Colliery. A Grant Ritchie steam winding machine is one of many attractions of the pithead tour. The visitor centre contains an introductory lifelike display describing the life of a Victorian pit village through the eyes of a typical miner. A self-drive coal heritage trail links Lady Victoria Colliery to the museum's other site at Prestongrange.

Lennoxlove House
On B6369, 1m S of Haddington. Easter Weekend and May-Sept, Wed, Sat, Sun 14.00–17.00; groups at other times by arrangement. (Duke of Hamilton). Tel: Haddington (062 082) 3720.
Originally named Lethington, it was owned for centuries by the Maitlands, one of whom was Secretary to Mary, Queen of Scots. In 1672 the Duchess of Lennox, (La Belle Stewart who was the model for Britannia on the coinage), bought and bequethed it to Lord Blantyre, stipulating that it be renamed "Lennoxlove" in memory of her devotion to her husband. House has a threefold interest: its historic architecture; the association of the proprietors with the Royal House of Stewart; and the Hamilton Palace collection of portraits, furniture and porcelain. Gardens. Tearoom.

Linlithgow Palace
S shore of loch, Linlithgow. Opening standard. (HS). Tel: 031–244 3101.
The splendid ruined Palace overlooking the loch is the successor to an older building which was burned down in 1424. The Chapel and Great Hall are late 15th-century and the fine quadrangle has a richly-carved 16th-century fountain. In 1542 Mary, Queen of Scots was born here while her father, James V, lay dying at Falkland Palace. In 1746 the palace was burned, probably by accident, when occupied by General Hawley's troops. George V held a court in the Lyon Chamber here in 1914. This now roofless palace still represents one of the most remarkable achievements in Scottish mediaeval architecture.

Livingston Mill Farm
Off A705 Kirkton, Livingston village. Apr-Sept, daily 10.00–17.00. Oct-Mar, first Sat & Sun each month, 13.00–16.00. Admission charge. Groups rates. Parking available. Tel: (0506) 414957.
Restored 18th-century farm steading and watermill. Small agricultural museum, children's farm, play area, animal paddock, picnic/barbecue site and nature walks along the banks of the River Almond. Oil Museum. Farm Kitchen 95% access for disabled. Home baking.

Luffness
1m E of Aberlady on A198. By arrangement. Free. Parking available. (Luffness Ltd). Tel: Aberlady (087 57) 218.
A 16th-century castle with a 13th-century keep built on the site of a Norse camp. There are extensive old fortifications, an old moat and gardens.

Malleny House Gardens
In Balerno, off A70, 7^1/$_2$m SW of Edinburgh. Gardens: open all year, daily 10.00 – sunset. Parking available. (NTS). Tel: 031-226 5922.
Adjoining a 17th-century house (not open) is a garden with many interesting plants including a good collection of shrub roses. The National Bonsai Collection for Scotland is housed here. No dogs.

John Muir House
High Street, Dunbar. Jun-Sept 10.00-12.30, 13.30-16.30. Daily except Wed & Sun. Free. Tel: Dunbar (0368) 63353.
Birthplace of John Muir, famous American conservationist and author. The top flat has been restored to the period (1838).

Museum of Flight
By East Fortune Airfield, off B1347, 4^1/$_2$m S of North Berwick. Apr-Sept, daily 10.30-16.30, and several open days. Free. (National Museums of Scotland). Tel: Athelstaneford (062 088) 308.
Aircraft on display at this World War II former RAF airfield range from a supersonic Lightening fighter to the last Comet 4 which was in airline service. The varied collection also includes a Spitfire, a 1930 Puss Moth and a 'Blue Streak' rocket. Special exhibitions relate to the development of fighter aircraft from 1914 to 1940 and to the airship R34 which flew from East Fortune to New York in 1919. Toilets, picnic area. Free car and coach park.

Myreton Motor Museum
Off A198, 17m from Edinburgh and 6m SW of North Berwick. May-Oct, daily 10.00-18.00; Nov-Apr, daily 10.00-17.00. Parking available. (M.J. Mutch). Tel: Aberlady (087 57) 288.
A varied collection of road transport from 1897, including motor cars, cycles, motorcycles, commercials, World War II military vehicles and automobilia. Catalogue and children's quiz book.

Niddry Castle
10m W of Edinburgh, turn off A89 1m W of Newbridge. May-Sept, Sun only 10.00-16.30. At other times by arrangement for groups. Donations. Tel: Winchburgh 890 753.
Late 15th-century Scottish Castle, a refuge for Mary, Queen of Scots, now being restored from a crumbling ruin to its former splendour. Also archaeological dig

North Berwick Law
S of North Berwick, off B1347. All times. Free
The 613-ft volcanic rock is a fine viewpoint and is crowned by a watch tower dating from Napoleonic times, and an archway made from the jawbone of a whale.

North Berwick Museum
School Road. Easter-end May, Sat and Mon 10.00-13.00, 14.00-17.00, Fri and Sun 14.00-17.00. Jun-Sept, Mon-Sat 10.00-13.00, 14.00-17.00, Sun 14.00-17.00. Free. (East Lothian District Council). Tel: (062 082) 4161, ext 298 or 342.
A compact museum with galleries devoted to natural history, archaeology and the life of the North Berwick area, housed on the upper floor of a former school. Special exhibitions are arranged in June to August.

Pinkie House
At E end of Musselburgh. Mid Apr-mid Jul, mid-Sept-mid Dec, Tues 14.00-17.00. Appointments necessary. Free. Parking available. (Loretto School). Tel: 031-665 2059.
Early 17th-century building with many later additions. It is best known for its painted gallery (c 1630) and plaster ceilings.

Polkemmet Country Park
From Whitburn take B7066 W for 2m. Signposted on right-hand side. All year. Facilities vary according to season and weather. Free. Parking available. Tel: (0501) 43905.
Converted stables and barn. Remnants of old mansion house owned previously by the Baillie family. Restaurant, bar, visitor centre. 9-hole golf course and floodlit driving range. Woodland walks.

Preston Market Cross

1/2m S of Prestonpans, 8m E of Edinburgh. All times. Free. (HS). Tel: 031-244 3101.

An outstanding Scottish market cross, the only one that still stands where and as it was built. The tall shaft, surmounted by a unicorn, stands on a circular structure with niches and a parapet. It was probably erected by the Hamiltons of Preston after they obtained the right to hold a fair in 1617.

Preston Mill and Phantassie Doocot

Off A1 at East Linton, 6m W of Dunbar. 1 Apr-30 Sept, Mon-Sat 11.00-13.00, 14.00-17.00, Sun 14.00-17.00; 1-31 Oct, Sat 11.00-13.00, 14.00-16.30, Sun 14.00-16.00 (last tour 20 mins before closing). Parking available. (NTS) Tel: (0620) 860426.

A picturesque water-mill, possibly the only one of its kind still in working condition in Scotland. Nearby is Phantassie Doocot (dovecot), originally containing 500 birds, and the Rennie Memorial, which contains a part of John Rennie's Waterloo Bridge.

Rosslyn Chapel

At Roslin, off A703, 7 1/2m S of Edinburgh. 1 Apr-31 Oct, Mon-Sat 10.00-17.00, Sun 12.00-16.45. Tel: 031 440 2159.

This 15th century chapel is one of Scotland's lovliest and most historic churches, renowned for its magnificent sculpture and Prentice Pillar. It is situated in a beautiful wooded setting near the village of Roslin. Coffee shop and craft shop.

St. Mary's Pleasance

Sidegate, Haddington. Open at all reasonable times. Free, but donations welcome. Gardens (Haddington Garden Trust). Tel: Haddington (062082) 3738 (Mon-Fri incl, 10.00-13.00 and 14.00-17.00). Parking available.

These gardens of Haddington House have been restored as a 17th-century garden, with rose and herb, meadow, cottage and sunken gardens. The Pleached Alley leads to St. Mary's Gate and the restored medieval church of St. Mary's.

St. Michael's Parish Church

Beside Linlithgow Palace, on S shore of the loch, Linlithgow. Oct-May, Mon-Fri 10.00-12.00, 14.00-16.00. Jun-Sept, daily 10.00-12.00, 14.00-16.00, and by arrangement. Free. Parking available. Tel: Linlithgow (0506) 842188.

One of the finest examples of a medieval parish church in Scotland. Contemporary 'golden' crown by Geoffrey Clarke replaced the medieval crown which collapsed in 1820.

Scottish Mining Museum

At Morrisons' Haven, on B1348, 8m E of Edinburgh, on the E.Lothian coast at Prestongrange. All year, Tues-Fri 10.00-16.30, Sat & Sun 12.00-17.00; closed Mon. Guided tours, refreshments. Free. (Scottish Mining Museum Trust). Tel: 031 663 7519.

A former colliery site with 800 years of mining history. Visitor Centre provides audio-visual programme plus walk-through exhibition and displays concerning mining and related industries at site. Cornish Beam Pumping Engine House and Exhibition Hall containing mining artefacts. Self-drive Coal Heritage Trail to Lady Victoria Colliery. Also on view are three steam locomotives, a steam navvy, a colliery winding engine and remains of a Hoffman Kiln. Special 'Steam Days' on first Sunday of each month Apr-Oct. Organised parties must book. Refreshments, free car parking, picnic area, free leaflets.

South Queensferry Museum

Old Burgh Chambers, High Street. Mon, Thurs-Sat 10.00-13.00, 14.15-17.00, Sun 12.00-17.00. Free. Tel: 031-225 2424, ext. 6689 (Huntly House Museum).

Displays relating to the former Royal Burgh of Queensferry, local crafts and industries, the Burry Man, the Queensferry Passage and the two great bridges across the Forth.

Stevenson House

Near Haddington, East Lothian. House and garden: Jul-mid Aug, Thurs, Sat & Sun 14.00-17.30; other times by arrangement. Groups welcome by special appointment. (Mrs J C H Dunlop). Tel: Haddington (062 082) 3376.

Although the mansion house dates from the 13th century, the present house dates mainly from the 16th century. It was altered both structurally and in decoration during the 18th century. The guided tour includes details of the history, furniture, pictures and china. Well landscaped gardens (both House Garden and Walled Kitchen Garden).

Suntrap

At Gogarbank, between A8 and A71, 6m W of Edinburgh. Garden all year, daily 09.30-dusk. Advice centre all year, Mon-Fri 09.30-16.30; except when staff member is on holiday. 1 Apr-30 Sept, Sat and Sun 14.30-17.00. Parking available. Tel: 031-339 7283.

A gardening advice centre, of particular interest to owners of small gardens, offering courses of instruction. Outlying department of Oatridge Agricultural College. Special section for disabled gardeners.

Tantallon Castle
A198, 3m E of North Berwick. Opening standard,
except Oct-Mar closed Wed and Thurs am. (HS).
Tel: 031-244 3101.
Very impressive fortification in magnificent
clifftop setting. Earliest parts date from 14th
century. Associated with the Earls of Douglas.
Although the castle withstood a regular siege by
James V in 1528, it was eventually destroyed by
General Monk in 1651.

Torness Power Station
By A1, 6m SE of Dunbar. May-Sept. Guided tours,
weekdays and Sats, between 10.00 and 16.00. Free.
Refreshments available. Parking available. Tel:
(0368) 63500, ext. 3871/2.
Nuclear Power Station. This plant, the most
modern power station in Britain, is operated by
Scottish Nuclear Ltd and produces a quarter of all
the electricity consumed in Scotland.

Torphichen Preceptory
B792, 5m SSW of Linlithgow. Open summer
standard, closed in winter. (HS). Tel: 031-244
3101.
Once the principal Scottish seat of the Knights
Hospitallers of St. John. An exhibition depicts the
history of the Knights in Scotland and overseas.

Victoria
Manse Road Basin, Linlithgow. Easter-end Sept.
Sat and Sun 14.00-17.00. Also day and evening
charters by arrangement. (Mrs. A. Lamb). Tel:
Linlithgow (0506) 842575.
Replica of a Victorian steam packet boat offering
half-hour pleasure cruises on the Union Canal.
Special rates for school parties during the week.
Disabled visitors must be able to get out of
wheelchairs.

Whitekirk
St. Mary's Parish Church: on A198 approach from
A1 or from North Berwick. Free. Early-morning-
late evening. Sunday worship: 11.30 (unless stated
otherwise). Visitors welcome. Parking available.
Printed guide available.
The history and architecture of the church date
back to 6th century. Large red sandstone building
with high square tower (Norman). Famed for
pilgrimages in medieval times and a healing well.
The tithe barn behind the church is one of the
oldest still standing. Its history is linked to St.
Baldred.

Winton House
B6355, 6m SW of Haddington. Open by prior
arrangement to parties of 10 and over and

exceptionally to others. (Sir David and Lady
Ogilvy). Tel: Pencaitland (0875) 340222.
A gem of Scottish Renaissance architecture dating
from 1620. Associations with Charles I and Sir
Walter Scott. Beautiful plaster ceilings, unique
carved stone chimneys, fine pictures and furniture.
Terraced gardens, fine trees, in springtime masses
of daffodils. Personally conducted tours.

Yester Parish Church
Gifford, B6369, 5m SSE of Haddington. Apr-Oct
incl. All reasonable times. Free.
The Dutch-looking church dates from 1708, and in
it is preserved a late medieval bell, and also a 17th
century pulpit. A tablet near the church
commemorates the Rev John Witherspoon (1723-
94), born at Gifford, principal of Princeton
University, USA, and the only cleric to sign the
American Declaration of Independence. No guide
dogs.

FIFE

Aberdour Castle
At Aberdour, A921, 5m E of Forth Bridge. Opening
standard, except closed Thurs pm & Fridays in
winter. (HS) Tel: 031–244 3101.
Overlooking the harbour at Aberdour, the oldest
part is the tower, which dates back to the 14th
century. To this other buildings were added in
succeeding centuries. A fine circular doocot stands
nearby, and here also is St. Fillan's Parish Church,
part Norman, part 16th century.

Sir Douglas Bader Garden for the Disabled.
Duffus Park, Cupar. Daily during daylight hours.
Tel: Cupar (0334) 53722 ext 437.
The garden has raised beds, rock gardens, shrub
border, fountains, waterfalls and sheltered seating.

Balbirnie Craft Centre
In Balbirnie Park, Markinch, on eastern outskirts
of Glenrothes New Town. All year. Tue-Sat
10.00-17.30. Sun 13.30-17.30. Free. Tel:
Glenrothes (0592) 755975.
Craft Centre has seven workshops of potter,
leatherworker, jeweller and silversmith, modern
furniture maker, stained glass artist, fashion
designer and original paintings.

Balgonie Castle
By Markinch Fife. 2m E of Glenrothes on B921 off
A911. All year. Resident. 14.00–17.00. Parking
available. Tel: (0592) 750119.
14th-century castle with additions to 1702. 17th-
century home of Field Marshall Sir Alexander

Leslie, made Lord General of the Scottish Covenanting Army and 1st Earl of Leven. Garrisoned by Rob Roy McGregor with 200 clansmen in January 1716. Recently restored 14th-century chapel. 2-acre wildlife garden. Leather carver's workshop and tapestry weaver's studio. Continuing restoration of this family home, and living museum. Educational centre for school visits (no charge).

Balmerino Abbey

On S shore of River Tay on unclassified road 5m W of Newport. View from outside only. Free. (NTS). Tel: 031–336 2157.
Cistercian abbey founded in 1229 by Queen Ermingade, second wife of William Lyon. Ruined during period of reformation. Set in particularly peaceful gardens.

British Golf Museum

Opposite Royal & Ancient Golf Club in St. Andrews. June-Oct, daily 10.00–17.30; Nov, Tues-Sun 10.00–17.00; Dec, Tues-Sat 10.00–16.00. Parking available. Tel: (0334) 73423.
Interesting memorabilia for all golfing enthusiasts dating back to the time when the now world-famous game was originated in this historic town.

Burntisland Museum

Above library, High Street. Open library hours. Parking nearby. Free. Tel: Burntisland (0592) 260732.
New display – "Burntisland Edwardian Fair". Walk through the sights and sounds of the town's Fair as it was in 1910. Also view local history gallery.

Cambo Country Park

Kingsbarns, 3m N of Crail. Easter-end Sept every day 10.00–18.00. Parking available. Tel: Crail (0333) 50810.
Nature trails, woodland walk, indoor and outdoor play areas, farm animals. Cafeteria, restaurant, shop. Rocky and sandy seashores to explore.

Andrew Carnegie Birthplace Museum

Moodie Street, Dunfermline. Apr-Oct, Mon-Sat 11.00–17.00, Sun 14.00–17.00; Nov-Mar, daily 14.00–16.00. Free. Parking available. Tel: Dunfermline (0383) 724 302.
Weaver's cottage, birthplace of Andrew Carnegie in 1835, and linked Memorial Hall. The displays tell the fascinating story of the weaver's son who emigrated to America and became one of the world's richest men and who then gave away 350 million dollars for the benefit of mankind.

Craigtoun Country Park

Situated 2¹/₂m SW of St. Andrews. Easter-early Oct, daily, 10.30–18.30 (last admission 17.30). Parking available. Tel: (0334) 73666.
Miniature railway, crazy golf, trampolines, boating, bowling green, putting green, picnic areas. Open-air theatre, garden/glasshouses. Restaurant/cafeteria.

Crail Museum and Heritage Centre

62 Marketgate, Crail. Easter (2 weeks), Jun-Sept. Parking available. Tearooms and restaurants nearby. Tel: Crail (0333) 50869.
Exhibits include relics of golf, HMS Jackdaw, the Royal Burgh, the Collegiate Church, local architecture, the old harbour, crafts and Crail past and present. Heritage Centre and Information Office.

Crail Tolbooth

Marketgate, Crail. 9m SE of St. Andrews.
The Tolbooth dates from the early 16th century, displaying a fish weather vane, and a coat of arms dated 1602. In the striking Dutch Tower is a bell dated 1520, cast in Holland. There have been 18th and 19th century additions. Elsewhere in this picturesque fishing village which is the oldest Royal Burgh in the East Neuk of Fife, see the Collegiate Church dating back to the 13th century, the Mercat Cross topped by a unicorn, the harbour and the crowstepped, red-tiled houses. The Tolbooth is a library and Town Hall.

Crawford Arts Centre

93 North Street, St. Andrews. Gallery. All year. Mon-Sat 10.00–17.00, Sun 14.00–17.00. Gallery free. Tel: St. Andrews (0334) 74610.
Arts Centre with exhibition galleries and Studio Theatre. Children's workshops are regularly organised and exhibitions change monthly. Coffee available in galleries. Sculpture Court.

Culross Abbey

7¹/₂m W of Dunfermline. All reasonable times. Free. (HS). Tel: 031244 3101.
The remains of a 13th-century Cistercian Monastery. The choir of the Abbey Church is the present Parish Church.

Culross Palace

Culross, 7¹/₂m W of Dunfermline. Opening standard. (HS). Tel: 031–244 3101.
Culross, on the north shore of the River Forth, is a most remarkable example of a small town of the 16th and 17th centuries which has changed little in 300 years. The small 'palace' was built between

1597 and 1611 by Sir George Bruce, who developed the sea-going trade in salt and coal from Culross. With crow-stepped gables and pantiled roofs, the 'palace' also has outstanding painted ceilings. Other buildings which must be seen include the Study, the Town House, the Ark and the Nunnery.

Dunfermline Abbey and Palace

Monastery Street, Dunfermline. Apr-Sep, Mon-Sat 09.30–17.00, Sun 14.00–17.00; Oct-Mar, Mon-Sat 09.30–16.00, Sun 14.00–16.00. (HS). Tel: 031–244 3101.

This great Benedictine house owes its foundation to Queen Margaret, wife of Malcolm Canmore (1057–93) and the foundations of her modest church remain beneath the present nave, a splendid piece of late Norman work. At the east end are the remains of St. Margaret's shrine, dating from the 13th century. Robert the Bruce is buried in the choir, his grave marked by a modern brass. Of the monastic buildings, the ruins of the refectory, pend and guest-house still remain. The guest-house was later reconstructed as a royal palace, and here Charles I was born.

Dunfermline District Museum

Viewfield Terrace, Dunfermline. All year except public and local holidays. Mon-Sat 11.00–17.00. Free. Small shop. Parking available. (Dunfermline District Council). Tel: Dunfermline (0383) 721814.

The museum, housed in a Victorian villa, has an interesting local history collection, particularly of weaving and linen damask material, the industry that made Dunfermline famous. Special exhibitions are on show regularly. The small gallery which is contained in this museum has a monthly turnover of photographic, art and crafts exhibitions.

Earlshall Castle & Gardens

1m E of Leuchars, 6 miles from St.Andrews. Open Easter, Fri, Sat, Sun & Mon, thereafter 1 June-3rd Sun in Sept. Gardens, tearoom, picnic facilities, woodland walks. Tel: Leuchars (033483) 205.

Built in 1546 by Sir William Bruce, ancestor of present owners – private family home. Jacobite relics, military trophies and special exhibitions.

East Sands Leisure Centre

In St. Andrews immediately adjacent to East Sands beach. Parking available. Tel: (0334) 76506.

Leisure centre and pool with 50-metre water slide and all facilities.

Falkland Palace and Gardens

A912, 11m N of Kirkcaldy. 1 Apr-31 Oct, Mon-Sat 10.00–18.00, Sun 14.00–18.00; last admission

17.00. (NTS). Tel: Falkland (033 757) 397.

A lovely Royal Palace in a picturesque little town. The buildings of the Palace, in Renaissance style, date from 1501–41. This was a favourite seat of James V, who died here in 1542, and of his daughter Mary, Queen of Scots. The Royal Tennis Court of 1539 is still played on. The gardens are small but charming.

Fife Folk Museum

At Ceres, 3m SE of Cupar. Apr-Oct, daily (except Tue) 14.15–17.00. Small Museum Shop. (Central & North Fife Preservation Society). Tel: Ceres (033 482) 380 (outwith opening hours).

Situated in the 17th-century Weigh House, near an old bridge in an attractive village, this museum is a growing collection in a unique setting, showing the agricultural and rural life of Fife in bygone times. Countryside annexe opened in 1983. Nearby is the attractive Ceres Church (1806) with a horse-shoe gallery. Alternative wheelchair entrance.

Hill of Tarvit

A916, 2m S of Cupar. House: open weekends during Easter weekend & Apr, Sat & Sun 14.00–18.00; 1 May-30 Sep, daily 14.00–18.00 (last admission 17.30). Garden: grounds open all year, 10.00-sunset. (NTS). Tel: Cupar (0334) 53127.

An Edwardian country house of 1696, designed by Sir Robert Lorimer for Mr. Frederick Boner Sharp, an art collector of note. Fine collection of furniture, portraits, paintings, tapestries, chinese porcelain and bronzes. Tearoom (weekends only, Apr, May, Jun, Sep, Oct and daily July, Aug). Lovely gardens, woodland walk to hilltop viewpoint.

Kellie Castle and Gardens

On B9171, 3m NNW of Pittenweem, 10m S of St. Andrews. (Castle) Easter weekend, Apr, Sat, Sun 14.00–18.00; 1 May-31 Oct, daily 14.00–18.00 (last admission 17.30). (Gardens) all year, daily, 10.00-sunset. (NTS). Tel: Arncroach (033 38) 271.

Fine architecture of the 16th/17th centuries, though the earliest parts date from the 14th century. Owned by the Oliphants for over 250 years, then by the Earls of Mar and Kellie, it was restored nearly a century ago by Professor James Lorimer. His grandson, the sculptor Hew Lorimer, is resident custodian. Notable plaster work and painted panelling. 4 acres of fine Victorian gardens.

Kirkcaldy Museum and Art Gallery

By railway station. All year, Mon-Sat 11.00–17.00, Sun 14.00–17.00. Free. Tel: Kirkcaldy (0592) 260732.

Visit this award-winning museum to see the

heritage of Kirkcaldy District in a unique collection of fine Scottish paintings, a fascinating new historical display and a full programme of changing art, craft and local history exhibitions. Gallery shop for crafts, cards and local publications.

Largo
Birthplace of Alexander Selkirk 'Robinson Crusoe'. Statue of Crusoe at Lower Largo.

Leuchars Norman Church
A919, 5¹/₂m NW of St. Andrews. All reasonable times, Mar-Oct. Free.
Beautifully decorated 12th-century Norman chancel and apse, with unique 17th-century belltower.

Lochty Private Railway
On B940 (Cupar-Crail road) 7m W of Crail. Mid Jun-early Sept each Sun 13.45–17.00. A steam-hauled passenger service is operated on a half-hourly basis (approx). Free admission to site and free car/coach parking.
This private railway is run by the volunteers of the Fife Railway Preservation Group who operate and maintain the railway and run a steam-hauled passenger train service between Lochty and Knightsward. Steam and diesel locomotives, passenger coaches and goods wagons. Souvenir shop/visitor centre.

Monarch Deer Farm
Naemoor Road, Crook of Devon, Kinross. Dawn-dusk, 7 days a week. Tel: (05774) 310.
Red deer, rare breeds, riverside walk, waterfall, waterfowl. Picnic & play areas. Farmshop, venison & crafts, farmhouse teas. B. & B., farmhouse holidays, Caravan Club of G.B. site. Car parking & toilet facilities.

Pittencrieff House Museum
Pittencrieff Park, Dunfermline. May-Oct, daily except Tues 11.00–17.00. Tel: Dunfermline (0383) 722935 (May-Oct only) or Dunfermline (0383) 721814. Contact Ms. Lin Collis, Curator.
The house, standing in a fine park, was built in 1610 for the Lairds of Pittencrieff, and was bought by Andrew Carnegie in 1902. There are displays of local history, costumes, and an art gallery.

Ravenscraig Castle
On a rocky promontory between Dysart and Kirkcaldy. Opening standard. (HS). Tel: 031–244 3101.
Imposing ruin of a castle founded by James II in 1460. Later it passed into the hands of the Sinclair Earls of Orkney. It is perhaps the first British castle to be symmetrically designed for defence by firearms.

St. Andrews Botanic Garden
Open Apr and Oct, 10.00–16.00. May-Sept, 10.00–19.00.
Botanic Garden established on present site in 1960; best known for its Rock Garden and Peat Garden.

St. Andrew's Castle
Shore at St. Andrews. Opening standard. (HS). Tel: 031–244 3101.
This ruined castle, which has been rebuilt at several periods, overlooks the sea and was founded in 1200 as a fortress and principal residence of the Bishop of St. Andrews. Here Cardinal Beaton was murdered in 1546, and the first round of the Reformation struggle was fought out in the siege that followed. The impressive bottle dungeon and secret passage – a mine and counter-mine – are notable features.

St. Andrew's Cathedral
In St. Andrews. Charge for museum and St. Rule's (Regulus') Tower. Opening standard. (HS). Tel: 031–244 3101.
Founded in 1160 and consecrated in 1318, St. Andrew's Cathedral was once the largest church in the country. Its design is said to have exceeded the capacity of the builders of the day to construct it. The remains include parts of the east and west gables, the south wall of the nave, and portions of the choir and south transept. There is a fascinating museum and St. Rule's Tower, dating from 1127, gives a magnificent view of the town.

St. Andrews Preservation Trust Museum
12 North Street, St. Andrews. 1 Jul-31 Aug, daily 14.00–16.30. Donations. Parking available. Tel: (0334) 72152.
Converted fishermen's houses. Collection comprises items of interest from St. Andrews including displays from a well-known grocer's shop and also a chemist, fishing equipment and photographs. Features work of the Trust in conservation and renovation.

St. Andrews Sealife Centre
The Scores, St. Andrews. Open from 09.00, 7 days a week, throughout most of the year. Education – Teachers' notes and worksheets available. Parking available. Tel: (0334) 74786.
A new world beneath the waves. The superb setting of St. Andrews Bay makes the Sealife Centre an experience for anyone visiting the east coast of

Scotland. Hundreds of exciting sea creatures are on display and multi-level viewing gives the chance to come face to face with them, in displays designed to recreate their natural environment. There is now also an outdoor seal pool and British shark display. Oysters, the restaurant, offers meals throughout the day with panoramic views of the sea.

St Andrews University

St Andrews town centre. Tel: St Andrews (0334) 76161.
The oldest university in Scotland, founded in 1412. See the 15th-century Church of St Salvator, now the chapel for the united colleges of St Salvator (1455) and St Leonard (1512); St Mary's College (1537) with its quadrangle; and the 16th-century St Leonard's Chapel. Also in the town are St Mary's House built in 1523 and now St Leonard's School Library, and Holy Trinity Church with a 16th century tower and interesting interior features. Guided tours operate twice daily through the summer.

St. Fillan's Cave

Cove Wynd, Pittenweem, near harbour, 9m SSE of St. Andrews. All year, 10.00–13.00, 14.30–17.30. (St. John's Episcopal Church). Tel: (0333) 311495.
St Fillan's Cave gave Pittenweem (Pictish for The Place of The Cave) its name. Situated behind the harbour and now surrounded by houses, with tiny well and stone staircase. Augustinian monks from the Isle of May established the Priory, the Great House and the Prior's lodging above the cave, cutting through the rock from the garden to the holy cave-shrine below. Restored and rededicated in 1935.

St. Monan's Church

In St. Monan's, A917, 12m S of St. Andrews. All reasonable times. Free. Tel: St. Monan's (03337) 258.
Possibly a Ninianic foundation, c 400 AD. A place of healing from early times. David I was reputedly cured of an arrow wound here. It became a Royal Votive Chapel perhaps at that time. Alexander III initiated new building work c 1265. David II repaired and remodelled the Choir area in 1362 as a thanksgiving for deliverance from a storm at sea. James III gifted it to the Dominicans c 1460 and it became the Parish Church in 1646.

Scotstarvit Tower

Off A916, 3m S of Cupar. Opening standard. Free. (HS). Tel: 031–244 3101.
A fine tower known to have been in existence in 1579.

Scottish Deer Centre

On A91, 3m W of Cupar, 12m W of St. Andrews. All year except Christmas and New Year. Apr-Oct 10.00–17.00. Later in summer, weekends only. Nov-Mar: special openings Christmas and Easter. Parking available. Tel: (033781) 391.
The centre offers a unique opportunity to see many species of deer: feed, stroke and photograph during a ranger-led tour. Audio-visual show and walk through multi-media exhibition. Giant outdoor adventureland, treetop canopy walk and maze. Rare breeds of deer. Farm walk and picnic sites. Winery and wine exhibition, craft centre, restaurant and snack bar. Free parking, modern toilets.

Scottish Fisheries Museum

At Anstruther harbour, 10m SSE of St. Andrews. All year, daily Apr-Oct, 10.00–17.30, Sun 11.00–17.00. Nov-Mar, daily 10.00–17.00, Sun 14.00–17.00. Tel: Anstruther (0333) 310628.
16th to 19th century buildings housing marine aquarium, fishing and ships' gear, model and actual fishing boats (including 'Fifie' and 'Zulu' in harbour). Well presented museum documenting the life of the east coast fisher folk. Reference library, tearoom.

Silverburn

1/2m E of Leven, off the A915. Gardens open at all times. Mini-farm open Mon-Fri in Summer (Apr-Sept) 08.30–16.30. Winter open Mon-Fri 08.30–15.30. Sat/Sun, all year round 14.00–16.00. Free. Parking available. Tel: (0333) 27890, ext 214, or (0333) 27568.
The estate consists of gardens, old flax mill, children's mini-farm, children's play area, display of old farm implements, sea-shore trail, tree trail, nature trail and craft centre.

Adam Smith Theatre

Bennochy Road, Kirkcaldy. Tel: Kirkcaldy (0592) 260498.
Theatre with performances all year, named after Adam Smith, the economist who was born in Kirkcaldy in 1723.

John McDouall Stuart Museum

Rectory Lane, Dysart, 2m N of Kirkcaldy. 1 Jun-31 Aug, daily 14.00–17.00. Free. (Kirkcaldy District Council). Tel: Kirkcaldy (0592) 260732.
A 17th-century building restored by the NTS as part of their 'little houses' scheme. Birthplace of the explorer John McDouall Stuart (1815–1866) who crossed Australia's desert heart in 1861. Permanent display relating to the explorer. Nearby are other NTS 'little houses' and the picturesque harbour.

The Study

In Culross. All year by arrangement: Apr, Jun, Jul, Aug and Oct, Sat & Sun 14.00–16.00. (The Study, Town House and audio-visual). (NTS). Tel: Newmills (0383) 880359.

Built in 1633, the tower contains a turnpike stair and a large room on the first floor houses a museum. Fine views of the Forth. Tearoom.

Tentsmuir Point National Nature Reserve

S and E of Tayport between estuaries of rivers Tay and Eden. A919, B945 from St. Andrews or Tayport. (NCC) Tel: (0334) 54038.

An area of foreshore (Abertay Sands) and inland area of dunes, trees and marsh.

Town House, Culross

Sandhaven, Culross. Easter weekend, 1 May-30 Sept, daily 11.00–13.00, 14.00–17.00, Sat, Sun 14.00–17.00, or by arrangement. (Town House, The Study and audio-visual). (NTS). Tel: New Mills (0383) 880 359.

Built in 1526, with a double stair on the outside, it has a prison (criminals on the ground floor, witches in the attic) and was a meeting place for the Town Council. Audio-visual presentation.

Vane Farm Nature Reserve

On the S shore of Loch Leven, on B9097, off M90 and B996, 4¹/₂m S of Kinross. Apr-Oct, daily 10.00–17.00, Nov-Mar, daily 10.00–16.00, except Christmas/New Year. (RSPB). Tel: Kinross (0577) 62355.

The Nature Centre is a converted farm building equipped with displays designed to interpret the surrounding countryside and the loch. Between the last week of September and April, the area is a favourite feeding and resting place for vast numbers of wild geese and duck, and binoculars and telescopes are provided for observation. Also observation hide and nature trail. Shop selling wide range of RSPB gifts. Car park with picnic space. Path up Vane Hill through birchwoods with impressive views.

The West Port

St. Andrews, at W end of South Street. All times. Free. (HS). Tel: 031–244 3101.

One of the few surving city gates in Scotland. Its building contract is dated 1589 although it was completely renovated in 1843. It now consists of a central archway protected from above by battlements between two semi-octagonal turrets with gun loops.

PERTHSHIRE

Aberfeldy Distillery

On A827 E of Aberfeldy. Easter-Oct, Mon-Fri 10.00–16.00. Free. Parking available. Tel: (0887) 20330.

Malt distillery and maturation warehouse built by the Dewar family in 1898 in their home town of Aberfeldy. Shop and reception.

Abernethy Round Tower

At Abernethy, A913, 9m SE of Perth. Free apply to keykeeper. (HS). Tel: 031–244 3101.

A round tower, 74 feet high, dating from the 11th century. Tradition has it that Malcolm Canmore did homage to William the Conqueror here. Beside it is a Pictish symbol stone.

Achray Forest Drive

Off A821, 4m N of Aberfoyle. Easter-end Sep, daily 1000–1800. Tel: Aberfoyle (087 72) 383.

Scenic drive on Forestry Commission roads with fine views of the Trossachs. Walks, picnic places, play area and toilets.

Ardblair Castle

On A923 1m W of Blairgowrie. Open to parties by arrangement. Parking available. Tel: (0250) 3155. (Mr. L. Blair Oliphant).

Mainly 16th-century castle on 12th-century foundations, home of the Blair Oliphant family. Jacobite relics and links with Charles Edward Stuart. Room containing relics of Lady Nairne (nee Oliphant), author of Charlie is My Darling and other songs.

Atholl Country Collection

Blair Atholl. Open every afternoon 1330–1730 during the summer season, also weekday mornings from 0930 during Jul, Aug & Sept, or by arrangement. Group rates on application to John Cameron. Tel: Blair Atholl (079681) 232.

Folk museum with blacksmith's 'smiddy' and crofter's stable and byre. Emphasis on the importance of flax growing and spinning to the economy of the district. Road, rail and postal services, the school, the kirk, the vet and gamekeeper are all featured. Picnic area and adjacent to Blair Castle Craft Centre.

Balhousie Castle (Black Watch Museum)

Facing North Inch Park, Perth. Entrance from Hay Street. Mon-Fri 10.00–16.30 (Winter 10.00–15.30), Sun and public holidays (Easter-Sept) 14.00–16.30. Free. Closed 23 Dec-3 Jan incl. Parking available. Advance notice required for groups. Tel: Perth (0738) 21281, ext. 8530.

The castle houses the regimental headquarters and museum of The Black Watch (Royal Highland Regiment) and displays in chronological order the history of the famous Regiment from 1740 to the present time. Garden, museum shop.

Beech Hedge
A93, just S of Meikleour, 12m NNE of Perth.
Listed as the highest of its kind in the world the Beech Hedge was planted in 1746 and is now 600 yards long and 85 feet high. Information board.

Ben Lawers
Off A827, 14m WSW of Aberfeldy. Visitor Centre open 13 Apr-30 Sep, daily, 1000–1700. Visiting groups should make prior booking with the Ranger Naturalist. (NTS). Tel: Killin (056 72) 397.
Visitor Centre has information on botany, geology, history of the Ben Lawers, Perthshire's highest mountain (3,984 feet) noted for its variety of alpine flowers. There is a Nature Trail and a variety of guided walks in summer.

Blair Atholl Distillery Visitor Centre
S of Pitlochry centre. Open all year round, Mon-Sat 09.30–17.00. Sundays, Easter to Oct 12.00–17.00. Seating up to 90 persons. Licensed. Parking available. Tel: Pitlochry (0796) 2234.
Attractive group of distillery buildings with new Visitor Centre, audio-visual and shop. Restaurant.

Blair Castle
Near A9, 6m NNW of Pitlochry. 1 Apr-late Oct, every day 1000–1700; Sun in Apr, May and Oct 1400–1700. (Duke of Atholl). Tel: Blair Atholl (079 681) 207.
A white turreted baronial castle, seat of the Duke of Atholl, chief of Clan Murray. The oldest part is Cumming's Tower, 1269. Mary, Queen of Scots, Prince Charles Edward Stuart and Queen Victoria stayed here. When the castle was in Hanoverian hands in 1746, General Lord Murray laid siege to it on the Prince's behalf, making it the last castle in Britain to be besieged. The Duke is the only British subject allowed to maintain a private army, the Atholl Highlanders. There are fine collections of furniture, portraits, lace, china, arms, armour, Jacobite relics and masonic regalia. Licensed restaurant, gift shop, deer park, pony-trekking, nature trails, picnic areas and caravan park. Free car and coach parks.

Branklyn Garden
Dundee Road (A85) Perth. 1 Mar-31 Oct, daily 0930-sunset. (NTS). Tel: Perth (0738) 25535.
Described as the finest two acres of private garden in the country, this outstanding collection of plants, particularly rhododendrons, alpines, azaleas, herbaceous and peat garden plants, attracts gardeners and botanists from all over the world. Worth visiting for the Meconopsis blue poppies alone!

Caithness Glass (Perth)
Inveralmond, Perth. On A9 north of the town. All year. Free. Factory shop: Mon-Sat 0900–1700, Sun 1300–1700, Sun 1100–1700 (Easter-end Sep). Factory viewing: Mon-Fri 0900–1630. Open until 1800 7 days a week during Jul and Aug. (Caithness Glass plc.). Tel: Perth (0738) 37373.
Visitors are welcome at the factory to see the fascinating process of glass-making. Factory shop, paperweight museum and gallery, and licensed restaurant. Ample car/coach parking.

Castle Menzies
On B846, Weem, 1m W of Aberfeldy. In process of restoration by Menzies Clan Society. Apr-mid Oct, Mon-Sat 10.30–17.00, Sun 14.00–17.00. (Menzies Clan Society). Tel: Aberfeldy (0887) 20982.
Fine example of 16th-century Z-plan transitional fortified tower house with elaborately carved dormers added in 1577. Castle also houses Clan Menzies Museum.

Clan Donnachaidh Museum
Calvine, A9, 4m W of Blair Atholl. Mid Apr-mid Oct, weekdays (ex Tues) 10.00–13.00, 14.00–17.30, Sun 14.00–17.00. At other times by arrangement. Free. Parking available. Tel: Calvine (079 683) 264.
Clan Donnachaidh comprises Reid, Robertson, MacConnachie, Duncan, MacInroy and others. Old and new exhibits include items associated with the Jacobite Risings of 1715 and 1745. Restaurant nearby.

Crieff Visitors' Centre
On the A822 leading south from Crieff on Muthill Road. All year, daily 09.00-late, (09.00–16.00 winter). The factories are only open on working days. Free. Tel: Crieff (0764) 4014.
A large modern visitors' centre containing 180 seat restaurant, adjoining showroom and two walk round craft factories enabling visitors to see paperweights and pottery being made.

David Marshall Lodge
Off A821, 1m N of Aberfoyle. Mid Mar-mid Oct, daily 1000–1800. (FC).
Visitor Centre and starting point for walks in the Queen Elizabeth Forest Park. It commands wide views over the upper Forth Valley to the Menteith Hills, Campsie Fells and Ben Lomond.

The Dean's House

Cathedral Square, Dunblane. Easter weekend. June-Sept, Mon-Sat 10.30–12.30, 14.30–16.30. Also open first Sun of each month June-Sept 14.30–16.30. Free.

Garden. Parking available. Tel: Dunblane (0786) 824254.

Former dwelling house, built in 1624, of Dean James Pearson, housing a cathedral museum and library. Coffee lounge.

John Dewar & Sons

Dunkeld Road, Inveralmond, Perth. All year except holidays. Tours: Mon-Thur 1000 & 1115; 1400 and 1515. Fri 1000 and 1115. Free. (Mr. R. Keiller, visits organiser). Tel: Perth (0738) 21231.

During a conducted tour of 1^1/$_2$ hours visitors see the casks of matured whisky arriving for blending and follow the process through to bottling and despatch. Gift shop.

Drummond Castle Gardens

3m S of Crieff, W of Crieff/Muthill Road (A822) East Lodge. Apr-Sept, Wed, Sun 14.00–18.00, May-Aug, daily 14.00–18.00 (last admission 17.00). Parking available. Gardens only open to public. (Grimsthorpe and Drummond Castle Trust). Tel: (076481) 257.

The Gardens of Drummond Castle were originally laid out about 1630 by John Drummond, 2nd Earl of Perth. In about 1830, the parterre was Italianised and embellished with fine figures and statues from Italy. Probably one of the most interesting pieces of statuary is the Sundial, designed and built by John Mylne, Master Mason to King Charles I.

Dunkeld Bridge

Over the River Tay at Dunkeld. Free access at all times. Tel: (03502) 688.

One of Thomas Telford's finest bridges, built in 1809. An attractive riverside path leads from here downstream to the famous Birnam Oak, last relic of Macbeth's Birnam Wood, and then around the village of Birnam. Best view is from riverside garden. Wheelchair users should approach from the square through the archway. Hotel and tearoom adjacent.

Dunkeld Cathedral

High Street, Dunkeld, 15m NNW of Perth. Opening standard. Free. (HS). Tel: 031244 3101.

Refounded in the early 12th century on an ancient ecclesiastical site, this cathedral has a beautiful setting by the Tay. The choir has been restored and is in use as the parish church. The nave and the great north-west tower date from the 15th century.

Dunkeld Little Houses

Dunkeld, A9 15m NNW of Perth. Tourist Information Centre with audio-visual presentation. Open 2 Apr-22 Dec, Mon-Sat 1000–1300 and 1400–1700. Extended hours from 1 Jun-31 Aug; Mon-Sat 1000–1700, Sun 1400–1700. Free. (NTS). Tel: Dunkeld (03502) 460.

The houses date from the rebuilding of the town after the Battle of Dunkeld, 1689. Charmingly restored by NTS and Perth County Council, they are not open to the public but may been seen from the outside and information on them gained from the Visitor Centre or from the National Trust for Scotland's representative at the Ell shop.

Edradour Distillery

2^1/$_2$m E of Pitlochry. Mar-Oct, daily, 09.30–17.00. Nov-Feb-Mar, Sat 10.00–16.00 (shop only). Outside this by prior arrangement. Parking available. Tel: (0796) 2095.

The smallest distillery in Scotland, established 1825. A visit includes a guided tour, audio-visual presentation and tasting.

Elcho Castle

On River Tay, 3m SE of Perth. Opening standard. Closed in winter. (HS). Tel: 031–244 3101.

A preserved fortified mansion notable for its tower-like jambs or wings and for the wrought-iron grills protecting its windows. An ancestral seat of the Earls of Wemyss; another castle, on or very near the site, was a favourite hide-out of William Wallace.

Fair Maid's House Gallery

North Port, Perth. Scottish Craft Shop. Open daily 1000–1700 (except Sun) all year. Free. Tel: Perth (0738) 25976.

One of the oldest buildings in Perth, now housing contemporary Scottish crafts and a gallery. Exhibition changes each month, covering painting, embroidery, tapestry, sculpture, etching and print-making.

Fairways Heavy Horse Centre

Walnut Grove, by Perth. 2m E of Perth, off A85. Daily, Apr-Sept, 10.00–18.00. Free. Tel: (0738) 32561/25931.

This Centre is both a working and breeding establishment for Clydesdale horses. There are forty brood mares during the summer months and two premium stallions and newly born foals. Enjoy a ride in a wagon pulled by a team of Clydesdales. See a video show featuring the heavy horses at work throughout the year. A video shows the blacksmith at work at his anvil and the horses being shod.

Falls of Dochart
Killin. Free.
Dramatic waterfalls rushing through the centre of this picturesque highland village. On the island of Inchbuie on the river is the burial ground of Clan McNab. Access key to this island and to the graveyard available from Tourist Information Centre in Killin.

Fortingall Yew
Fortingall, 9m W of Aberfeldy
The great yew in an enclosure in the churchyard is over 3,000 years old, perhaps the oldest tree in Britain. The attractive village, which was rebuilt in 1900 with many thatched cottages is claimed to be the birthplace of Pontius Pilate.

Glengoulandie Deer Park
9m from Aberfeldy on B846 to Kinloch Rannoch. Daily, 09.00-one hour before sunset. Tel: Kenmore (08873) 261/306.
Native animals housed in a natural environment. Many endangered species are kept, and there are fine herds of red deer and Highland cattle. No guide dogs.

Glenturret Distillery
From Crieff take A85 to Comrie for 1m, then turn right at crossroads for $^1/_4$m. Mar to Dec. Tel: Crieff (0764) 2424.
Scotland's oldest distillery, with guided tour and free taste. Award-winning heritage centre, audio-visual and 3-D exhibition museum. Good facilites for blind visitors.

Great Scots Visitor Centre
In centre of Auchterarder, off High Street. Turn into Abbey Road opposite Craigrossie Hotel. Easter-June, 13.00–17.00; July-Oct, Mon-Sat 10.00–17.00; Sunday 13.00–17.00. Closed Oct-Easter. Parking available. Tel: (0764) 62079.
Last Scottish steam-driven factory steam engine and weaving display. Local history exhibition. Great Scots: the story of Scotland told by computerised lighting; special effects projected on a huge map of Scotland. The only Barrs Irn Bru bar in the world! Millshop: gifts, maps, books, tartan knitwear.

The Hermitage
Off A9, 2m W of Dunkled. All reasonable times. Car park. (NTS). Tel: (0796) 3233 or (03502) 667.
A picturesque folly, built in 1758, restored in 1952, and again in 1986. It is set above the wooded gorge of the River Braan. There are nature trails in the area.

Highland Motor Heritage Centre
Off A9 at Bankfoot, 6m N of Perth. Summer (and winter weekdays): daily 08.30–20.30, Sat evening until 23.00. Winter weekends: Nov-Easter, daily 10.00–18.00; Tel: Bankfoot (0738) 87696.
A collection of classic and vintage cars, costumes and memorabilia are displayed using authentic period settings. There are various other attractions in the museum such as a driving game, and free slot car racing and motor heritage videos. There is also a gift shop and licensed restaurant.

Huntingtower Castle
Off A85, 3m WNW of Perth. Opening standard. (HS). Tel: 031–244 3101.
A 15th century castellated mansion until 1600 known as Ruthven Castle. This was the scene of the Raid of Ruthven in 1582; James VI, then 16, accepted an invitation from the Earl of Gowrie to his hunting seat and found himself in the hands of nobles who demanded the dismissal of the royal favourites. When the king tried to escape, his way was barred by the Master of Glamis. The Ruthven conspirators held power for some months, but the Earl was beheaded in 1584. There are fine painted ceilings.

Inchmahome Priory
On an island in the Lake of Menteith, A81, 4m E of Aberfoyle. Access by boat from lakeside, Port of Menteith. Opening standard, except closed Oct-Mar. Admission free. (HS). Tel: Stirling (0786) 50000. Tel: 031–244 3101.
The ruins of an Augustinian house, founded in 1238, where the infant Mary, Queen of Scots was sent for refuge in 1547.

Innerpeffray Library
B8062, 4m SE of Crieff. All year. Mon-Sat 10.00–12.45, 14.00–16.45, Sun 14.00–16.00. Oct-Mar 10.00–12.45, 14.00–16.00, Sun 14.00–16.00. Closed all day Thurs. Parking available. Small tearoom. Tel: Crieff (0764) 2819.
The oldest library still in existence in Scotland, founded 1691, housed in a late 18th-century building. The nearby church was built in 1508.

Loch of the Lowes
Off A923, 2m NE of Dunkeld. Visitor Centre open Apr-Sept. Observation Hide is open permanently. (SWT). Tel: Dunkeld (035 02) 337.
This Scottish Wildlife Trust reserve is famous for its breeding osprey pair; visitors can watch these birds on the nest from a special hide. Visitor centre, staff ranger and observation hill. Wide range of provision for visitors with special needs.

Lower City Mills

Perth, near town centre. Signposted "Working Water Mill" from inner ring road. Easter-end Oct. Parking available. Tel: (0738) 30572.

18th/19th century water-powered town mill, restored to working order. Produces flour and oatmeal in the traditional manner. Craft Centre with workers in residence. Gift shop, unlicensed tearoom.

Megginch Castle Gardens

A85, 10m E of Perth. Apr-June and Sept, Wed only 14.00–17.00, Jul and Aug, Mon-Fri 14.00–17.00. Parking available. (Capt. Drummond of Megginch, the Rt. Hon. Lady Strange). Tel: (082 12) 222.

The gardens around the 15th-century castle have daffodils, rhododendrons and 1,000-year-old yews. There is a double-walled kitchen garden, 16th-century rose garden and 19th-century flower parterre as well as the Gothic courtyard with pagoda-roofed dovecote. There is also an interesting example of topiary, including a golden yew crown. An 18th-century physic garden is currently being restored and a new astrological garden has just been created.

Muthill Museum

In centre of Muthill Village beside Muthill Church and Tower. Easter and June-Sept, Tues, Thurs, Sat and Sun 14.30–17.00. Free.

Small Folk Museum/Heritage Centre housed in Georgian cottage (c.1760) in conservation village.

Pass of Killiecrankie

Off A9, 3m N of Pitlochry. NTS Visitor Centre: 1 Apr-21 Oct, daily 10.00–17.00. 1 Jun- 31 Aug, daily 09.30–18.00. Site open all day. (NTS). Tel: Pitlochry (0796) 3233.

A famous wooded gorge where in 1689 the Government troops were routed by Jacobite forces led by 'Bonnie Dundee'. Soldier's Leap. NTS centre features the battle, natural history and ranger services. The Pass is on the network of Garry-Tummel walks, which extend for 20 miles in the area. Snack bar.

Perth Art Gallery and Museum

George Street. All year, Mon-Sat 10.00–17.00. Free. Tel: Perth (0738) 32488.

Collections of local history, fine and applied art, natural history, archaeology and ethnography. Changing programme of temporary exhibitions.

Perth Repertory Theatre

High Street, Perth. Group concessions available, but variable. Tel: Perth (0738) 21031.

An intimate Victorian theatre, built in 1900 in the centre of Perth, offering a variety of plays, musicals, etc. Induction loop for hard of hearing. Coffee bar and restaurant open during day and for performances.

Pitlochry Festival Theatre

Off A9 bypass at Pitlochry local access. May-Oct, open all day for refreshments and art exhibitions. (Box Office) Tel: Pitlochry (0796) 2680.

Scotland's 'Theatre in the Hills' is now rehoused in a magnificent new building by the River Tummel. Opened by Prince Charles in 1981, it is a must for all holidaymakers. Catering and bar facilities. Coffee shop open from 10.00; lunch 12.00–14.00; restaurant 18.30–20.00. Magnificent view from foyer and restaurant.

Pitlochry Power Station and Dam

Off A9 at Pitlochry. Late Mar-late Oct, daily 09.40–17.30. (North of Scotland Hydro-Electric Board. Tel: (08824) 251.

One of nine hydro stations in the Tummel Valley. The dam created Loch Faskally where boating and fishing are available. Salmon can be seen through windows in the fish ladder. Exhibition and film inside power station.

Queen Elizabeth Forest Park Visitor Centre

Off A821, 1m N of Aberfoyle. Mid Mar-mid Oct, daily 10.00–18.00, also open December weekends up to 24th. (FC).

In this 45,000 acres of forest, moor and mountainside there are many walks. On A821 is the David Marshall Lodge, a picnic pavilion and information centre. 'Duke's Road' from Aberfoyle to the Trossachs has fine views.

Queen's View, Loch Tummel

On B8019, off A9, 8m NW of Pitlochry. Open at all times. Free. Parking available. Tel: (0796) 3123.

A magnificent viewpoint along Loch Tummel to the peak of Schiehallion, 3,547 feet. Queen Victoria visited it in 1866. Toilets, car park and seasonal cafe.

Rumbling Bridge

A823 at Rumbling Bridge. Free. All reasonable times.

The River Devon is spanned here by two bridges, the lower one dating from 1713, the upper one from 1816. A footpath from the north side gives good access to spectacular and picturesque gorges and falls, one of which is known as the Devil's Mill. Another, Cauldron Linn, is a mile downstream, whilst Vicar's Bridge is a beauty spot a mile beyond this.

Scone Palace
Off A93 (Braemar Road), 2m NE of Perth. Easter-Oct, Mon-Sat 09.30–17.00; Sun 13.30–17.00 (Jul & Aug 10.00–17.00), other times by arrangement. (Earl of Mansfield). Tel: Perth (0738) 52300.
The present castellated palace, enlarged and embellished in 1803, incorporates the 16th-century and earlier palaces. It has notable grounds and a pinetum and is still a family home. The Moot Hill at Scone, known in the 8th century and earlier, was the site of the famous coronation Stone of Scone, brought there in the 9th century by Kenneth MacAlpine, King of Scots. In 1296 the Stone was seized by the English and taken to Westminster Abbey. The ancient Abbey of Scone was destroyed by followers of John Knox. Magnificent collection of porcelain, furniture, ivories, 18th-century clocks and 16th-century needlework. Full catering facilites. Coffee shop, restaurant, produce and gift shop, gardens, playground, banqueting, pinetum. Parties of disabled visitors welcome.

The Scottish Horse Museum
The Cross, Dunkeld. Easter to end Sept, daily 10.30–12.00, 14.00–17.00. (Scottish Horse Trust). Tel: Dunkeld (035 02) 296.
Exhibits, uniforms, photographs, maps and rolls of all those who served in this Yeomanry Regiment.

Scottish Tartans Museum
Drummond Street, Comrie, 6m W of Crieff. Apr-Oct, Mon-Sat 10.00–17.00, Sun 11.00–15.00; Nov-Mar, check times with office. Tel: Comrie (0764) 70779.
The Scottish Tartans Society is the custodian of the largest collection in existence of material relating to tartans and Highland dress, historic costumes and artefacts; weavers cottage; dye plant garden. There is a research service on surnames, clans and tartans, and an archive of every known tartan.

Stuart Strathearn
Muthill Road, Crieff. June-Sept daily 09.00–19.00. Oct-May, daily 09.00–17.00. Free. Tel: (0764) 4004.
Manufacturer of Scottish crystal. Visit the factory to view the traditional skills involved in the production and decoration of the full lead crystal displayed in the factory shop. Video on glass making, picnic area and large car park.

Tullibardine Chapel
Off A823, 6m SE of Crieff. All reasonable times. Free. Apply adjacent farmhouse. (HS). Tel: 031–244 3101.
Founded in 1446, this is one of the few rural churches in Scotland which was entirely finished and still remains unaltered.

Tummel Forest Centre
On B8019, 6m NW of Pitlochry. Open from Mon before Easter-last Fri in Oct 10.00–17.30. Free. Parking available. (FC). Tel: (03502) 284.
Audio-visual slide show and presentation of various aspects of local history and industries. Forest walks, reconstructed Highland clachan and partly excavated ring fort.

Wade's Bridge
On B846, north of Aberfeldy. All times. Free. Parking available.
The bridge across the River Tay was begun in 1733 by General Wade with William Adam as architect. It is considered to be the finest of all Wade's bridges. The Black Watch Memorial is a large cairn surmounted by a kilted soldier, erected close to the bridge in Queen Victoria's Jubilee Year (1887). Easy access across lawn to river bank.

Weavers House and Highland Tryst Museum
64 Burrell Street, Crieff on the A822. Summer: 09.00–18.30 daily. Winter: 10.00–16.30; closed Sun. Parking available. Tel: (0764) 5202.
Award-winning museum in the historic capital of Strathearn, on the turbulent frontier where Highlands meet Lowlands. A 'Hands-on' museum where the dressing-up chest and Victorian games are a favourite with children. In a row of 18th and 19th century weavers houses, visitors can see working tartan handloom weavers, spinners and cordwainers produce yarn, yardage and cordwain for sale. Open air activities and tea garden. Coffee parlour (seats 20) in the old weavers house. Shop. Extensive Scottish clan and family archive with records of over 2,000 tartans. More than just a museum!

ANGUS

Aberlemno Sculptured Stones
At Aberlemno, B9134, 6m NE of Forfar. All times. Free. (HS). Tel: 031–244 3101.
In the churchyard is a splendid upright cross-slab with Pictish symbols; three other stones stand beside the road.

Angus Folk Museum
Off A94 at Glamis, 5m SW of Forfar. 13 Apr-30 Sept daily 11.00–17.00, last tour 16.30. Parking available. (NTS). Tel: (030 784) 288.
Kirkwynd Cottages, a row of 19th century cottages with stone-slabbed roofs, containing relics of domestic and agricultural life in the county in the

19th century and earlier. In the agricultural annexe are farming implements and a Bothy Exhibition, including tape recorded information.

Arbroath Abbey

In Arbroath. Opening standard. (HS). Tel: 031–244 3101.

Founded in 1178 by William the Lion and dedicated to St Thomas of Canterbury, it was from here that the famous Declaration of Arbroath asserting Robert the Bruce as King was issued in 1320. Important remains of the church survive; these include one of the most complete examples of an abbot's residence.

Arbroath Art Gallery

Arbroath Library, Hill Terrace. All year, Mon-Fri 09.30–18.00, Sat 09.30–17.00. Free. (Angus District Council). Tel: Arbroath (0241) 72248.

Changing exhibitions of paintings by local artists and others. Special interest exhibits.

Arbroath Cliffs Nature Trail

Starts from north east end of promenade. 3 miles of cliff scenery, well-defined footpath. Descriptive booklets from local tourist information centre.

Arbroath Signal Tower Museum

Signal Tower, Ladyloan, Arbroath. All year, Nov-Mar, Mon-Fri 14.00–17.00, Sat 10.30–13.00 and 14.00–17.00; Apr-Oct, Mon-Sat 10.30–13.00 and 14.00–17.00 also in Jul-Aug, Sun 14.00–17.00. Free. Pre-booking for groups essential. (Angus District Council). Tel: Arbroath (0241) 75598 or Montrose (0674) 73232.

Part of Scotland's Fishing Heritage Trail, this museum is housed in a tower formerly used to communicate with the Bell Rock lighthouse offshore.

Ardestie and Carlungie Earth-Houses

N of A92, Ardestie: about 6m E of Dundee, at junction with B962. Carlungie: 1m N on unclassified road to Carlungie. All times. Free. (HS). Tel: 031–244 3101.

Two examples of large earth-houses attached to surface dwellings. At Ardestie the gallery is curved and 80 feet in length: the Carlungie earth-house is 150 feet long, and is most complex; used in first centuries AD.

Barrack Street Museum, Dundee

City centre. All year, Mon-Sat 10.00–17.00. Free (prior notice of groups preferred). (City of Dundee District Council). Tel: Dundee (0382) 23141, ext. 65152.

Dundee's museum of natural history. Main displays on wildlife of Tayside including highlands. Also geology. Also on show the skeleton of the Famous Tay Whale. New Art and Nature Gallery devoted to temporary exhibitions exploring the influence of nature on the Arts. Small shop, toilets.

Barrie's Birthplace

9 Brechin Road, Kirriemuir. Easter weekend, 28 Apr-30 Sep, Mon-Sat 11.00–17.30, Sun 14.00–17.30, last admission 30 mins before closing. (Mrs. Elizabeth M Drainer). Tel: Kirriemuir (0575) 72646 or 72538 (Home). (NTS).

Here in this white-washed cottage playwright, Sir John M Barrie was born in 1860. Manuscripts, personal possessions and mementoes of actors and producers associated with his plays are shown in the museum.

Braes of Angus

Forest walks, picnic areas etc, at Glen Doll, 18 miles NW of Kirriemuir, N to Clova, then unclassified road.

Brechin Museum

In Library, St. Ninian's Square. All year, Mon-Tues-Wed-Fri 09.30–18.00, Thur 09.30–19.00, Sat 09.30–17.00. Free. (Angus District Museums). Tel: Montrose (0674) 73232.

Housed in Public Library. New displays include archaeology, medieval burgh and Cathedral, civic and industrial history, folk life and paintings by local artist David Waterson.

Brechin Round Tower

At Brechin. Viewed from the churchyard. All reasonable times. (HS). Tel: 031–244 3101.

12th century cathedral, partially demolished in 1807, restored 1900–02. Attached to the cathedral are one of the two remaining round towers of the Irish type in Scotland, dating back to the 11th or 12th century.

Broughty Castle Museum, Dundee

Broughty Ferry, 4m E of city centre. Mon-Thu & Sat 10.00–13.00 and 14.00–17.00 (closed Fri). Sun, (Jul-Sep only) 14.00–17.00. Free. Booking essential for large groups. (City of Dundee District Council). Tel: Dundee (0382) 23141 or 76121.

Former estuary fort, now museum. Local history gallery includes sections on fishing, lifeboat, ferries and growth of town. Important collection of relics from Dundee's former whaling industry including harpoons, knives and scrimshaw. Wildlife of seashore. Display of arms and armour, and military history of castle. Small shop.

The Caledonian Railway
Preserved at Brechin, this fine Caledonian terminus is open to visitors. Part of the former Caledonian main line is in the process of restoration.

Camperdown House and Country Park, Dundee
Off A923, near junction with A972, 3m NW of city centre. Tel: Dundee (0382) 23141.
A mansion of c. 1829 for the 1st Earl of Camperdown, son of Admiral Lord Duncan, victor of the Battle of Camperdown, 1797. The Mansion is situated in 395 acres of beautiful parkland containing many rare trees (including Camperdown Elm). Golf, tennis, horseriding, putting, caravan park. Mansion houses a self-service restaurant. Award-winning "Battle of Camperdown" Adventure Play Park and Wildlife Centre in grounds too.

Camperdown Wildlife Centre
Off A923, near junction with A972, 3m NW of Dundee. Open all year. 10.00–16.00. (City of Dundee District Council). Parking available. Tel: Dundee (0382) 623555.
Indigenous wildlife collection including deer paddocks, wildcats, pinemartens, European brown bear, lynx, wolves, arctic foxes, pheasants, golden eagle and buzzards. Wildfowl ponds, bantams and large selection of domestic stock. Guided tours for educational parties. Snack bar and souvenir shop, restaurant 250 yards away, large play complex adjacent (free). Free parking.

Clatto Country Park, Dundee
Dalmahoy Drive, off A972 from Dundee city centre. All year, 10.00–dusk. Free. Parking available. Tel: Dundee (0382) 89076.
Reservoir area with 24 acres of water protected by a shelter belt of conifer and mixed woodland. Particularly popular for windsurfing, canoeing and dinghy sailing (instruction available). Rowing boats, windsurfing, canoeing and sailing equipment for hire. Barbecue facilities. Children's adventure play area.

Crombie Country Park
On B961, 3½m NE of Newbigging. All year, 10.00–dusk. Free. Free car parking available. Buses by appointment. (Tayside Regional Council). Tel: Carmyllie (024 16) 360.
Victorian reservoir with the appearance of a natural loch. Extensive conifer woodland and some broadleaf and specimen trees in 250 acres of land. Wildlife hides, trails, display and interpretation centre. Ranger Centre with environmental displays, woodland and lochside walks. Guided walks, talks,

picnic and barbecue areas, children's play park and conservation areas.

Damside Garden Herbs and Arboretum
Situated 2 miles inland off the A92 between Montrose and Stonehaven by Johnshaven. Follow signs. May-Oct, 11.00–19.00 (closed Mon). Apr and Nov, Dec, weekends only 11.00–19.00. Closed Jan, Feb and March. Parking available. Tel: (0561) 61498.
Herb garden of over 8 acres showing the history of Celtic, Roman, Monastic and Formal Herbs. Newly planted arboretum. Information area. Tearoom seating 36. Shop (not licensed).

Edzell Castle and Garden
Off B966, 6m N of Brechin. Opening standard. Daily, Sun pm only. (HS). Tel: 031–244 3101.
The beautiful pleasance, a walled garden, was built by Sir David Lindsay in 1604; the heraldic and symbolic sculptures are unique in Scotland, and the flower-filled recesses in the walls add to the outstanding formal garden, which also has a turreted garden house. The castle itself, an impressive ruin, dates from the early 16th century, with a large courtyard mansion of 1580.

Glamis Castle
A94, 5m SW of Forfar. Easter, 13 Apr-15 Oct, daily 12.00–17.30, other times by prior arrangement only. Parking available. (Earl of Strathmore and Kinghorne). Tel: Glamis (030 784) 242.
This famous Scottish castle, childhood home of Her Majesty Queen Elizabeth The Queen Mother and birthplace of The Princess Margaret, owes its present appearance to the period 1675–87. Portions of the high square tower, with walls 15 feet thick, are much older. There has been a building on the site from very early times and Malcolm II is said to have died there in 1034. The oldest part of today's castle is Duncan's Hall, legendary setting of Shakespeare's famous play 'Macbeth'. There are also fine collections of china, painting, tapestry and furniture. Gift shop, gallery shop (selling pictures, prints and antiques); garden produce stall, self-service restaurant (serving light lunches and a range of home-baked items).

Glenesk Folk Museum
16m NNW of Brechin. Easter weekend and every weekend thereafter until 1 June, then Mon-Sat 14.00–18.00, Sun 13.00–18.00 until 30 Sept; daily June-Sept 14.00–18.00. Tel: (035 67) 236/254.
A series of displays shows everyday life in Glenesk from c. 1800 to the present day. Tearoom/craft/gift shop on the premises known as "the Retreat".

House of Dun

On A935 4m W of Montrose. Grounds and courtyard buildings open Easter weekend 21/22 Apr and 28 Apr-21 Oct, daily 11.00–17.30. Parking available. (NTS). Tel: Bridge of Don (067 481) 264.

Palladian house overlooking the Montrose Basin, built in 1730 for David Erskine, Lord Dun, to designs by William Adam. Exuberant plasterwork in the saloon. Courtyard buildings include a potting shed and gamekeeper's room. Also Angus Weavers giving displays of weaving linen tableware on traditional looms. Woodland walks.

Howff Burial Ground, Dundee

Meadowside. Daily, closes 17.00 or dusk if earlier. Tel: Dundee (0382) 23141.

Formerly the gardens of the Greyfriars' Monastery, the Howff was granted to Dundee as a burial ground by Mary, Queen of Scots. Used as a burial ground between the 16th and 19th centuries, it contains many finely carved tombstones. It was also used as a meeting place by Dundee's Incorporated Trades until 1778, hence the name 'howff'.

Kerr's Miniature Railway

In Arbroath, on the seafront 600 yds from parking beside Hotel Seaforth on A92. Apr-Sept, Sat and Sun 14.00–17.00. July and first half of Aug, daily 14.00–17.00. Tel: (0241) 79249.

Steam and petrol-hauled trains (four locos). Runs for 400yds alongside BR Edinburgh to Aberdeen main line. Tunnel, footbridge and platforms, turntable and loco shed. Miniature bus and fire engine give trips for children along promenade.

McManus Galleries, Dundee

Albert Square, city centre. All year, Mon-Sat 10.00–17.00. Free. (Prior notice of groups preferred). (City of Dundee District Council). Tel: Dundee (0382) 23141.

Dundee's principal museum and art gallery. Local history displays including major new galleries on trade and industry, social and civic history. Archaeology gallery under redevelopment. Art galleries contain important collection of Scottish and Victorian paintings; and silver, glass, ceramics, furniture. Regular touring exhibitions. Shop.

Meigle Museum

In Meigle, on A94, 12m WSW of Forfar. Opening standard. Closed Fri. (HS). Tel: 031–244 3101.

This magnificent collection of 25 sculptured monuments of the Celtic Christian period, all found at or near the old churchyard, forms one of the

most notable assemblages of Dark Age sculpture in Western Europe.

Mills Observatory, Dundee

Balgay Hill, north side of the city. Apr-Sep, Mon-Fri 10.00–17.00, Sat 14.00–17.00; Oct-Mar, Mon-Fri 15.00–22.00, Sat 14.00–17.00. Free. (Booking essential for large groups). (City of Dundee District Council). Tel: Dundee (0382) 67138.

A public astronomical observatory with telescopes, displays on astronomy and space exploration, lecture room with projection equipment, and small planetarium. Viewing of sky subject to weather conditions. Balcony with fine views over River Tay. Audio-visual programme. Small shop and toilets.

Monikie Country Park

Off B961, 1m N of Newbigging, 10m N of Dundee. All year, 10.00-dusk. Car parking is free. (Tayside Regional Council). Tel: Newbigging (082 623) 202.

Country park situated on a reservoir complex of three areas of water, constructed by the Dundee Water Company over a span of 20 years from 1845. Ground consists of parkland and mixed woodlands, and covers 185 acres. Countryside Ranger Service, woodland walks, watersports including canoeing, sailing and windsurfing courses. Children's play area, rowing, sailing and windsurf hire, picnic areas with barbecue sites. Tearoom in summer.

Montrose Basin

Important wildfowl refuge and nature reserve holding high populations of wintering birds. Estuary of the River Esk.

Montrose Museum

Panmure Place. Apr-Oct, Mon-Sat 10.30–13.00, 14.00–17.00; Jul and Aug: Sun 14.00–17.00; Nov-Mar, Mon-Fri 14.00–17.00, Sat 10.30–13.00 and 14.00–17.00. Tel: Montrose (0674) 73232.

Extensive local collections cover the history of Montrose from prehistoric times to local government reorganisation, the maritime history of the port, the natural history of Angus and local art. Pictish stones, Montrose silver and pottery; whaling artefacts; Napoleonic items (including a cast of his death mask). Paintings by local artists and local views, sculpture by W. Lamb.

Red Castle

Off A92, 7m S of Montrose. All times. Free.

This red stone tower on a steep mound beside the sandhills of Lunan Bay probably dates from the 15th century when it replaced an earlier fort built for William the Lion by Walter de Berkely. Robert the Bruce gave it to Hugh, 6th Earl of Ross, in 1328.

Royal Research Ship Discovery
On Waterfront, Victoria Dock. Apr-May, Sep, daily 13.00–17.00, Sat, Sun, Bank Holidays 11.00–17.00. Jun-Aug 10.00–17.00. Tel: Dundee (0382) 201175/25282.
Royal Research Ship Discovery is Captain Scott's famous antarctic exploration vessel, built in Dundee in 1901. The ship's crew welcomes visitors aboard. Final restoration by Dundee Heritage Trust.

St. Cyrus Nature Reserve
From Montrose take A92 north after crossing North Esk River and take first right for ¹/₂m. From St. Cyrus take A92 S for 1m, turn left before North Esk River and proceed for ¹/₂m. Apr-Oct, Tues-Sun 09.00–17.00. Free. Parking available. Tel: (06748) 3736.
The reserve has many botanical and ornithological interests while the visitor centre houses displays on local history, natural history, salmon fishing and wildlife. There are children's games, a salt water aquarium and an audio visual. Guide dogs not allowed.

St. Vigean's Museum
¹/₂m N of Arbroath (HS). Tel: 031–244 3101.
A cottage musum containing Pictish gravestones which are among the most important groups of early Christian sculpture in Scotland. Attractive St. Vigean's Church nearby.

Shaw's Sweet Factory, Dundee
Fulton Road, west end of Kingsway by NCR factory. Mar-mid June, every Thurs 13.30–16.30; mid June-mid Aug, Mon, Tues, Thurs, Fri 13.30–16.30; mid Aug to Christmas, Thurs 13.30–16.30. Free. Coach parties or large groups Mon-Fri any time by phone (1 hour's notice). Parking available. Tel: (0382) 610369.
1940's style sweet factory, producing old fashioned sweets using traditional methods. The sweet-maker will demonstrate and explain the precedure. Factory shop and mini-museum of sweet making.

Tay Bridges
The present Railway Bridge carries the main line from Edinburgh to Aberdeen. Built between 1883 and 1887, it replaces the first Tay Railway Bridge which was blown down by a storm in 1879 with the loss of a train and 75 lives after being in use for less than 2 years. The Rail Bridge is the longest in Europe. The Road Bridge was opened in 1966, spanning the River Tay from Dundee to Newport-on-Tay, a distance of 1¹/₂ miles. It is made of box girders resting on 42 concrete piers, and took over 3 years to build. No disabled access to Road Bridge walkway.

Unicorn, Dundee
Victoria Dock, just E of Tay Road Bridge. 1 Apr-mid Oct, every day. Sun-Fri 10.00–17.00, Sat 10.00–16.00. Open in winter, daily, 10.00–16.00. (The Unicorn Preservation Society). Tel: Dundee (0382) 200900.
The Unicorn is a 46-gun wooden frigate now in the course of restoration. She was launched at Chatham in 1824 and is Britain's oldest ship afloat. Displays on board of the history of the Unicorn, ship-building and the Royal Navy.

University Botanic Garden, Dundee
Off Riverside Drive. Open Mar-Oct 10.00–16.30, Nov-Feb 10.00–15.00. Free. Honesty box for donations. Tel: (0382) 66939.
A teaching collection of native and exotic plants in 9 hectares of naturalistically landscaped garden, tropical and temperate planthouses. Award winning visitors centre.

ABERDEEN

Aberdeen Art Gallery and Museums
Schoolhill. All year. Mon-Sat 10.00–17.00 (Thu 10.00–20.00), Sun 14.00–17.00. Free. Parking available. (City of Aberdeen District Council). Tel: Aberdeen (0224) 646333. Artline: 24-hour recorded information service, Tel: Aberdeen (0224) 632133.
Permanent collection of 18th, 19th and 20th century art with the emphasis on contemporary works. A full programme of special exhibitions. Music, dance poetry, events, film, coffee shop, gallery shop, reference library, print room. Disabled access: A lift is available in the Gallery for disabled visitors which takes them to the first floor galleries and also gives access to the McBey print room and reference library. Guide dogs permitted.

Bridge of Dee
Built in 1500 by Bishop Gavin Dunbar in James V's reign. Its seven arches span 400 feet and it formerly carried the main road south. The mediaeval solidity of the structure is enlivened by heraldic carvings.

Brig O'Balgownie
At Bridge of Don, N of Aberdeen, upstream of main

A92 bridge.
Also known as the 'Auld Brig o' Don', this massive arch, 62 feet wide, spans a deep pool of the river and is backed by fine woods. It was completed c. 1320 and repaired in 1607. In 1605 Sir Alexander Hay endowed the bridge with a small property, which has so increased in value that it built the New Bridge of Don (1830), a little lower down, at a cost of £26,000, bore most of the cost of the Victoria Bridge, and contributed to many other public works. Now closed to motor vehicles.

Cruickshank Botanic Gardens
Chanonry. All year, Mon-Fri 09.00–16.30, also May-Sep, Sat and Sun 14.00–17.00. Free. (City of Aberdeen). Tel: Aberdeen (0224) 272704/272664.
Extensive collection of shrubs, herbaceous and Alpine plants, heather and succulents. Rock and water gardens.

James Dun's House
Schoolhill. All year. Mon-Sat 10.00–17.00. Free. Tel: Aberdeen (0224) 646333.
This former residence of James Dun, master and rector of Aberdeen Grammar School, is now a museum featuring special temporary exhibitions of particular interest to families. Museum shop.

Duthie Park and Winter Gardens
Polmuir Road/Riverside Drive. All year inc. Public Holidays, daily, 10.00 until 30 mins before dusk. Free. Tel: Aberdeen (0224) 583155.
One of Aberdeen's many parks – and one of the favourites with the residents. It features an all-year round display of colour in the Winter Gardens, as well as the unique 'rose hill' where the city's enthusiasm for roses is best seen. Westburn, Seaton, Hazlehead also well worth a visit.

Fishmarket
Off Market Street. Tel: Aberdeen (0224) 897744.
Aberdeen is one of the major fishing ports of Britain, landing hundreds of tons of fish daily. Every morning (Mon-Fri) the fishing fleets unload their catches, which are auctioned off amid tense bustle. Best visited 0730–0930.

His Majesty's Theatre
Rosemount Viaduct in city centre. Dress circle bar and stalls bar. Parking available. Tel: Aberdeen Box Office (0224) 641122.
Aberdeen's main theatre, opened in 1906 to the designs of Frank Matcham, seats 1,500. It offers a varied programme of entertainment, including ballet, opera, musicals, plays and concerts. Lounge bars.

Jonah's Journey
Rosemount Place, Aberdeen. All year, Mon-Fri 10.00–16.00; Sat/Sun by arrangement. Closed public holidays. Parking available. Tel: (0224) 647614.
The Gallery forms activity-based learning centre on aspects of life in Bible times; ideal for children as they can dress-up, grind grain, spin, weave. Also they can visit a well, a nomad's tent, Israelite house, workshop, etc. Coffee lounge, shop (Mon-Sat 1000–1200). Street market Sat 1000–1200.

Kings College/Marischal College
Contrasting colleges of the University of Aberdeen founded 1495. Kings's Buildings date from 16th century, interesting chapel and crown spire. Marischal spectacular granite frontage built in 1906.

Maritime Museum
Provost Ross's House, Shiprow. All year, Mon-Sat 10.00–17.00. NTS Visitor Centre open 1 May-30 Sept, Mon-Sat 10.00–16.00. Free. Tel: Aberdeen (0224) 585788.
Situated in one of Aberdeen's oldest buildings (1593), the museum uses models, paintings and audio-visual displays to tell the story of local shipbuilding, the fishing industry, the North Sea oil and gas developments. Museum shop.

Provost Skene's House
Guestrow, off Broad Street. All year. Mon-Sat 10.00–17.00. Free. Parking available. Tel: Aberdeen (0224) 641086.
Erected in the 16th century, this house bears the name of its most notable owner, Sir George Skene, Provost of Aberdeen 1676–1685. Remarkable painted ceilings and interesting relics. Period rooms suitably furnished and displays of local history. A video gives an introduction to the house and its history. Provost Skene's kitchen (for tea, coffee and light meals).

St. Andrew's Cathedral
King Street. May-Sept, Mon-Sat. 10.00–16.00. Sunday-Service Times. Gift shop. Coffee/tea and homebakes on Fridays 10.00–12.00. Tel: Aberdeen (0224) 640290.
Cathedral Church of Scottish Episcopal Diocese of Aberdeen & Orkney. Contains the Seabury Memorial, commemorating the consecration of Samuel Seabury of Connecticut in Aberdeen in 1784, the first Bishop of America (and of the Anglian Communion outside the British Isles). Also see the permanent exhibition Christian Heritage of North East Scotland, an ecumenical

exhibition showing some of the distinctive features of Christianity of North East Scotland. 4 Church Trails.

St. Machar's Cathedral
Chanonry. All year, 09.00–17.00. Free. Tel: Aberdeen (0224) 485988.
This granite cathedral was founded in 1131 on an earlier site, though the main part of the building dates from the mid-15th century. The west front with its twin towers is notable, and the painted wooden heraldic nave ceiling is dated 1520. The nave is in use as a parish church.

Satrosphere, The Discovery Place
West end of Union Street in Justice Mill Lane. Open all year. Mon-Sat 10.00–16.00, Sun 13.30–17.00, closed Tues. Parking available. Tel: (0224) 213232.
'Hands-on' Science & Technology Centre with between 70–100 do-it-yourself experiments, exploring sound, light, energy and the environment. Special events every 2/3 months. Small cafe and seating area. Shop selling science-based toys and gifts.

University Zoology Museum
Along King Street, left at roundabout, situated at corner of Tillydrone Avenue and St. Machar's Drive. All year (except Christmas and New Year), Mon-Fri 09.00–17.00. Free. Parking available. Tel: (0224) 272850.
A general collection of exhibits on the animal kingdom, with particular emphasis on British birds and insects. The Botany Department gardens are adjacent. Disabled visitors welcome, but prior notice required.

NORTH EAST

Aden Country Park
On A950 between Old Deer and Mintlaw, 30m N of Aberdeen. Park open all year. Heritage centre May-Sept 11.00–17.00. Apr and Oct weekends only 12.00–17.00. Unlicensed restaurant. Parking available. Tel: Mintlaw (0771) 22857.
Country Park of 230 acres containing woodland walks, picnic areas, caravan site etc. Ranger service and exhibitions, picnic areas, adventure playground, numerous walks and features. Restaurant, shop and tourist information centre. It is home of the award-winning North East of Scotland Agricultural Heritage Centre.

Alford Valley Railway
Murray Park, Alford. Weekends only Apr/May/Sept; daily 11.00–17.00 Jun/Jul/Aug. Parking available. Tel: Alford (09755) 62326.
Narrow gauge railway running from Alford Station and Museum to Haughton Country Park, approx. 1 mile and Haughton Country Park to Murray Park (1 mile). Terminus near Alford Transport Museum.

Anderson's Story Book Glen
At Maryculter, off Lower Deeside Road, 5m WSW of Aberdeen. 1 Mar-31 Oct, 10.00–18.00. 1 Nov-end Feb, Sat & Sun 11.00–16.00. Tel: Aberdeen (0224) 732941.
The Glen is the result of 11 years work by the Anderson family. Storybook characters and places come to life in a colourful outdoor setting of flowers, streams and waterfalls. There are seating areas and a restaurant seating 250 which serves snacks and 3-course meals.

Auchindoun Castle
In Glen Fiddich, 3m SE of Dufftown, $^1/_2$m off A941. All times: viewed from the outside only. Free. (HS). Tel: 031-244 3101.
A massive ruin on the summit of an isolated hill, enclosed by prehistoric earthworks. The corner stones were removed to Balvenie. In Queen Mary's wars the castle was the stronghold of the redoubtable 'Edom o'Gordon' who burned Corgarff. Jacobite leaders held a council of war there after Dundee's death at Killiecrankie.

Balmoral Castle
On A93, 8m W of Ballater. Grounds and exhibition of paintings and works of art in the Ballroom of the castle. May-Jun-Jul daily except Sun 10.00–17.00. Donations from entry fee to charities. Tel: Crathie (03397) 42334.
The family holiday home of the Royal Family for over a century. The earliest reference to it, as Bouchmorale, was in 1484. Queen Victoria visited the earlier castle in 1848; Prince Albert bought the estate in 1852; the castle was rebuilt by William Smith of Aberdeen with modifications by Prince Albert and was first occupied in 1855. Souvenir shops, refreshment room, country walks and pony-trekking.

Balvenie Castle
At Dufftown, A941, 16m SSE of Elgin. Apr.-Sept., standard opening; closed Oct.-Mar. Parking available. (HS). Tel: 031-244 3101.
Picturesque ruins of 13th century moated stronghold originally owned by the Comyns.

Visited by Edward I in 1304 and by Mary Queen of Scots in 1562. Occupied by Cumberland in 1746. The corner stones came from Auchindoun.

Banchory Woollen Mill
North Deeside Road (On A93). Open Mon.-Sat. 09.00–17.00 (Summer); 10.00–17.00 (Winter). Tel: (03302) 3231.
One of the finest selections in this area of pure wool knitwear, tweeds, tartans, travel rugs, gifts and souvenirs. For overseas visitors they operate VAT free shopping and "Post-it-Home" schemes. Enjoy a refreshing morning coffee, snack, lunch or afternoon tea (all with home-baking) in the 40-seat "Crofter's Kitchen" coffee shop. Large free car park to rear of Mill Shop.

Baxter's Visitor Centre
¹/₂m W of Fochabers on main Aberdeen-Inverness road (A96). 5 Mar-24 Dec, Mon-Fri 10.00–16.30 (Fri-last tour 14.00). Weekends 14 May-11 Sep (no tours). No Factory Tours during staff holidays or at weekends. Weekend opening 14/15 Apr, 19 May-30 Sept; Sat 1100–1730, Sun 1230–1630. Please book in advance. No coaches in Jul/Aug in afternoons. Tel: Fochabers (0343) 820 393, ext 241.
Slide show with commentary, Old Baxter Shop, replica of the original George Baxter and Sons establishment where Baxters of Speyside were formed. George Baxter cellar, shop and tearoom. Highland cattle nearby.

Bennachie Forest
Don View Visitor Centre. 4 miles north of Monymusk on minor road from Kemnay to Keig. Exhibits, picnic place, walks.

Braemar Castle
A93, at Braemar. May-early Oct, daily 10.00–18.00. (Farquharson of Invercauld). Tel: Braemar (03397) 41219. Out of season (03397) 41224.
This turreted stronghold, built in 1628 by the Earl of Mar, was burnt by Farquharson of Inverey in 1689. It was rebuilt about 1748 and garrisoned by Hanoverian troops. There is a round central tower, a spiral stair, barrel-vaulted ceilings and an underground pit prison. Fully furnished family residence. Interesting historical relics. Free car and bus park.

Brodie Castle
Off A96, 4¹/₂m W of Forres. Easter and 1 Apr-30 Sept. Mon-Sat 11.00–18.00, Sun 14.00–18.00. 6–21 Oct, Sat 11.00–18.00, Sun 14.00–18.00. Last admission 17.15. (NTS). Tel: Brodie (030 94) 371.
The castle, associated with the Brodie family for 500 years, was largely rebuilt after the earlier structure was burned in 1645; it is based on a 16th century 'Z' plan, with additions made in the 17th and 19th centuries. The house contains fine French furniture, English, Continental and Chinese porcelain, and a major collection of paintings. A woodland walk has been laid out in the gardens by the edge of a 4-acre pond. Picnic area, adventure playground, car park, shop and small tearoom.

Buckie Maritime Museum
Cluny Place. All year, Mon.-Fri. 10.00–20.00, Sat. 10.00–12.00. Free. Tel: Forres (0309) 73701.
Displays on fishing methods, coopering, lifeboats, navigation and local history. The Peter Anson Gallery houses watercolours of the development of fishing in Scotland. Sales point.

Bullars of Buchan
Off A975, 7m S of Peterhead. Tel: (02612) 2789.
A vast chasm in the cliffs, 200 feet deep, which no man can see with indifference said Dr Johnson in 1773. A haunt of innumerable seabirds.

Burns Family Tombstones and Cairn
Off A94, 8m SW of Stonehaven at Glenbervie Church. All times. Free.
The Burnes (Burns) family tombstones in the churchyard were restored in 1968 and a Burns memorial cairn is nearby.

Candacraig Gardens and Gallery
In Strathdon on A944 (formerly B973), 11m N of Ballater. Victorian walled garden: May-Oct., daylight hours: Gallery Cafe (licensed) open during garden season: evening illuminations by arrangement. Parking available.
Victorian walled garden with 1820 Gothic style summerhouse. Formal and modern rose gardens and period fountain. Visitor centre and tearoom. Plants for sale.

Castle Fraser
3m S of Kemnay off A944. Castle: 28 Apr-30 Sept, daily 14.00–18.00 (last tour 17.15). 6–21 Oct, Sat & Sun 14.00–18.00. Gardens and Grounds: all year, daily 09.30-sunset. (NTS). Tel: (033 03) 463.
Castle Fraser begun about 1575. It belongs to the same great period of native architectural achievements as Crathes and Craigievar Castles, and is the largest and grandest of the Castles of Mar. Two notable families of master masons, Bel and Leiper, were involved in its construction, completed in 1636. Noted for its great hall. Garden and picnic area and tearoom.

Cloverleaf Fibre Stud

8m N of Huntly. Take A97, then take turning to Netherdale on right. The farm is 300 yds from junction. Guided tours at 11.00, 13.00 and 15.00; other times by arrangement. Parking available. Tel: (04665) 879.

Working farm breeding llamas, alpacas, guanacos, reindeer, goats bearing cashmere, cashgora and mohair. Rare breeds of sheep. Garments for sale on display together with spinning and knitting fibres obtained from the animals.

Craigellachie Bridge

Near A941, just N of Craigellachie, 12m SSE of Elgin. Parking available.

One of Thomas Telford's most beautiful bridges. Opened in 1814, it carried the main road till 1973 when a new bridge was built alongside. It has a 152 ft. main span of iron, cast in Wales, and two ornamental stone towers at each end.

Craigievar Castle

On A980, 6m S of Alford, 26m W of Aberdeen. Castle: 28 Apr-30 June and 3–30 Sept, daily 14.00–18.00. 1 July-2 Sept, daily 11.00–18.00. (Last tour 17.15). Grounds: open all year 09.30-sunset. (NTS). Tel: Lumphanan (03398) 83635.

This masterpiece of Scottish baronial architecture stands on the Braes of Leochel-Cushnie in the midst of 100 acres of farm and parkland. Completed in 1626 for William Forbes (Willie the Merchant or Danzig Willie), it stands today virtually as the builders left it – a fairytale castle of turrets, chimney stacks, corbelling and gables. Famous for magnificent original plaster ceilings, carved panelling and all family contents. Picnic area, woodland walks.

Craigston Castle

Turriff-Fraserburgh road, 10m SE of Banff. Open 25 days in summer. Please make appointment. (Mr. Bruce Urquhart). Tel: King Edward (08885) 228.

Seat of the Urquhart family since its building 1604–07. Can be seen from the Turriff to Fraserburgh road. Adjacent woodlands of interesting species etc. Parking.

Crathes Castle and Gardens

Off A93, 3¹/₂m E of Banchory. Castle, Visitor Centre, Shop and Restaurant. 13 Apr.-28 Oct. daily 11.00–18.00: last tour of castle 17.15, booked parties at other times. Garden and Grounds all year 09.30 to sunset. Tearoom. Parking available. Ranger service and special event. No dogs in garden or restricted areas, please – dog trail available. Enquiries and bookings: Tel: (033 044) 525.

The double square tower of the castle dates from 1533 and the building, an outstanding example of a Scottish tower house, was completed in 1660. The notable interior includes the fascinating painted ceilings, dating from 1599, in the Chamber of the Nine Nobles, the Chamber of the Nine Muses and the Green Lady's Room. The Queen Anne and Victoria wings were destroyed by fire in 1966. The Queen Anne wing only was rebuilt and opened in 1972. Yew hedges dating from 1702 enclose a series of small gardens with fine collections of trees and shrubs. Nature trails designed for wheelchair users. Shop, licensed restaurant and snack bar; formal gardens, grounds with 7¹/₂ miles of wayfaring trails, visitor centre with exhibition rooms and field study centre. Ample parking, cars and coaches.

Crathie Church

Crathie, 8m W of Ballater. 1 Apr.-31 Oct., daily 09.30–17.30. Sun 14.00–17.00 (services held at 11.30, Sun). Free. Tel: Crathie (03384) 208.

This small church, built in 1895, is attended by the Royal Family when in residence at Balmoral.

Creative Cask Company

On B9102, 14m S of Elgin. All year, daily (except Wednesdays). Free. Tel: Carron (03406) 273/456.

Craft workshop manufacturing furniture from oak whisky casks.

Cullen Old Church

Signposted in Cullen. Apr-Sept, daily 14.00–16.00. Free. Parking available. Tel: (0542) 40757.

12th-century parish church with 16th and 17th century additions. Although essentially 14th century, this church with its fine sacrament house still incorporates some 12th-century work.

Delgatie Castle

Off A947, 2m E of Turriff. Fri, Sat, Sun 14.00–17.00. (Capt. Hay of Hayfield). Tel: Turriff (0888) 63479 (09.00–12.00).

Tower house, home of the Hays of Delgatie, dating back to the 11th century with additions up to the 17th century. Its contents include pictures and arms; the notable painted ceilings were installed c. 1590. Mary, Queen of Scots stayed here for three days in 1562; a portrait hangs in the room she used. Turnpike stair of 97 steps.

Drum Castle

Off A93, 10m W of Aberdeen. 13 Apr-30 Sep, daily 14.00–18.00. 6–21 Oct, Sat & Sun 14.00–18.00 (last admission 17.15). Grounds open all year, 09.30-sunset. (NTS). Tel: (03308) 204.

A massive granite tower built towards the end of

the 13th century adjoins a mansion of 1619. The Royal Forest of Drum was conferred in 1323 by Robert the Bruce on his armour-bearer and clerk-register, William de Irwin. The family connection remained unbroken until the death of Mr H Q Forbes Irvine in 1975. The house stands on a 400 acre estate with lawns, rare trees and shrubs, and inside are antique furniture and silver, family portraits and relics. Coffee room, adventure playground and wayfaring course.

Drummuir Castle
Just off B9014 between Keith and Dufftown. May-Sept, Sun 14.00–16.00. Parking available. Tel: (054 281) 225.
Victorian castle with magnificent Lantern Tower. Recently restored home of the Duff family. Tours provided by owners. Garden and grounds.

Duff House
At Banff. Apr-Sept, Mon-Sat 09.30–19.00, Sun 14.00–19.00; closed in winter. Parking available. (HS). Tel: 031–244 3101.
Although incomplete, William Adam's splendid and richly detailed mansion is among the finest works of Georgian Baroque architecture in Britain. There is an interpretative exhibition.

Dufftown Museum
The Tower, The Square, Dufftown. Apr, May, Oct, Mon-Sat 10.00–12.30, 13.30–17.30; June, Sept, Mon-Fri 10.00–18.00, Sat 10.00–12.30, 13.30–18.00, Sun 14.00–17.00; July, Aug, Mon-Fri 09.30–12.30, 13.30–18.30, Sun 14.00–18.00. Free. Tel: Forres (0309) 73701.
Displays on local and social history themes. Tourist Information Office.

Duffus Castle
Off B9012, 5m NW of Elgin. Opening standard. Free. (HS). Tel: 031–244 3101.
Massive ruins of a fine motte and bailey castle, surrounded by a moat still entire and water-filled. A fine 14th century tower crowns the Norman motte. The original seat of the de Moravia family, the Murrays, now represented by the Dukedoms of Atholl and Sutherland.

Dunnottar Castle
Off A92, S of Stonehaven. Apr-Oct, Mon-Sat 09.00–18.00. Sun 14.00–17.00. Last entry half hour before closing. Nov-Mar 09.00-Dusk. Sat & Sun closed. Tel: Stonehaven (0569) 62173.
An impressive ruined fortress on a rocky cliff 160 feet above the sea, a stronghold of the Earls Marischal of Scotland from the 14th century.

Montrose besieged it in 1645. During the Commonwealth wars, the Scottish regalia were hidden here for safety. Cromwell's troops occupied the castle but in 1652 this treasure was smuggled out by the wife of the minister at Kinneff, 7 miles south, and hidden under the pulpit in his church.

Elgin Cathedral
North College Street, Elgin. Opening standard. (HS). Tel: 031244 3101.
When entire, this was perhaps the most beautiful of Scottish cathedrals, known as the lantern of the North. It was founded in 1224, but in 1390 it was burned by the Wolf of Badenoch. It did not fall into ruin until after the reformation. Much 13th-century work still remains; the nave and chapter house are 15th-century. There is a 6th-century Pictish slab in the choir.

Elgin Museum
High Street, Elgin. Apr-Sept, Tues-Fri 10.00–17.00, Sat 11.00–16.00. Admission charges. Tel: (0343) 543675.
An award-winning museum housing a world famous collection of Old Red Sandstone, Permian and Triassic fossils. Also exhibited are items ranging from prehistoric to modern times and natural history specimens of the area.

Finzean Bucket Mill
From Banchory take B974 to Strachan, continue on B976 (Aboyne road) as far as Finzean Stores. Take left (To Forest of Birse) for 3m. May-Oct 11.00–17.00; closed Thurs. Out of season by arrangement. Parking available. Tel: (033 045) 633.
Mid 19th century, water powered, wood turning mill with 13½-ft waterwheel. Visitors can see mill in operation (milling conditions permitting). Shop, Information Centre.

Fochabers Folk Museum
Fochabers. All year. Winter, daily 09.30–13.00, 14.00–17.00. Summer, daily 09.30–13.00, 14.00–18.00. Parking available. (Christies (Fochabers Ltd.). Tel: Fochabers (0343) 820362.
An interesting conversion of an old church housing a large collection of horse-drawn carts on the top floor, and on the ground floor a varied collection of local items, giving the history of Fochabers over the past 200 years.

Fordyce
Unclassified road off A98, 3m SW of Portsoy. Parking available. Tel: (02612) 2419.
Award-winning conservation village built around a

16th-century castle and an early church containing splendid canopied tombs.

Fowlsheugh Nature Reserve
Access along cliff-top path north from small car park at Crawton, signposted from A92, 3m S of Stonehaven. All times. Free. (RSPB). Tel: 031–557 3136.
Large and spectacular seabird colony, best seen April-July. Small visitor centre in car park is open Apr-Aug, with information warden.

Fyvie Castle
Off A947, 8m SE of Turriff and 25m NW of Aberdeen. 28 Apr and 3–30 Sept, daily 14.00–18.00. 28 May-2 Sept daily 11.00–18.00. 6–21 Oct, Sat & Sun 14.00–18.00 (last admission 17.15). (NTS). Tel: Fyvie (065 16) 266.
The five towers of Fyvie Castle enshrine five centuries of Scottish history, each being built by the five families who owned the castle. The oldest part dates from the 13th century and it is now one of the grandest examples of Scottish baronial architecture. Apart from the great wheel stair, the finest in Scotland, and the 17th century morning room, with its contemporary panelling and plaster ceiling, the interior as created by the 1st Lord Leith of Fyvie reflects the opulence of the Edwardian era. There is an exceptionally important collection of portraits including works by Batoni, Raeburn, Ramsay, Gainsborough, Opie and Hoppner. In addition, there are arms and armour and 16th century tapestries. Tearoom, grounds including loch.

Glendronach Distillery
On B9001, between Huntly and Aberchirder, 19m N of Inverurie. All year, Mon-Fri 10.00 or 14.00 (by arrangement only). Free. Tel: Forgue (046682) 202 (08.30–16.30).
Visitor Centre and guided tour around malt whisky distillery dating from 1826.

Glenfarclas Distillery
Off A95, 17m WSW of Keith and 17m NE of Grantown-on-Spey. All year. Mon-Fri 09.00–16.30. Closed 25, 26 Dec and 1,2 Jan. June-Sept, every day. Sat 10.00–16.00, Sun 13.00–16.00. Other times by arrangement; groups by arrangement. Tel: Ballindalloch (08072) 257/245.
Tours of a well-known malt whisky distillery, visual exhibition and museum of old illicit distilling equipment in Reception Centre.

Glenfiddich Distillery
Just N of Dufftown on A941, 16m S of Elgin. All year, weekdays 09.30–16.30 (except between Xmas and New Year). Also Easter-mid Oct, Sat 09.30–16.30, Sun 12.00–16.30. Free. Tel: Dufftown (0340) 20373.
After an audio-visual programme available in six languages, visitors are shown around the distillery and bottling hall and are then offered a complimentary dram. Picnic area, gift shop at car park.

The Glenlivet Distillery Visitor Centre
B9008, 10m N of Tomintoul. Easter-end Oct, Mon-Sat 10.00–16.00. Free. Coach parties by arrangement. Tel: Glenlivet (08073) 427 (during season) and Keith (05422) 6294 (during winter).
Guided tours of distillery. Exhibits of ancient whisky tools and artefacts and life-size reproduction of Landseer's painting 'The Highland Whisky Still'. Free whisky sample. Children under 8 not admitted to production areas but welcome to Reception Centre.

Glenshee Chairlift
Off A93, 10m S of Braemar. Daily, 09.00–17.00. Charge for chairlift. Tel: Braemar (033 83) 320/(03397) 41320.
Ascends the Cairnwell mountain (3,059 feet) from the summit of the highest main road pass in Britain (2,199 feet). Restaurant.

Grampian Transport Museum
At Alford, 25m W of Aberdeen on A944. 1 Apr-30 Sep, daily 10.30–17.00 also first two weekends in Oct. Tel: Alford (09755) 62292.
A large independent transport museum, opened in April 1983. Extensive collection of road vehicles, including horse drawn, steam, commercial and vintage motor cars. Pedal cycles and motorcycles also well represented. Highland rail transport is described in the railway museum in Alford's former railway station.

Haddo Country Park
B999 Aberdeen-Pitmeddan road, signposted to right between Pitmedden and Tarves. All year. Discovery Room open daily, 11.00–18.00 during summer season and at various other times. Free. Parking available – charge. (NTS). Tel: (065 15) 489.
180 acres, including woodland walks, lake, ponds, bird hides, picnic areas, adventure playground and Discovery Room. Ranger service.

Haddo House
Off B999, 4m N of Pitmedden, 19m N of Aberdeen. (House) 13 Apr-28 Oct, daily 14.00–18.00. (Shop

& restaurant) 13 Apr-28 Oct, daily 11.00–18.00. (NTS). Tel: (06515) 440.

Designed in 1731 by William Adam, a pupil of Sir William Bruce and father of the Adam brothers, for William, second Earl of Aberdeen, Haddo House replaced the old House of Kellie, home of the Gordons of Methlick for centuries. Much of the interior is 'Adam Revival' carried out about 1880 for John, seventh Earl and first Marquess of Aberdeen and his Countess, Ishbel. Garden, Trust shop and tearoom.

Haughton Country Park
25m W of Aberdeen on A944, 1/2m N of the village of Alford. All year. Free. Parking available. Tel: (09755) 62453 or 62107.

Country Park with visitor centre and caravan site.

Huntly Castle
Castle Street, Huntly. Opening standard. (HS). Tel: 031244 3101.

An imposing ruin which replaced mediaeval Strathbogie Castle which, until 1544, was the seat of the Gay Gordons, the Marquesses of Huntly, the most powerful family in the north until the mid-16th century. There are elaborate heraldic adornments on the castle walls. The castle, now stands in a wooded park, was destroyed by Moray in 1452, rebuilt, then rebuilt again in 1551–54, burned 40 years later and again rebuilt in 1602.

Huntly Museum
In the Library, Main Square. All year Tues-Sat 10.00–12.00, 14.00–16.00. Free. (North East of Scotland Museums Service). Tel: Peterhead (0779) 77778.

Permanent local history exhibitions and temporary thematic exhibitions twice a year.

Inverurie Museum
Inverurie. All year, Mon, Tues, Thurs, Fri 14.00–17.00, Sat 10.00–13.00, 14.00–16.00. Free. (North East of Scotland Museums Service). Museum shop. Tel: Peterhead (0779) 77778.

Permanent display of local archaeology and thematic exhibitions three times a year. Just outside the town, on B993, is a 60 foot high motte, the Bass.

Kildrummy Castle
A97, 10m W of Alford. Opening standard. Weekends only in winter. (HS). Tel: 031–244 3101.

The most extensive example in Scotland of a 13th century castle. The four round towers, hall and chapel remains belong in substance to the original. The great gatehouse and other work is later, to the

16th century. It was the seat of the Earls of Mar, and played an important part in Scottish history until 1715 when it was dismantled.

Kildrummy Castle Gardens Trust
A97, off A944, 10m W of Alford, Aberdeenshire. Apr-Oct, daily 10.00–17.00. Children must be accompanied. Parking available. Tel: (09755) 71264/71277.

The shrub and alpine garden in the ancient quarry are of interest to botanists for their great variety. The water gardens lie below the ruined castle. Specimen trees are planted below it in the Back Den. Play area, video room, woodland walk. Plants for sale. Interesting old stones displayed. Museum opens on request. Dogs must be kept on leash.

Kinneff Old Church
Off unclassified road, E of A92, 2m N of Inverbervie. All reasonable times. Free. Parking available. (Kinneff Old Church Preservation Trust).

Part of this historic church formed the original building in which the Crown Jewels of Scotland were hidden for nine years after being smuggled from Dunnottar Castle through Cromwell's besieging army in 1651. In the present church, which dates from 1738, are the recently restored memorials to the parish minister, Rev. James Grainger, who concealed the regalia under the flagstones of the church; and to the governor of the castle, Sir George Ogilvy of Barras.

Lecht Ski Tow
Off A939, 7m SE of Tomintoul. During ski-ing season only. (Lecht Ski Co Ltd.). Tel: (09756) 51440.

Ski tows operating to slopes on both sides of the Lecht Road which here is a section of the military road built in the mid-18th century from Perth to the Moray Firth. Famous for its snowfalls. Licensed cafeteria, ski hire, ski school. Free car park.

Leith Hall
B9002, 7m S of Huntly. (House) 28 Apr-30 Sept, daily 14.00–18.00; 6–21 Oct, Sat & Sun 14.00–18.00 (last admission 17.15). (Garden) all year 09.30-sunset. (NTS). Tel: (04643) 216.

The mansion house of Leith Hall is at the centre of a 263-acre estate which was the home of the head of the Leith and Leith-Hay family from 1650. The house contains personal possessions of successive lairds, most of whom followed a tradition of military service. The grounds contain varied farm and woodlands. There are two ponds, a bird observation hide and three countryside walks, one leading to a hilltop viewpoint. Unique 18th century stables; Soay sheep; ice house. Extensive and interesting informal garden of borders, shrubs and rock garden. Picnic area and tearoom.

Loanhead Stone Circle
1/4m NW of Daviot, 5m NW of Inverurie, off B9001. All reasonable times. Free. (HS). Tel: 031–244 3101.
The best known example of a widespread group of recumbent stone circles in east Scotland.

Lossiemouth Fisheries and Community Museum
Situated at the harbour, East Basin, Lossiemouth. Apr-Sept, Mon-Sat 11.00–13.00 and 14.00–17.00. Parking available. Tel: (0343 81) 3772.
Permanent features include Memorial Room for lost/drowned, killed in active service, fishermen and study of the late J. Ramsay McDonald, Prime Minister.

McEwan Gallery
On A939, 1m W of Ballater. Open all year, 10.00–18.00; other times by arrangement. Free. Parking available. Tel: Ballater (03397) 55429.
An unusual house built by the Swiss artist Rudolphe Christen in 1902, containing works of art, mainly of the Scottish school. Also natural history and sporting books. Occasional special exhibitions are held. Full advisory and restoration services.

Mill of Towie
Drummuir, Keith, Banffshire. Mill: Easter and May-Oct 10.30–16.30. (Mr. Rod Stewart). Tel: Drummuir (054 281) 274.
Nestling in the hills beside the River Isla, the Mill of Towie has been restored to full working order. Tours of the 19th-century oatmeal mill by the miller. Picnic and play area beside the river.

Moray Motor Museum
Take the Lossiemouth Road (A941) from Elgin centre bypass; 800yds on right. Apr-Oct 11.00–17.00. Parking available. Tel: (0343) 544933.
Unique collection of over 40 cars and motor cycles housed in an old mill building.

Mortlach Church
Dufftown. Easter-Oct, daily 10.00–16.00 (except during services). Donations. Tel: Dufftown (0390) 20380.
Founded c 566 AD by St. Moluag. Part of present building dates from 11th/12th centuries. In 1016 it was lengthened by 3 spears length on the command

of King Malcolm after his victory over the Danes. Believed to be one of the oldest churches in continual use for public worshop. Sculptured stones in vestibule and very fine stained glass. Battle stone in churchyard; old watch tower.

Muchalls Castle
Off A92, 11m S of Aberdeen. Open last week of June to end of first week in Sept. Sun and Tues 14.30–16.30. Any other date or time: written arrangement only. Parking available. (Mr. & Mrs. A.M. Simpson).
Overlooking the sea, this tiny 17th-century castle was built by the Burnetts of Leys in 1619. Ornate plasterwork ceilings and fine fireplaces are features and there is also a secret staircase. Gardens.

Muir of Dinnet Nature Reserve
Midway between Aboyne and Ballater on A97, 1m N of junction with A93. Mid-May-Sept, Thurs-Mon between 10.00–18.00. Visitor Centre closed Tues and Wed; Reserve open at all times. Free. Parking available. Tel: (03398) 81667 or 81669.
Visitor information centre, nature trails and walk to spectacular rocky setting of the Vat Burn.

Nairn Fishertown Museum
Laing Hall, King Street. May-Sept, Mon-Sat 14.30–16.30; Mon, Wed & Fri 18.30–20.30. Parking available. Tel: Nairn (0667) 53331.
A collection of photographs and articles connected with the Moray Firth and herring fishing industries during the steam drifter era. Exhibits on domestic life of the fishertown. Model boats.

North East Falconry Centre
4m S of Banff on A97 to Aberchirder. Centre on right. All year, daily 10.00–17.00. Parking available. Tel: (02616) 602.
Flying displays of owls, hawks and falcons at 11.00 and 14.00. Coffees, teas and soft drinks available.

North East of Scotland Agricultural Heritage Centre (Aden Country Park)
On A950 between Old Deer and Mintlaw, 30m N of Abrdeen. Parking available. Tel: Mintlaw (0771)22857.
Housed in the carefully restored Aden Home Farm, the Centre imaginatively interprets 20th-century estate life with audio-visual programme, horseman's house and costume guide. Additionally, NE farming life and innovation over 200 years are highlighted in the award-winning (2nd Prize Scottish Museum of the Year Awards 1988 and Certificate of Distinction in the British Tourist Authorities "Come to Britain" Awards 1988)

"Weel Vrocht Grun" exhibition by use of special dioramas, atmospheric soundtrack and video film.

Northfield Farm Museum
10m W of Fraserburgh. From A98 follows signs for New Aberdour. From B9031 follow New Pitsligo signs. May-30 Sept, daily 13.30–17.30. Parking available. Tel: (07717) 504.
A large collection of farm equipment including tractors, implements, stationary engines, household bric-a-brac from the 1870's.

The Old Manse Herb Garden
10m N of Huntly on A97 take B9117 left for 1m. Garden is on left. May-Sept, daily, 10.00–17.00. Parking available. Tel: (0466) 780873.
Small display garden containing 80–90 specimens of culinary, aromatic and medicinal herbs. Pot-grown herbs are for sale.

Old Mills
W end of Elgin off the A96. Tue-Sun 09.00–17.00 (closed Mon). Parking available. (Moray District Council). Tel: Elgin (0343) 540698.
The oldest and only remaining meal mill on the River Lossie. Its history can be traced back to a Royal Charter of 1230 granting its rights to the monks of Pluscarden Priory. Visitor Centre, coffee shop, craft centre and picnic area.

Old Semeil Herb Garden
Just off the A944 Aberdeen-Corgarff road. May-mid Oct, daily 10.00–17.00; closed Thurs. Free. Parking available. Tel: (09756) 51343.
Specialist Herb Plant Nursery. Plant sales, display herb garden, garden pottery, books, seeds, gifts, unusual plants, etc. The Garden Room (seating 24) for teas, home baking.

Pennan
10m E of MacDuff on B9031.
Coastal fishing village which provided location for film Local Hero.

Peterhead
St. Peter Street, Peterhead. All year, daily except Sun, 10.00–12.00, 14.00–17.00. Free. (North East of Scotland Museums Service). Tel: Peterhead (0779) 77778.
The development of fishing and whaling, with Arctic exhibits, is featured. Local history, photographic and coin exhibitions.

Pitmedden Garden and Museum of Farming Life
Outskirts of Pitmedden village on A920, 14m N of Aberdeen, off B999. Garden, Museum and Visitor Centre: 28 Apr-30 Sept, daily 10.00–18.00. Last tour 17.15. (NTS). Tel: Udny (065 13) 2352.
The highlight is the 17th century Great Garden originally laid out by Sir Alexander Seton, with elaborate floral designs, pavilions, fountains and sundials. The 'thunder houses' at either end of the west belvedere are rare in Scotland. The Museum of Farming Life contains a collection of agricultural and domestic implements. On the 100-acre estate is a woodland and farmland walk. Visitor Centre, tearoom, exhibition on formal gardens, picnic area.

Pluscarden Abbey
From B9010 at Elgin take unclassified road to Pluscarden, 6m SW. All year daily 05.00–20.30. Free. Tel: (034 389) 257/388 (09.00–11.00 and 14.30–17.00).
Originally a Valliscaulian house, the monastery was founded in 1230. In 1390 the Church was burned, probably by the Wolf of Badenoch who burned Elgin about the same time. It became a dependent priory of the Benedictines' Abbey of Dunfermline in 1454 until the suppression of monastic life in Scotland in 1560. Thereafter the buildings fell into ruins until 1948 when a group of Benedictine monks from Prinknash Abbey, Gloucester, returned to restore it. Monastic church services open to the public.

Randolph's Leap
Off B9007, 7m SW of Forres. Parking available.
The River Findhorn winds through a deep gorge in the sandstone, and from a path above are impressive views of the clear brown water swirling over rocks or in still dark pools. Randolph's Leap is the most striking part of this valley.

'Remains to be seen'
From Ellon take B9005 to Methlick until Quilquox sign on right. Cross river and bear left up hill. Quilquox croft on left approx. 1½m. All year. Apr-Oct, daily 10.00–19.00; Nov-Mar 11.00–16.00. Parking available. Tel: (03587) 229.
An exhibition of period clothes and accessories, lace and jewellery and a porcelain room. Gardens planted by ornithologist to attract birds. Children's play area. Complimentary tea and coffee.

Rob Roy's Statue
Peterculter by A93. All times. Free.
Statue of Rob Roy standing above the Leuchar Burn can be seen from the bridge on the main road.

St. Ninian's Chapel, Tynet
Tynet, 3m E of Fochabers on A98. All year, dawn-dusk. Free. Parking available. The Church is in use

weekly and is open daily. Visitors are requested to respect its character as a place of worship. The access road is single-track and is unsuitable for coaches. Tel: (0452) 32196.
Built about 1755 by the Laird of Tynet, ostensibly for his own use as a sheepcote but in reality as a Mass centre for the Catholics of the neighbourhood. It has undergone many extensions and alterations since, the latest being in the 1950s under the direction of Ian G. Lindsay, RSA. St. Ninian's has the distinction of being the oldest post-Reformation Catholic church still in use. Mass 17.30 Saturday, all year.

Seamen's Memorial
Buckie. Key at 6 New Street. Free. Parking available. Tel: (0542) 32426.
A small chapel with beautiful stained glass windows dedicated to local fishermen who lost their lives at sea since 1946. Opened by HM The Queen in 1982.

Speyside Heather Garden Centre
From Aviemore take B9152 (old A9) approx 4½ miles N until you turn right onto A95 Elgin/Grantown-on-Spey road. Continue on A95 for approx 4m. Watch for 'Thistle' signs to Heather Centre. Turn left on Skye of Curr road. Heather Centre is 200 yds up on right-hand side. Closed Jan, except by appointment. Mar-Oct, Mon-Sat 09.00–17.00/18.00 (Sun 10.00–17.00/18.00); Nov-Feb, Mon-Sat 09.00–17.00 (closed Sun). Garden and Craft Shop – Free. Parking available. Tel: (047 985) 359.
Centre consists of Heather Heritage Centre which houses an exhibition on historical uses of heather, eg thatching, weaving ropes doormats, baskets; its uses in medicine, drinks, dyeing wool, etc. Heather Craft Shop. Tearoom. Plant sales and gift shop. Ornamental garden and landscaped show garden displaying approx. 300 varieties of heathers.

Stonehaven Tolbooth Museum
At quay at Stonehaven. Jun-Sep, daily (except Tue) 14.00–17.00, plus Mon, Thu, Fri and Sat 10.00–12.00. Free. (North-East of Scotland Museums Service). Tel: Peterhead (0779) 77778.
This 16th-century former storehouse of the Earls Marischal was later used as a prison. In 1748–49 Episcopal ministers lodged inside and baptised children through the windows. The museum displays local history, archaeology and particularly fishing.

The Tomnavulin-Glenlivet Distillery
Tomnavoulin, 3½m NNE of Tomintoul on B9008. 26 Mar-3 Nov, Mon-Sat 09.30–16.30; June-Aug;

Sun 10.00–16.00. Free. (Lt. Col. R. Maddison). Tel: Glenlivet (080 73) 442.
Opened in May 1984, a visitors' centre has been created by converting the old carding mill from which the distillery took its name. It comes from the Gaelic for 'mill on the hill'. The picnic area is well furnished in a level secluded area by the River Livet, close to walks.

Tolquhon Gallery
From Pitmedden take B999 N for 2m, turn left onto unclassified road, continue 1m to end of road (500 yds. beyond Tolquhon Castle). Mar-Dec. Mon-Sat 11.00–18.00, Sun 13.00–18.00. Closed Thurs. Free. Parking available. Tel: (065 13) 2343.
A changing programme of exhibitions of paintings, original prints and selected ceramics and glass by artists from throughout Scotland. Sculpture garden.

Tomintoul Museum
The Square, Tomintoul. Apr, May, Oct, Mon-Sat 09.30–13.00, 14.00–17.30, Sun 14.00–17.30; June, Sept, Mon-Fri 09.30–18.00, Sat 09.30–13.00, 14.00–18.00, Sun 14.00–18.00; July, Aug, Mon-Fri 09.00–18.30, Sat 09.00–13.00, 14.00–18.30, Sun 11.00–13.00, 14.00–18.30. Free. Tel: Forres (0309) 73701.
At 1160 feet Tomintoul is the highest village in the Highlands. Museum has displays on local history, folklife, a reconstructed farm kitchen, wildlife, climate, landscape and geology. Tourist Information Centre.

Ugie Salmon Fish House
At the mouth of the River Ugie across from the golf course in Peterhead. Mon-Sat 09.00–12.00 and 14.00–17.00. Free. Parking available. Tel: (0779) 76209.
The oldest Salmon Fish House in Scotland dating from 1585. Built for George Keith, 5th Earl Marischal of Scotland. Fresh and smoked salmon always available.

The Village Store
In centre of Aberlour on main street. Mar-end Oct, daily 10.00–18.00. Nov-Feb restricted hours. Free. Parking available. Tel: (03405) 243.
This old village general store has all the original fittings, records and stock dating back to the 1920's. A fascinating insight into shopping history. Scottish crafts, cards, preserves and sweets on sale.

THE NORTHERN HIGHLANDS

Ardvreck Castle
A837, 11m E of Lochinver, on Loch Assynt. All

reasonable times. Free.
Built in 1490 by the MacLeods, who in the mid-13th century obtained Assynt by marriage; the three-storeyed ruins stand on the shores of Loch Assynt. After his defeat at Culrain, near Bonar Bridge, in 1650, the Marquess of Montrose fled to Assynt but was soon captured and confined here before being sent to Edinburgh and executed.

Beauly Priory
At Beauly, A9, 12m W of Inverness. Apr-Sep standard opening, closed Oct-Mar. (HS). Tel: 031–244 2903.
Ruins of a Valliscaulian Priory founded in about 1230. Notable windows and window-arcading.

Beinn Eighe National Nature Reserve
W of A896/A832 junction at Kinlochewe. (NCC). Tel: Kinlochewe (044 584) 258.
The first National Nature Reserve in Britain, of great geological and natural history interest. Car park and nature trails on A832 NW of Kinlochewe. Aultroy Cottage Visitor Centre on A832, 1m nearer Kinlochewe. Car park, toilets.

Caithness Glass
Harrowhill, Wick. All year. Free. Factory shop: Mon-Fri 09.00–17.00, Sat 09.00–13.00 (all year), Sat 09.00–16.00 (summer only). Factory viewing: Mon-Fri 09.00–16.30 (all year). (Caithness Glass plc). Tel: Wick (0955) 2286.
See hand-made glass blowing from the raw materials stage through all the processes to the finished article. Cafe and factory shop. Ample car/coach parking.

Cape Wrath
12m NW of Durness.
The most northerly point of Scotland's north-west seaboard. A passenger ferry (summer only) connects with a minibus service to the cape.

Castle of Old Wick
Off A9, 1¹/₂m S of Wick.
On a headland above the sea, over a deep cleft in the rocks, this almost windowless square tower of the Cheynes dates back to the 14th century.

Castle Stuart
5m E of Inverness on B9039. 1 May-30 Sept, daily 10.30–17.30. Parking available. Tel: (0463) 790 745.
Built in 1625 by James Stuart, 3rd Earl of Moray, on land bestowed by Mary Queen of Scots to her half-brother James, Regent and 1st Earl of Moray. Small, attractive garden. Gift shop.

Castles Girnigoe and Sinclair
3m N of Wick. Take airport road towards Noss Head Lighthouse. All times. Free. Care to be taken in wet weather. Parking available. Tel: (0955) 3761.
Two adjacent castles on a cliff-edge above Sinclair's Bay, one time strongholds of the Sinclairs, Earls of Caithness. Girnigoe is the older, dating from the end of the 15th century; Sinclair was built 1606–07. Both were deserted c. 1679 and 20 years later were reported in ruins.

Cawdor Castle
At Cawdor on B9090, 5m SW of Nairn. May-Sep, 10.00–17.00 (Rt Hon The Earl of Cawdor). Tel: Cawdor (06677) 615.
The old central tower of 1372, fortified in 1454 (a family home for over 600 years), is surrounded by 16th-century buildings, remodelled during the following century. Notable gardens surround the castle. Shakespeare's Macbeth was Thane of Cawdor, and the castle is one of the traditional settings for the murder of Duncan. Licensed restaurant, snack bar and picnic area in grounds; beautiful gardens and extensive nature trails; 9-hole pitch and putt golf course and putting green.

Corrieshalloch Gorge
A835 at Braemore, 12m SSE of Ullapool. All times. Free. Parking available. (NTS). Tel: (0463) 232084.
This spectacular gorge, 1m long and 200 feet deep, contains the Falls of Measach which plunge 150 feet. Suspension bridge viewpont.

Dornoch Cathedral
In Dornoch. All year. 09.00-dusk. Free. Tel: (0862) 810325.
Founded in 1224 by Gilbert, Archdeacon of Moray and Bishop of Caithness. this little cathedral was partially destroyed by fire in 1570, restored in the 17th century, in 1835–37, and again in 1924. The fine 13th-century stonework is still to be seen.

Dornoch Craft Centre
Town Jail. All year. Summer, Mon-Sat 09.30–17.00, Sun 12.00–17.00; Winter, Mon-Fri 09.30–17.00. Free. Tel: Dornoch (0862) 810555.
Weaving of tartans on Saurgr power looms, kilt making and soft toy making. Small exhibition in Jail cells. Coffee room (Apr-Sep).

Dounreay Nuclear Power Development Establishment
Dounreay, 10m W of Thurso. Easter-Sep, daily 09.00–16.30. Free. No dogs. Tours (free) by

arrangement through the exhibition, Tel: Thurso (0847) 62121, ext 656. (United Kingdom Atomic Energy Authority).

An interesting exhibition giving visitors a general conception of nuclear power and of the activities and work taking place at the establishment. Conducted tours of the prototype Fast Reactor every afternoon (over 14's only). Picnic area.

Duirinish Lodge
4 miles from Kyle of Lochalsh. Follow signs for Plockton and turn right at Duirinish. Lodge is on left hand side at the top of the hill. Open Mar-Oct, Mon-Sat, dawn-dusk. Nursery on site – plants for sale. Voluntary contributions go to charity. Parking available. Tel: (059 984) 268.

Duirinish Lodge has a wild woodland garden which hosts a wide variety of trees, rhododendrons, azaleas and heathers, as well as a small shrubbery. There are excellent views of Applecross and the Isles of Skye and Raasay.

Duncansby Head
The NE point of mainland Scotland, 18m N of Wick. All times. Free.

The lighthouse on Duncansby Head commands a fine view of Orkney, the Pentland Skerries and the headlands of the east coast. A little to the south are the three Duncansby Stacks, huge stone 'needles' in the sea. The sandstone cliffs are severed by great deep gashes (geos) running into the land. One of these is bridged by a natural arch.

Dun Dornaieil Broch
20m N of Lairg. A836, then on Loch Hope road. All times. Free. (HS). Tel: 031–244 3101.
Notable example of a prehistoric broch.

Dunrobin Castle
Off A9, $12^1/_2$m NNE of Dornoch. May, Mon-Thurs 10.30–12.30. June-Sept, Mon-Sat 10.30–17.30, Sun 13.00–17.30. Last admission 17.00. (Countess of Sutherland). Tel: (04083) 3177.

Magnificently set in a great park and formal gardens, overlooking the sea. Dunrobin Castle was originally a square keep built about 1275 by Robert, Earl of Sutherland, from whom it got its name Dun Robin. For centuries this has been the seat of the Earls and Dukes of Sutherland. The present outward appearance results from extensive changes made 1845–50. Fine paintings, furniture and a steam-powered fire engine are among the miscellany of items to be seen. Beach and tearoom.

Durness Old Church
At Balnakeil, $^1/_2$m W of Durness, near Craft

Village. All reasonable times. Free.
Built in 1619, now a ruin.

Eas Coul Aulin Falls
At the head of Loch Glencoul, 3m W of A894. Contact Mr. Moffat, Tel: Kylestrome (097 183) 239 or Mr. Watson, Tel: (05714) 446.

The tallest waterfall in Britain, dropping 658 feet (200 metres). There are occasional cruises to the waterfall.

Falls of Glomach
NE off A87, 18m E of Kyle of Lochalsh. (NTS).
One of the highest falls in Britain, 370 feet, set in a steep narrow cleft in remote country. The best approach is from the Dorusdain car park (Forestry Commission), $2^1/_2$ miles off the north section of the loop in the old A87. Path 5 miles; allow 5 hours for round trip. Stout footwear, protective clothing, food and compass essential.

Falls of Shin
A836, 5m N of Bonar Bridge.
Spectacular falls through rocky gorge; famous for salmon leap.

Fearn Abbey
Take A9 N from Alness for 12m, turn right onto B9165. Open all year. Free. Parking available.
The Abbey was founded in the 13th century. It was converted into a parish church, but in 1742 the roof fell in during a service killing 42 people, a disaster prophesied by the Brahan Seer. The restored church (the nave and choir of the Abbey) is still a parish church, but the North and South Chapels are still roofless.

Fortrose Cathedral
At Fortrose, 8m SSW of Cromarty. Opening standard. Free. (HS). Tel: 031–244 3101.
The surviving portions of this 14th-century cathedral include the south aisle with its vaulting and much fine detail.

Gairloch Heritage Museum
In Gairloch, on A832. Easter-end Sep, Mon-Sat 10.00–17.00. Tel: Badachro (044 583) 243.
Award-winning museum with displays of all aspects of the past life in the West Highland area from prehistoric times to the present day. Licensed restaurant attached.

Grey Cairns of Camster
6m N of Lybster on Watten Road, off A9. All reasonable times. Free. (HS). Tel: 031–244 3101.
Two megalithic cairns: a round cairn and a long

cairn containing chambers, probably 4th millenium BC.

Groam House Museum
High Street, Rosemarkie. 1 May-1 Oct, Mon-Sat 11.00–17.00, Sun 14.30–16.30. (Groam House Museum Trust). Tel: Fortrose (0381) 20961.
This small museum, now a Pictish Centre for Ross and Cromarty, contains a splendid Pictish symbol stone, c. 750 AD. and other fragments, all found in Rosemarkie. Also hangings and representations of other Pictish stones with video programmes on the Picts and the Brahan Seer with a selection of photos and a shop.

Handa Island Nature Reserve
Handa Island, 3m NW of Scourie. Access: day visits by local boatmen from Tarbet. Apr-mid Sep, Mon-Sat 10.00–17.00. Accommodation is well equipped, bothy available to members of RSPB only (contact RSPB, 17 Regent Terrace, Edinburgh). Warden on island. (RSPB). Tel: 031-557 3136.
An island seabird sanctuary with vast numbers of fulmars, shags, gulls, kittiwakes and auks. Arctic and great skuas on moorland. Shelter for visitors with displays.

Highlands at War
2m S of Castletown on B876 E of Thurso. Apr-Oct, daily 09.00–17.00; closed Mon. Parking available. Tel: (0847 85) 607.
An exhibition showing a World War II bunker, Anderson air-raid shelter, revolving Allen-Williams machine-gun turret and a World War I trench.

The Hydroponicum
Achiltibuie. Open Apr-10 Oct, 7 days a week, tours at 10.00, 12.00, 14.00 and 17.00. Closed 11 Oct-end Mar. Parking available. Tel: (085 482) 202.
Informative, thought-provoking, 90-minute story about the evolution of Robert Irvine's prophetic "Garden of the Future"; a garden without soil. The spectacle of strawberries hanging overhead, ripening bananas, figs, vines, lemons, flowers and vegetables in the far north-west of Scotland is astounding. Hydroponic growing kits and souvenirs available in the shop.

The Indian Temple
Above Evanton on Fyrish Hill off A9.
Erected by General Sir Hector Munro (1726–1805) and said to represent the gates of Seringapatan, the town he captured in the Indian campaign of 1781.

Inverewe Gardens
On A832, 6m NE of Gairloch. (Gardens) all year, daily 09.30-sunset. (Visitor Centre and Shop) 1–29 Apr and 3–28 Oct, Mon-Sat 10.00–17.00, Sun 12.00–17.00. 30 Apr-2 Sept, Mon-Sat 09.30–18.00, Sun 12.00–18.00. Licensed Restaurant open 1 Apr-12 May and 3 Sept-15 Oct, Mon-Sat 10.30–16.30, Sun 12.00–16.30. 13 May-2 Sept, Mon-Sat 10.00–17.00, Sun 12.00–17.00. Guided garden walks with head gardener, 1 Apr-28 Oct, Mon-Fri at 13.30. Tel: Poolewe (044 586) 200.
Plants from many countries flourish in this garden created by Osgood MacKenzie over 120 years ago, giving an almost continuous display of colour throughout the year. Eucalyptus, rhododendrons, and many Chilean and South American plants are represented in great variety, together with Himalayan lilies and giant forget-me-nots from the South Pacific. Garden for disabled, shop, restaurant, caravan and camp site, petrol, plants sales. Groups of disabled visitors welcome.

Langwell Gardens
Off A9 at Berriedale. Open June-Oct (inc) 10.00–18.00, daily. Parking available. Tel: Caithness (059 35) 237/278.
Walled garden in its present form laid out in 1916. Herbaceous borders and unexpected views along paths backed by evergreen hedges. As well as the rose garden there is a new rockery/specimen plant area, herb and kitchen garden. An adjacent nursery provides access to the garden, via a pleasant woodland walk and carries a large stock of heathers, alpine/rockery plants, trees and shrubs.

Lhaidhay Caithness Croft Museum
On A9, 1m N of Dunbeath. Easter-30 Sep, daily 09.00–17.00. Tel: Dunbeath (05933) 244.
An early 18th-century croft complex with stable, dwelling house and byre under one thatched roof with adjoining barn. Completely furnished in the fashion of its time. The barn has a notable crux roof. Picnic area.

Lyth Arts Centre
Signposted 4 miles off A9 between Wick and John O'Groats. 26 Jun-6 Sep, daily 10.00–18.00. (Mr W Wilson). Tel: Lyth (0955 84) 270/031–226 6424.
Travelling exhibitions including Scottish fine art, crafts and tapestry. Snack bar, gardens.

MacDonald Tower
Mitchell Hill, Dingwall.
Impressive monument to General Sir Hector MacDonald who was born near Dingwall. There is a special exhibit recalling his military career in the museum at Town House.

Sir John MacDonald Monument
Rogart
Birth place of the first Prime Minister of Canada. Unveiled by John Diefenbaker in 1963.

Hugh Miller's Cottage
Church Street, Cromarty, 22m NE of Inverness via Kessock Bridge. 13 Apr-30 Sept, Mon-Sat 10.00–12.00, 13.00–17.00; Sun 14.00–17.00. (NTS). Tel: Cromarty (03817) 245.
The birthplace of Hugh Miller (1802–56) – stonemason – became eminent geologist, naturalist, theologian and writer. The furnished thatched cottage, built c 1711 by his great grandfather, contains an exhibition and video programme on his life and work.

John Nicolson Museum
On the A9 between Wick and John O'Groats. June-Aug 10.00–12.00, 14.00–16.00, Mon-Sat. Closed Sun. Parking available. Picnic site. Tel: (0955) 3761, ext. 242.
The display tells the archaeological history of Caithness, concentrating on the Iron Age brochs of the county and on John Nicolson, a Victorian antiquarian. Of special interest is a 4,000-year-old beaker which would have contained food or drink to sustain the dead person on his or her journey to the afterlife.

St. Andrew's Church, Golspie
Early 18th century. Built on the site of an ancient chapel to St. Andrew.

St. Duthus Chapel and Collegiate Church
Tain. Chapel: All reasonable times. Free. Church: Open daily, enquire locally. Free. Tel: Tain (0862) 2140.
The chapel was built between 1065 and 1256. St. Duthus died in 1065 and was buried in Ireland, but 200 years later his remains were transferred to Tain. The chapel was destroyed by fire in 1427. St. Duthus Church was built c 1360 by William, Earl and Bishop of Ross, in Decorated style, and became a notable place of pilgrimage. Folk museum and Clan Ross Centre in grounds.

St. Mary's Chapel, Crosskirk
Off A836, 6m W of Thurso. All reasonable times. Free. (HS). Tel: 031-244 3101.
A rudely-constructed chapel with very low doors narrowing at the top in Irish style. Probably 12th century.

St. Peter's Church
Near the Harbour at Thurso. All reasonable times. Free.

Ruins situated in the attractively restored old part of Thurso. Of mediaeval or earlier origin; much of the present church dates from the 17th century.

Smoo Cave
A838, 1 1/2m E of Durness. All reasonable times. Free. Tel: Durness (097 181) 259.
Three vast caves at the end of a deep cleft in the limestone cliffs. The entrance to the first resembles a Gothic arch. The second cavern, access difficult, has a waterfall. The third is inaccessible.

Strathnaver Museum
Off A836, at Farr, near Bettyhill. Summer, Mon-Sat, 14.00–17.00. Donations (J and R McKay). Tel: Mrs.Rudie, Bettyhill (06412) 330.
The former Farr Church (18th century) now houses this museum of local history. This is historic Clan MacKay country and is associated with the Sutherland Clearances.

Struie Hill
6m SE of Bonar Bridge on A836.
Viewpoint with magnificent panoramas east and west of Dornoch Firth.

Tain Museum
Next to Tolbooth Tower, 2nd right off High Street. Easter-end Sept, 10.00–16.30. Parking available. Tel: (0862) 3054 or 2140.
The museum is in the grounds of a medieval church and is the centre for the Clan Ross.

Thurso Heritage Museum
Town Hall, Jun-Sep, Mon-Sat 10.00–13.00, 14.00–17.00. Tel: Thurso (0847) 62459/62692.
Exhibition of agricultural and domestic life, local trades and crafts with a room of an old Caithness cottage.

Torridon
Off A896, 9m SW of Kinlochewe. Deer Museum and audio-visual display, 25 May-30 Sept, Mon-Sat 10.00–18.00, Sun 14.00–18.00. Parking available. (NTS). Tel: Torridon (044587) 221.
About 16,000 acres of some of Scotland's finest mountain scenery whose peaks rise over 3,000ft. Of major interest also to geologists: Liathach (3,456 ft) and Beinn Alligin (2,232 ft) are of red sandstone, some 750 million years old and are topped by white quartzite some 600 million years old. The NTS Visitor Centre at the junction of A896 and Diabaig road has audio-visual presentations of wild life. At the Mains nearby is a static display of the life of the red deer. Disabled access to visitor centre and deer museum only.

Ullapool Museum
Quay Street, Ullapool. Apr-Oct, Mon-Sat 09.00–18.00. Free (donations appreciated). Tel: Ullapool (0854) 2356.
A collection of items of both local and general interest.

Whiten Head
5m N of A838 and 6m E of Durness. No road access; boat trips from Durness in summer.
A splendid perpendicular cliff with a fine series of caves.

Wick Heritage Centre
Bank Row, Wick. Jun-Sep, Mon-Sat 10.00–12.30, 14.00–17.00, or by arrangement for groups. (Wick Society). Tel: Wick (0955) 3385.
Prize-winning exhibition of the herring fishing industry; also displays of domestic and farming life. Gardens and tearoom.

WESTERN AND CENTRAL HIGHLANDS

Achnacloich Woodland Garden
N of Oban on A85, 3m E of Connel Bridge. 7 Apr-22 June and 4 Aug-15 Oct, 10.00–18.00. Tel: Connel (063 171) 221.
Achnacloich is situated on a promontory on the south side of Loch Etive. From the lawns round the castellated mansion the view west is to Mull and east to Ben Cruachan. This large woodland garden is protected by oak woods, tall larch and slopes southwards with paths, steps and bridges. It is free of frost-pockets and bursts into life early with daffodils, primulas, magnolias and shrubs.

Appin Wildlife Museum
On A828 at Appin Home Farm, 25m N of Oban. All year, daily 10.00–18.00. Donations. Tel: Appin (063 173) 308.
The Forest Ranger (John Scorgie) has over the years collected specimens of the local wildlife, to let visitors know what to look for in the area.

Ardanaiseig Gardens
E of B845, 22m E of Oban. 31 Mar-31 Oct, daily 10.00-dusk. Tel: Kilchrenan (08663) 333.
Rhododendrons, azaleas, rare shrubs and trees. Magnificent views across Loch Awe and of Ben Cruchan. The hotel restaurant is open for morning tea, luncheon and afternoon tea.

Ardchattan Priory
On the N side of Lower Loch Etive, 6¹/₂m NE of Oban. Open all times. Free. (HS). Tel: 031–244 3101
One of the Valliscaulian houses founded in Scotland in 1230, and the meeting place in 1308 of one of Bruce's Parliaments, among the last at which business was conducted in Gaelic. Burned by Cromwell's soldiers in 1654, the remains include some carved stones. The gardens of Ardchattan House, adjoining the Priory, are open Apr-Sep; admission charge. Achnaba Church, near Connel, has notable central communion pews.

Ardnamurchan Natural History and Vistor Centre
From Salen take the B8007 for 7m to Glenborrodale. The Centre is 2m further on. Apr-Oct, Mon-Sat 10.30–17.30; Sun 12.00–17.30. Admission free. Parking available. Tel: (097 24) 254 or 263.
Designed for the Glasgow Garden Festival, this attractive Douglas fir building houses static displays of local geology and wildlife plus stone byre converted to audio-visual building for 13-minute film of local ecology. Coffee shop, books and gifts.

Arduaine Gardens
20m S of Oban on the A816, joint entrance with Loch Melfort Hotel. Apr-end Sept 10.00–18.00, Sat-Wed, closed Thurs and Fri. Parking available. Tel: (08522) 298.
Noted west coast garden of particular interest to plantsmen and garden enthusiasts.

Argyll Wildlife Park
Dalchenna, Inveraray, Argyll. On A83, 2 miles from Inveraray. Tea room. Open all year 09.30–18.00/dusk. Tel: (0499) 2264.
60 acre site, with one of Europe's largest collection of wildfowl, a large owl collection, with an emphasis on Scottish wildlife.

Auchindrain Old Highland Township
On A83, 5¹/₂m SW of Inveraray. Easter-Sept 30. Apr,May, Sept: 11.00–16.00 (not Sat); June, Jul, Aug: 10.00–17.00. Tel: Furnace (049 95) 235.
Auchindrain is an original West Highland township, or village of great antiquity and the only communal tenancy township in Scotland to have survived on its centuries old site much in its original form. The township buildings which have been restored and preserved are furnished and equipped in the style of various periods to give the visitor a living experience of what life was really like for the Highlander in past centuries. Visitor centre; shop; refreshments; picnic area; car park and toilets.

Aviemore Centre

Off A9, 32m S of Inverness. All year, daily 10.00 onwards. Admission free (charge for facilities). Group rates on request from Sales Dept. Stakis plc. Tel: (03552) 47177. Tel: Aviemore (0479) 810624.

Leisure, sport and conference centre with wide range of recreational and entertainment facilities, including: cinema/theatre, swimming pool, ice rink, saunas, artificial ski slope, go-karts, discos, restaurants, and many more.

Ballachulish Interpretative Centre

In Ballachulish

Opened in 1981. Displays and information about immediate area, including the 200 year history of the local slate industry.

Ben Nevis

Near Fort William.

Britain's highest mountain (4,406 ft/1,344 m) and most popular mountain for both rock-climber and hillwalker. It is best seen from the north approach to Fort William, or from the Gairlochy Road, across the Caledonian Canal.

Ben Nevis Woollen Mill

Belford Road, Fort William (On A82). Mill Shop open 7 days per week. Tel: (0397) 4244.

Nestling in the shadow of the world famous Ben Nevis, you can browse through a very large choice of pure wool Scottish knitwear, tartans, tweeds, gifts and souvenirs. Do you claim Scottish descent? Then have your own Clan History gone into by computer, and take home a real memento of your visit. They operate VAT free shopping and "Post-it-Home" schemes for overseas visitors. The 200-seat Licensed Restaurant offers a wonderful selection of Taste of Scotland dishes, wholesome snacks, morning and afternoon coffee and tea. Large free car park.

Bernera Barracks

At Glenelg, on unclassified road W of A87 at Shiel Bridge. All times. Free.

The remains of Bernera Barracks, erected c 1722 and used continuously until after 1790.

Bonawe Iron Furnace

At Bonawe, 12m E of Oban, off A85. Opening standard, Apr-Sep only. (HS). Tel: 031244 3101.

The restored remains of a charcoal furnace for iron-smelting, established in 1753, which worked until 1876. The furnace and ancillary buildings are in a more complete state of preservation than any other comparable site.

Cairngorm Chairlift

A951 from A9 at Aviemore, then by Loch Morlich to car park at 2,000 feet. All year, daily 09.00–16.30, depending on weather. (Cairngorm Chairlift Company Limited). Tel: Cairngorm (047 986) 261.

At the car park is a large Day Lodge containing restaurant, bar, shop and snack bar. At the top of the chairlift is the Ptarmigan snack bar, the highest observation building in Great Britain at 3,600 feet with magnificent views to west and north-east. Also alpine garden.

The Cairngorm Reindeer Centre

Reindeer House, Loch Morlich. A951 from Aviemore. All year, daily (subject to weather), 11.00 departure. Extra afternoon trips at peak times. Parking available. Tel: Cairngorm (047 986) 228.

Visitors may accompany the guide to see the reindeer herd free-ranging in their natural surroundings. Also visit the Reindeer Centre at Reindeer House. Disabled visitors welcome, prior notice would be helpful.

Cairngorm Whisky Centre

1m from Aviemore. Mon-Sat 10.00–18.00 and later during season. Sun 12.30–14.30. Video and tasting – children not normally allowed due to licensing laws. Parking available. Tel: Aviemore (0479) 810574.

A video presentation, tasting room, displays on the making of whisky and a small museum of distillery relics is available at the centre which is also part of the Rothiemurchus Visitor Centre.

Castle Stalker

On a tiny island offshore from A828, 25m NNE from Oban. Mar-Sept, open by appointment. Charges include boat trip. Parking available. (Lt. Col. D.R. Stewart Allward). Tel: Upper Warlingham (088 362) 2768.

This picturesque ancient home, c. 1500, of the Stewarts of Appin, and associated with James V, has recently been restored.

Clan Cameron Museum

Achnacarry, Spean Bridge. Turn off A82 before Commando Monument, turn right after crossing canal. Easter-Oct, 14.00–17.00. Parking available. Tel: (0397) 7473.

A reconstructed 17th-century croft house. Memorabilia of Bonnie Prince Charlie, the Commandos, the Camerons and Queen's Own Cameron Highlanders.

Clan MacPherson Museum
In Newtonmore on A9/A86, 15m S of Aviemore. May-Sep, Mon-Sat 10.00–17.30, Sun 14.30–17.30. Free. Tel: Newtonmore (054 03) 332.
Relics and memorials of Clan Chiefs and other MacPherson families. Exhibits include a letter to Prince Charles Edward Stuart from his father, a massive silver epergne depicting an incident in the life of Cluny of the '45 after the Battle of Culloden, green banner of the clan, Victorian royal warrants, crests, James MacPherson's fiddle and other historical relics.

Clava Cairns
Near Culloden, off B9006, 6m E of Inverness. All reasonable times. Free. (HS). Tel: 031-244 3101.
Late Neolithic or Early Bronze Age chambered cairns with standing stone circles.

Cobb Memorial
Between Invermoriston and Drumnadrochit by A82. All times. Free.
A cairn commemorates John Cobb, the racing driver, who lost his life near here in 1952 when attempting to beat the water speed record, with his jet speedboat, on Loch Ness.

Combined Operations Museum
Cherry Park, near Inveraray Castle, Inveraray. Mid-May-end Sept daily 10.00–13.00, 14.00–18.00, Sun 13.00–18.00, closed Fri. Jul-Aug, daily 10.00–18.00 incl. Fri, Sun 13.00–18.00. Last admissions: 12.30 & 17.30. Parking available. Tel: Inveraray (0499) 2203.
The museum sets out to show by means of photographs, models, posters and displays, the work of the Combined Training Centre at Inveraray during World War II.

Commando Memorial
Off A82, 11m NE of Fort William
An impressive sculpture by Scott Sutherland, erected in 1952 to commemorate the Commandos of World War II who trained in this area. Fine views of Ben Nevis and Lochaber.

Cruachan Pumped Storage Power Station
Off A85, 18m E of Oban. Easter-Oct, daily 09.00–16.30. Parking available. Tel: Cruachan (086 62) 673.
In a vast cavern inside Ben Cruachan is Scottish Power's 400,000 kilowatt pumped storage power station which utilises water pumped from Loch Awe to a reservoir 1,200 feet up the mountain. New Visitors' Centre, guided minibus tour, picnic area and snack bar. Car park.

Culloden Moor
B9006, 5m E of Inverness. Site open all year. Visitor Centre: 1 Apr-25 May and 10 Sept-21 Oct, daily 09.30–17.30; 26 May-9 Sept, daily 09.00–18.30. Visitor Centre (NTS). Tel: Inverness (0463) 790607.
Here Prince Charles Edward's cause was finally crushed at the battle on 16 April 1746. The battle lasted only 40 minutes: the Prince's army lost some 1,200 men, and the King's army 310. Features of interest include the Graves of the Clans, communal burial places with simple headstones bearing individual clan names alongside the main road; the great memorial cairn, erected in 1881; the Well of the Dead, a single stone with the inscription 'The English were buried here'; Old Leanach farmhouse, now restored as a battle museum; and the huge Cumberland Stone from which the victorious Duke of Cumberland is said to have viewed the scene. Information available on cassette programme for groups in French, German, Gaelic, Italian and Japanese. Study room, bookshop and self-service restaurant. Induction Loop.

Darnaway Farm Visitor Centre
Off A96, 3m W of Forres. 1 Jun-mid Sept, daily 10.00–17.00. Also available estate tours including Darnaway Castle (Jul, Aug, Wed, Thurs & Sun 13.00–15.30 with estate ranger). Tel: Moray Estates – Forres (0309) 72213.
At the Visitor Centre, an exhibition of the farms and forest of Moray Estates, with audio-visual programme. Viewing platform to watch cows being milked. Nature trails and woodland walks, picnic areas, tearoom and play area.

Dochfour Gardens
Approx. 6m SW of Inverness on the A82 Inverness-Fort William road. The entrance is near the south end of Loch Dochfour. 1 Apr-31 Oct, daily 14.00–17.00. Parking available. Tel: Inverness (046 386) 218.
Fifteen acres of terraced gardens are set against the background of Loch Dochfour in the famous Great Glen. Special features are the magnificent specimen trees, naturalised daffodils, rhododendrons, water garden and extensive yew topiary. The large kitchen garden has soft fruit in season.

Easdale Island Folk Museum
Easdale Island, 16m S of Oban, take B844 then ferry. Apr-Oct, Mon-Sat 10.30–17.30, Sun 10.30–16.30, or by arrangement. Tel: Balvicar (08523) 370 evenings.
A pictorial history of life on the Slate islands in the

1800's, showing the industrial and domestic life of the villagers. Scenic walks around the island and panoramic views from the hill.

Eden Court Theatre
Bishops Road, Inverness. Parking available. Tel: Inverness (0463) 239841.
An 800-seat, multi-purpose Theatre, Conference Centre and Art Gallery, completed in 1976 and situated on the banks of the River Ness. Part of the complex is the 19th-century house built by Robert Eden which houses the new luxury cinema – The Riverside Screen. There is a wide variety of entertainment throughout the year including classical concerts, drama, variety shows, films, pantomime and art exhibitions. The Theatre Restaurant is open for morning coffees, lunch, afternoon teas, dinner and late suppers.

Eilean Donan Castle
Off A87, 9m E of Kyle of Lochalsh. Easter-Sep, daily 10.00–18.00. (The Conchra Charitable Trust). Tel: Kyle (0599) 85 202.
On an islet (now connected by a causeway) in Loch Duich, this picturesque castle dates back to 1220. It passed into the hands of the MacKenzies of Kintail who became Earls of Seaforth. In 1719 it was garrisoned by Spanish Jacobite troops and was blown up by an English man o'war. Now completely restored, it incorporates a war memorial to the Clan MacRae, who held it as hereditary Constables on behalf of the MacKenzies. Gift Shop.

Falls of Foyers
Foyers 17m SW of Inverness B852.
Upper fall is 30 feet and lower 90 feet.

Farigaig Forest Centre
Off B862 at Inverfarigaig, 17m S of Inverness. Easter-mid Oct 09.30–19.00. Free. (FC). Tel: (0463) 791 575.
A Forestry Commission interpretation centre in a converted stone stable, showing the development of the forest environment in the Great Glen. Forest walks.

Fort George
B9039, off A96 W of Nairn. Opening standard. (HS). Tel: 031–244 3101.
Begun in 1748 as a result of the Jacobite rebellion, this is one of the finest late artillery fortifications in Europe, which is still in use. There is also the Regimental Museum of the Queen's Own Highlanders.

Garvamore Bridge
6m W of Laggan Bridge, on unclassified road, 17m SW of Newtonmore. All times. Free.
This two-arched bridge at the south side of the Corrieyarick Pass was built by General Wade in 1735.

Glencoe and Dalness
A82, 3m E of Glencoe Cross, runs through the glen. (Visitor Centre) 1 Apr-25 May, 10 Sept-21 Oct, daily 10.00–17.30; 26 May-9 Sept, daily 09.30–18.30. (NTS). Tel: Ballachulish (085 52) 307.
The finest and perhaps the most famous glen in Scotland through which a main road runs. Scene of the Massacre of Glencoe, 1692, and centre for some of the best mountaineering in the country (not to be attempted by the unskilled). Noted for wildlife which includes red deer, wildcat, golden eagle, ptarmigan. NTS owns 14,200 acres of Glencoe and Dalness. Ski centre, chairlift and ski tows (weekends and New Year and Easter holiday periods only, other times by charter arrangement) at White Corries. Visitor Centre gives general information, particularly on walks. Visitor Centre, special presentation, Ranger Service, walks and trails, shop, picnic area and tea bar.

Glencoe and North Lorn Folk Museum
In Glencoe Village, off A82, on S shore of Loch Leven. May-Sep, Mon-Sat 10.00–17.30.
Clan and Jacobite relics, also domestic implements, weapons, costumes, photographs, dolls' houses and dolls, agricultural tools, dairy and slate quarrying equipment are included in this museum housed in a number of thatched cottages.

Glencoe Chairlift
Off A82 by Kingshouse. Jan-Apr, Thurs to Mon inclusive of Easter; June-Sept, daily 10.00–17.00. Tel: Kingshouse (08556) 226.
Chairlift to 2,100 feet offers magnificent views of the areas around Glencoe and Rannoch Moor. Summer: access chairlift, snack bar, car park, toilets. Winter: two chairlifts and three tows for ski-ing, car park, toilets and snack bars.

Glenelg Brochs
Unclassified road from Eilanreach, 12m W of Shiel Bridge. All times. Free. (HS). Tel: 031–244 3101.
Two Iron Age brochs, Dun Telve and Dun Troddan, have walls still over 30 feet high.

Glenfeochan House Gardens
Kilmore, 5m S of Oban, A816. Daily, 1 Apr-31 Oct, 10.00–18.00. Parking available. Tel: (063177) 273.

Glenfeochan House, built in 1875, is surrounded by six acres of mature gardens. Many of the trees were planted in the 1850's. A wide variety of rhododendron are on view, including a Loderi Collection. Walled garden with herbaceous borders, vegetables and large greenhouse (containing peaches, nectarines) and herb beds.

Glenfinnan Monument
A830, 18¹/₂m W of Fort William. 1 Apr-25 May, 10 Sept-21 Oct, daily 10.00–13.00 and 14.00–17.30; 26 May-9 Sept 09.30–18.30. (NTS). Tel: (039783) 250.
The monument commemorates the raising of Prince Charles Edward Stuart's standard at Glenfinnan on 19 August 1745. It was erected by MacDonald of Glenaladale in 1815; a figure of a Highlander surmounts the tower. The Visitor Centre tells of the Prince's campaign from Glenfinnan to Derby and back to the final defeat at Culloden. Audio-visual programme, snack bar and viewpoint.

Glengarry Forest
Off A82 2m W of Glengarry Village.
Picnic Place, walks. Also picnic place on shore of Loch Oich, on A82 at south end of loch.

Glen Grant Distillery
Rothes. Late Apr-end Sep, Mon-Fri 10.00–16.00. Free. Tel: Rothes (034 03) 413 (during season) and Keith (05422) 8924 (during winter).
Tours of the distillery, with Reception Centre and whisky sample. Children under 8 not admitted to production areas but welcome in Reception Centre.

Glenmore Forest Park
7m E of Aviemore, off B9152. Open all year. (FC). Tel: Kincraig (05404) 223 or Cairngorm (047986) 271.
Over 12,000 acres of pine and spruce woods and mountainside on the north-west slopes of the Cairngorms, with Loch Morlich as its centre. This is probably the finest area in Britain for wildlife, including red deer, reindeer, wildcat, golden eagle, ptarmigan, capercailzie, etc. Remnants of old Caledonian pinewoods. Well-equipped caravan sites and hostels open all year, canoeing, sailing, fishing, swimming, forest trails and hillwalking, and an Information Centre. Campsite, forest walks, toilets, picnic area, shop, cafe and wayfaring trail.

Highland Folk Museum
A9 at Kingussie, 12m SW of Aviemore. All year, Apr-Oct, Mon-Sat 10.00–18.00, Sun 14.00–18.00; Nov-Mar, Mon-Fri 10.00–15.00; closed Xmas & New Year. (Highland Regional Council). Tel: Kingussie (0540) 661 307.

The open air museum includes an 18th century shooting lodge, a 'Black House' from Lewis, a Clack Mill, a turf-walled house from the Central Highlands and exhibits of farming equipment. Indoors, the farming museum has fine displays of a barn, dairy, stable and an exhibition of Highland tinkers; and there are special features on weapons, costume, musical instruments and Highland furniture. Picnic garden. Special events Easter-September.

Highland Wildlife Park
Off A9 (B9152), 7m S of Aviemore. Open daily 10.00–17.00 (closing times vary during spring and autumn); closed winter season. Tel: Kincraig (054 04) 270. Office open 09.00–17.00.
This notable wildlife park features breeding groups of Highland animals and birds in a beautiful natural setting. Drive-through section has red deer herd, bison, Highland cattle, etc. Aviaries display capercailzie, eagles; also wolves, wildcats and nearly 60 other species. There is an exhibition on 'Man and Fauna in the Highlands', and a children's animal park. Also souvenir shop, cafeteria and picnic area.

Highland Wineries
Moniack Castle, Kirkhill, 7m W of Inverness off the A862. All year, 10.00–17.00; closed Sun. Free. Parking available. Tel: (0463 83) 283.
Winery making country wines and liqueurs. Tours of the winery show the processes involved in wine making. Free tasting, tours, shop and licensed restaurant.

Inveraray Bell Tower
In Inveraray. Early May-late Sep, Mon-Sat 10.00–13.00, 14.00–17.00; Sun 14.00–17.00. (Scottish Episcopal Church of All Saints). Tel: Inveraray (0499) 2433.
The 126-feet high granite tower houses Scotland's finest ring of bells and the world's third-heaviest ring of ten bells, which are rung regularly. Excellent views, pleasant grounds.

Inveraray Castle
¹/₂m N of Inveraray. Apr-Jun, Sep-mid Oct, Mon-Sat (not Fri) 10.00–12.30, 14.00–17.30, Sun 13.00–17.30; Jul-Aug, Mon-Sat 10.00–17.30, Sun 13.00–17.30. (Argyll Estates). Tel: Inveraray (0499) 2203.
Inveraray has been the seat of the chiefs of Clan Campbell, Dukes of Argyll, for centuries. The present castle was started in 1743 when the third Duke engaged Roger Morris to build it. Subsequently the Adam family, father and sons, were also involved. The magnificent interior

decoration was commissioned by the fifth Duke from Robert Mylne. In addition to many historic relics, there are portraits by Gainsborough, Ramsay and Raeburn. Tearoom and craft shop. Gardens open on selected weekends.

Inveraray Jail
In the centre of Inveraray. All year, 09.30–18.00 (last admission 17.00). Parking available. Tel: (0499) 2381.
The living 19th-century prison. Trained 'prisoners' and 'warders', lifelike figures, imaginative exhibitions, sounds, smells and trials in progress all bring the 1820 courtroom and former county prison back to life. Shop.

Inverawe Smokery & Fisheries
All year, daily. 09.00–17.00 Smokehouses. Apr-Oct (incl) 09.00–18.00 Fisheries. Tel: (08662) 446.
A detailed exhibition of how fish is cured & smoked in the old traditional fashion. Fisheries: 3 lochs stocked with trout for fishing. Good walks. Toilets, light refreshments, children's play area.

Inverliever Forest
B845 Lochawe.
Forest trail, walks, picnic places, camp site.

Inverness Museum & Art gallery
Castle Wynd, Inverness. Mon-Sat 09.00–17.00; Jul & Aug, Sun 14.00–17.00. Free. (Inverness District Council). Tel: Inverness (0463) 237114.
The museum interprets the social and natural history, archaeology and culture of the Highlands, with fine collections of Highland silver, bagpipes, and Jacobite relics. Special exhibitions, performances and talks. Coffee shop. Museum shop.

Jacobite Cruises
From Inverness centre on A82, 1¹/₄m at roadside. Easter-mid Oct. Cruises at 10.00, 14.00 and 18.30. Parking available. Tel: (0463) 233999.
Cruises on the Caledonian Canal and Loch Ness. Bar and light refreshments available on board.

Kilchurn Castle
N tip of Loch Awe, 21m E of Oban. Access at all reasonable times. (HS). Tel: 031–244 3101.
The keep was built in 1440 by Sir Colin Campbell of Glenorchy, founder of the Breadalbane family. The north and south sides of the building were erected in 1693 by Ian, Earl of Breadalbane, whose arms and those of his wife are over the gateway. Occupied by the Breadalbanes until 1740, in 1746 it was taken by Hanoverian troops. A gale in 1879 toppled one of it towers.

Kilmory Castle Gardens
Off A83 road to Inveraray, on outskirts of Lochgilphead. Parking available. Tel: (0546) 2127.
The garden was started in the 1770's and included around 100 varieties of rhododendron, supplied plants for Kew Garden and contained a collection of hardy ferns and alpines. The gardens are being restored with woodland walks and a nature trail. There are also footpaths and a herbaceous border.

Kilravock Castle
12m E of Inverness 6m W of Nairn off the B9091. Tel: Croy (066 78) 258.
The extensive grounds and garden of this 15th-century castle are noted for a large variety of beautiful trees, some centuries old and unique in this country. The tree garden, nature trails and river host an abundance of wildlife. A plan location of trees is available on request. Guided tours of the castle and afternoon tea are available on Wednesdays. Lunch is available by prior request daily except Sundays.

Kinlochlaich House Gardens
Midway between Oban and Fort William on A828. Entry by police station. Parking available. Tel: (063) 173 342.
Walled garden, incorporating West Highland's largest nursery garden centre. There are display beds of primulas, alpines, rhododendrons, heathers as well as fruiting and flowering shrubs and trees.

Kintail
N of A87 between Lochs Cluanie and Duich, 16m E of Kyle of Lochalsh. (NTS). Tel: (059 981) 219.
Magnificent Highland scenery including the Five Sisters of Kintail, peaks rising to 3,500 feet. Red deer and wild goats. Visitor Centre at Morvich open 1 Jun to end Sep Mon-Sat 0900–1800, Sun 1300–1800.

Kyle House
¹/₂m from jetty at Kyleakin. Open 1 May-31 Aug, daily. 13.00-dusk. Free. Tel: Isle of Skye (0599) 4517.
Situated by Loch Alsh the garden is protected in winter by the Gulf Stream. This allows many tender plants to attain quite large sizes. Most of the garden was planted around 30 years ago by the late Mr. Colin Mackenzie. It covers about 3 acres. Also a kitchen garden and a viewpoint from which can be seen the Cuillin Hills on the Isle of Skye, the Isle of Raasay and many other small islands.

Lady Rowena, Steam Launch
Sails from BR Station Pier at Lochawe Village on A85. 28 May-Sept 10.30–16.00, 7 days a week. Last

cruise 15.30 unless pre-booked. Tel: 041–334 2529 or (08382) 440/449.

Restored Edwardian launch with genuine steam engine and peat-fired boiler. Cushioned seating and enclosed cabin. Variety of cruises (50 mins. to 3 hrs.) to places of interest on Loch Awe. Comfortable Pullman Carriage Tearoom on the pier with superb views of Kilchurn Castle. Ferry to castle.

Ladycroft Agricultural Museum

At Archiestown, by Aberlour, on the B9102 Grantown Scenic route whisky trail. All year, 10.00-dusk. (Mr & Mrs C W Spence). Tel: Carron (034 06) 274.

A museum of the time when all the farm implements were worked by horses. There are life-size models of men and horses.

Landmark Visitor Centre

Carrbridge, 6m N of Aviemore on old A9. All year. Open 09.30–17.30 in winter, 09.30–20.30 in summer. Tel: Carrbridge (047 984) 613.

This 'Landmark' Visitor Centre was the first of its kind in Europe. Ten thousand years of Highland history are shown in the triple-screen audio-visual theatre and a dramatic exhibition interprets the history of Strathspey. Now has sculpture park, tree-top trail and woodland maze. Adventure playground with giant slides and aerial net walkways. Also new pine forest nature centre. Craft and bookshop, restaurant, bar, snack bar, picnic area and plant centre. Free parking.

Lochalsh Woodland Garden

Off A87, 3m E of Kyle of Lochalsh. All year, daily. (NTS). Tel: Balmacara (059 986) 207.

A wide variety of native trees and shrubs and more exotic plants from Tasmania, New Zealand, the Himalayas, Chile, Japan and China in the grounds of Lochalsh House (not open to the public). There are pleasant walks and an ecology display in the coach house.

Loch-an-Eilean Visitor Centre

B970, 2½m S of Aviemore. All year. Free. (Rothiemurcus Estate) Tel: Aviemore (0479) 810 858.

This exhibition which is held in a cottage by the loch and a beautiful ruined castle, traces the history of the native Scots Pine forest from the Ice Age until today, its management and conservation. Good local interest for birdwatchers.

Loch Garten Nature Reserve

Off B970, 8m NE of Aviemore. If Ospreys present, daily mid Apr-Aug 10.00–20.00 along signposted

track to Observation Post. Other access into bird sanctuary strictly forbidden Apr-Aug but elsewhere on the reserve access unrestricted throughout the year. (RSPB). Tel: Aviemore (0479) 83694 or 031–557 3136.

Ospreys, extinct in Scotland for many years, returned here to breed in 1959. Their treetop eyrie may be viewed through fixed binoculars from the Observation Hut. Other local specialities include crested tits, crossbills and capercailzies. The surrounding area owned by the RSPB, includes extensive stretches of old Caledonian Pine forest with rich and varied wildlife.

Loch Morar

SE of Mallaig

Said to be the deepest loch in Scotland and the home of Morag, a monster with a strong resemblance to the Loch Ness Monster.

Loch Nan Uamh Cairn

Off A830, S of Arisaig.

The loch is famous for its association with Bonnie Prince Charlie. The memorial cairn on the shore marks the spot from which Prince Charles Edward Stuart sailed for France on 20 September, 1746 after having wandered round the Highlands as a fugitive with a price of £30,000 on his head.

Loch Ness

SW of Inverness

This striking 24-mile long loch in the Great Glen forms part of the Caledonian Canal which links Inverness with Fort William. For much of its length it is over 700 feet deep. The loch contains the largest volume of fresh water of any lake in the British Isles. Famous world wide for its mysterious inhabitant, the Loch Ness Monster. It is also ideal for cruising and sailing.

The Official Loch Ness Monster Exhibition

At Drumnadrochit on A82, 14m SW of Inverness. Peak season daily 09.00–21.30, off season times vary, please check. Tel: Drumnadrochit (04562) 573 or 218.

A revised and greatly extended exhibition presents evidence of the existence of unknown creatures in Loch Ness. Also explains some dubious early pictures. Sales counter.

Loch Ness Lodge Visitor Centre

A82 S from Inverness to Drumnadrochit, turn onto A831 to Cannich 50 metres on right. All year 09.00–18.00, June-Sept 09.00–21.00. Parking available. (Loch Ness Lodge Hotel Co. Ltd.) Tel: (04562) 342.

Large screen cinema on Loch Ness, its history and

myth. Pictorial display of local culture and items of interest. Gift shop. Coffee shop specialising in home baking. Loch Ness sonar scanning cruises.

Loch Ness Monster Video Show
4/9 Huntly Street, Inverness. 1 June-30 Sept, 09.30–21.30, Mon-Sat (10.00–17.30 Sun). 1 Oct-30 May 09.00–17.00, Mon-Sat. Parking available. Tel: Inverness (0463) 222781.
A thirty to forty minute video show on the art of kiltmaking and the Loch Ness Monster search and preview of the Loch Ness Monster Exhibition at Drumnadrochit.

McCaig's Tower
On a hill overlooking Oban. All times. Free. Tel: Oban (0631) 63122.
McCaig was a local banker who tried to curb unemployment by using local craftsmen to build this tower from 1897–1900 as a memorial to his family. Its walls are two feet thick and from 30–47 feet high. The courtyard within is landscaped and the tower is floodlit at night in summer. An observation platform on the seaward side was added in 1983.

Flora MacDonald's Monument
Inverness Castle. All times. Free.
Monument to Flora MacDonald (1722–1790) on the esplanade of the Victorian castle. Flora MacDonald is famed for the help she gave to the Young Pretender in June 1746, enabling him to escape from Benbecula to Portree.

Neptune's Staircase
3m NW of Fort William off A830 at Banavie.
A series of 8 locks, built between 1805 and 1822, which raises Telford's Caledonian Canal 64 feet.

Nevis Range Gondola
On A83 3m W of Fort William. Take A82 N from Fort William for 4m. Turn right onto unclassified road marked Torlundy. Jan-Apr, daily 08.30–16.30; May-Dec 09.00–16.00. Parking available. Tel: (0397) 5825/6.
In summer the Gondola with six-seater cabins travels 2.3km. There is a 50-seat cafe at the bottom station and a 150-seat licensed mountain restaurant at the upper station. There are forestry walks and mountain bikes for hire and a shop. In winter there is an extensive ski area, a ski school and ski hire.

Oban Glass
Lochavullin Estate, Oban. All year. Free. Factory Shops: Mon-Fri 09.00–17.00 (all year); Sat 09.00–13.00 (Summer only). Factory viewing:
Mon-Fri 09.00–17.00 (all year). Parking available. (Caithness Glass plc). Tel: Oban (0631) 63386.
See paperweight making from the raw materials stage through all the processes to the finished article. Visit the factory shop with an extensive range of glassware. Ample car/coach parking.

Queen's Own Highlanders Regimental Museum
Fort George, near Ardersier. Apr-Sept, Mon-Fri 10.00–18.00, Sat 10.00–18.00 (provisional), Sun 14.00–18.00. Oct-Mar, Mon-Fri 10.00–16.00. Free. Parking available. Tel: Inverness (0463) 224380.
Regimental museum with collections of medals, uniforms and other items showing the history of the Queen's Own Highlanders, Seaforth Highlanders and The Queen's Own Cameron Highlanders and Lovat Scouts.

Parallel Roads
Glen Roy, unclassified road off A86, 18m NE of Fort William.
Unusual parallel lines conspicuous on both sides of picturesque glen north of Fort William. These 'parallel roads' are hillside terraces marking levels of lakes dammed by glaciers during the Ice Age.

Roderick MacKenzie Memorial
1m E of Ceannacroc on A887, 13m W of Invermoriston. All times. Free.
A cairn on the south of the road commemorates the heroic action of Roderick MacKenzie, a supporter of Prince Charles Edward Stuart who drew off pursuit by pretending to be his leader. He was shot dead by pursuing soldiers and in the resulting confusion of identity, the real Prince Charlie was able to flee from the area.

Rothiemurchus Estate Visitor Centre
1m from Aviemore. All year, 09.00–17.00. Parking available. Tel: Aviemore (0479) 810858.
Highland cattle, red deer, Caledonian pine forest, Cairngorms National Nature Reserve, trout farm (feed the fish), fresh and smoked trout for sale. Designer knitwear and crafts, estate tours, tractor and trailer rides, Land Rover safaris, clay pigeon shooting range, loch and river fishing.

St. Benedict's Abbey
Fort Augustus, A82.
Former fort takes its name from William Augustus, Duke of Cumberland, who made it his headquarters after the Battle of Culloden in 1746. Abbey built in 19th-century. Now houses a boys' school run by Benedictine monks.

Scot II Cruises

Departure point: top of Muirton Locks, Inverness. Signposted with thistle. Morning Cruise: 10.15. Afternoon Cruise: 14.15. All cruises run from 30 Apr-28 Sept. Group rates available on request. (British Waterways Board). Tel: Inverness (0463) 232955.

Scot II was built in 1932 originally as a Canal Tug. She now cruises on the Caledonian Canal and Loch Ness, offering an interest-packed voyage past Tomnahurich Hill through swing bridges and locks, past a lighthouse and out on to the beautiful Loch Ness to historic Urquhart Castle. Licensed bar, snack bar, toilets.

Scottish Crafts and Ben Nevis Exhibition

Fort William. Easter-June 09.00–17.40; Jul & Aug 09.00–22.00; Sept-Nov 09.00–17.30. Tel: Fort William (0397) 4406.

A visual exhibition and large-scale model of Ben Nevis, presented to explain all about Britain's highest mountain.

Sea Life Centre

Barcaldine, on A828, 11m N of Oban. Mar-Nov, daily. Tel: (0631) 72386.

Centre houses a large and exciting display of native marine life. Visitors can experience the feeling of being on the sea-bed without getting wet and come face to face with octopus, catfish and seals. Both the aquarium and restaurant have a beautiful lochside setting.

James Stewart Tablet

2m SW of Ballachulish on shores of Loch Linnhe. Commemorates James Stewart who was tried and unjustly hanged for the Appin murder in 1752 and made famous in R L Stevenson's 'Kidnapped'.

Strathspey Railway

Aviemore (Speyside) to Boat of Garten. Access at Aviemore: cars B970 then Dalfaber Road, pedestrians take underpass from Main Road at Bank of Scotland. Train Services Easter weekend, 22 April, Suns 1 Apr-28 Oct. Sats 5 May-27 Oct. Weds 4 Apr-28 May. Daily 28 May-30 Sept. Stations open 09.30–18.00. 1st and 3rd class single and returns fares. (Strathspey Railway Co. Ltd). Tel: Aviemore (0479) 810725.

The line is part of the former Highland Railway (Aviemore-Forres section) closed in 1965 and reopened 1978 after restoration work begun in 1972. Passenger steam train service run entirely by volunteers. Station buildings at Aviemore (Speyside) were brought from Dalnaspidal and the footbridge from Longmorn. Timetables available.

Museum of small relics and other static rolling stock on display at Boat of Garten.

Strone House Gardens

A83, 12m E of Inveraray. Apr-Oct, daily 09.00–21.00. Tel: Cairndow (049 96) 284.

Rhododendrons, azaleas, daffodils and exotic shrubs. The Pinetum contains the tallest tree in Britain.

Urquhart Castle

2m SE of Drumnadrochit, on W shore of Loch Ness. Opening standard. (HS). Tel: 031–244 3101.

Once one of the largest castles in Scotland, the castle is situated on a promontory on the banks of Loch Ness, from where sitings of the 'monster' are most frequently reported. The extensive ruins are on the site of a vitrified fort, rebuilt with stone in the 14th century. The castle was gifted by James IV, in 1509, to John Grant of Freuchie, whose family built much of the existing fabric and held the site for four centuries. The castle was blown up in 1692 to prevent its being occupied by Jacobites.

West Highland Museum

Cameron Square, Fort William. All year, Mon-Sat 10.00–13.00, 14.00–17.00 (Jun and Sep 09.30–17.30, Jul and Aug 09.30–21.00). Tel: Fort William (0397) 2169.

Historical, natural history and folk exhibits, local interest and a tartan section. Jacobite relics including a secret portrait of 'Bonnie Prince Charlie'.

White Corries Chairlift

Off A82 by Kinghouse.

Chairlift to 2,100 feet offers magnificent views of Glencoe and Rannoch Moor.

A World in Miniature

North Pier, Oban, Argyll. Easter-mid Oct, 10.00–17.30, daily except Sun 12.00–17.30. Tel: 085 26 272 or Oban (0631) 66300.

Exhibition of 1/12 scale miniature rooms, furniture, dioramas, etc.

CENTRAL AND SOUTH WEST SCOTLAND

Ailsa Craig

Island in Firth of Clyde, 10m W of Girvan. Contact Mr. McCrindle for party rates, Tel: Girvan (0465) 3219. Visitors must obtain permission from the Marquis of Ailsa, the Factor, Cassillis Estates, Maybole Castle, 4 High Street, Maybole. Tel: Maybole (0655) 82103.

A granite island rock, 1,114 feet high with a circumference of 2 miles. The rock itself was used to make some of the finest curling stones and the island has a gannetry and colonies of guillemots and other seabirds.

Alloway
Southern suburb of Ayr.
Birth place of Robert Burns. Location of Burns Interpretation Centre. Burns Cottage and other sites associated with the poet.

Alloway Kirk
In Alloway. 2¹/₂m S of Ayr. All reasonable times. Free. Tel: Alloway (0292) 41252 (mornings).
Ancient church, a ruin in Burns' day, where his father William Burns is buried. Through its window, Tam saw the dancing witches and warlocks in the poem Tam o'Shanter. Adjacent to Burns Centre, Burns Monument Hotel and ¹/₂ mile from Burns Cottage/Tearoom.

Antartex Village
Loch Lomond, By Balloch, just off A82. Open daily 10.00–18.00 (closed Christmas & New Years Day).
Plenty of free parking. Seating capacity for over 150 within the Spinning Wheel Coffee Shop. Disabled facilities. Situated at the Southernmost tip of Loch Lomond, which enjoys the most dramatic scenery in the West of Scotland. It features a variety of craft workshops, where crafts-people work and sell their goods. Aspects of the famous Antartex Sheepskin processing and manufacturing make up an interesting factory tour, finally leading into the newly extended retail area, full of Antartex sheepskins and leathers. The full range of the Edinburgh Woollen Mill garments, knitwear, tartans and tourist lines plus something for the teenagers in the trading post.

Arbigland Gardens
By Kirkbean, off A710, 12m S of Dumfries. May-end Sep: Tue, Thu, Sun 14.00–18.00. House open afternoons Whit Week. (Captain J.B. Blackett). Tel: Kirkbean (038788) 283.
These extensive woodlands, formal and water gardens are arranged round a sandy bay which is ideal for children. John Paul Jones' birthplace is nearby, and his father was the gardener at Arbigland. Tearoom.

Ardrossan Castle
Ardrossan, on a hill overlooking Ardrossan Bay. All year, all reasonable times. Free. Tel: Saltcoats (0294) 602617.
Mid 12th-century castle on a hill with fine views of

Arran and Ailsa Craig. Castle was destroyed by Cromwell and only part of the north tower and two arched cellars remain. Car park.

Ardwell House Gardens
Ardwell, 11m SSE of Stranraer. Mar-Oct, daily 10.00–18.00. Parking available.
Daffodils, rhododendrons, crazy paving, foliage and flowering shrubs. Also pond walks with sea view. Plants for sale.

Argyll's Lodging
Castle Wynd, Stirling. Seen from the outside.
This fine example of an old town residence was built c. 1632 by Sir William Alexander of Menstrie, later Earl of Stirling, who eleven years earlier helped to found Nova Scotia (New Scotland). It is now a youth hostel.

Argyll and Sutherland Highlanders' Museum
In Stirling Castle. Easter-end Sept, Mon-Sat 10.00–17.30, Sun 11.00–17.00. Oct, Mon-Fri 10.00–16.00. Free. Parking available. Tel: Stirling (0786) 75165.
Fine regimental museum, with a notable silver and medal collection.

Auchentoshan Distillery
A82, NW of Glasgow. All year. Mon-Fri 09.00; last tour 15.30. Parking available. Tel: Duntocher (0389) 79476.
Guided tours showing production of lowland single malt whisky. Unusually, this spirit is triple distilled. Enjoy a dram and visit the shop. Duration of visit: approx. 45 minutes. (It is always advisable to telephone in advance to avoid unnecessary delays).

Bachelors' Club
Tarbolton, B744, 7¹/₂m NE of Ayr off A758. 1 Apr-28 Oct, daily 12.00–17.00; other times by arrangement. Tel: (0292) 541940.
A 17th-century house where in 1780 Robert Burns and his friends founded a literary and debating society, the Bachelors' Club. In 1779, Burns attended dancing lessions here, and in 1781 he was initiated as a Freemason. Period furnishings, with reminders of Burns' life at Lochlea Farm. Small coffee shop.

Bannockburn Heritage Centre
Off M80, 2m S of Stirling. 1 Apr-28 Oct, daily 10.00–18.00. Audio-visual presentation (last showing 17.30). (NTS). Tel: Bannockburn (0786) 812664.
The audio-visual presentation tells the story of the events leading up to the significant victory in

Scottish history (1314). In June 1964 the Queen inaugurated the Rotunda and unveiled the equestrian statue of Robert the Bruce. Information available on cassette.

Barsalloch Fort
Off A747, 7¹/₂m WNW of Whithorn. All reasonable times. Free. (HS). Tel: 031–244 3101.
Remains of an iron-age fort on the edge of a raised beach bluff. 60–70 feet above the shore, enclosed by a ditch 12 feet deep and 33 feet wide.

Ben Lomond
B837, 11m beyond Drymen. Parking available. (NTS). Tel: 041–552 8391.
Probably Scotland's most beloved mountain. Rising from the east shore of Loch Lomond to a height of 3,194ft, the Ben offers exhilarating walking and spectacular views all round. The summits of Ptarmigan (2,398ft), Sron Aonaich (1,893ft) and Beinn Uird (1,955ft) are within the property, comprising 5,423 acres. The hills are used for sheep-farming and visitors are asked to observe the Country Code. Dogs MUST be kept on a lead at all times, especially during the lambing season, as a lot of damage can be done in a very short time.

Blacksmith's Shop Visitor Centre
Gretna Green, just off A74 at Scottish/English border. Daily, all year. Tel: Gretna (0461) 38363/38224.
The old Blacksmith's Shop, famous for runaway marriages, has a museum with anvil marriage room and coach house. Gretna was once a haven for runaway couples seeking to take advantage of Scotland's then laxer marriage laws, when couples could be married by a declaration before witnesses; this was made illegal in 1940. Elopers can still, however, take advantage of Scots law permitting marriage without parental consent at 16. Among places where marriages took place were the Old Toll Bar (now bypassed) when the road opened in 1830, and the Smithy. Restaurant, bar and souvenir shop.

Bladnoch Distillery
1m S of Wigtown on A714. Apr-end Oct, Mon-Fri 10.00–16.00. Free. Parking available. Tel: (09884) 2235/2236.
Most southerly distillery in Scotland, built 1814. Original buildings still in use based around a central courtyard. Licensed shop and visitor centre. Free taste of Bladnoch 8-year-old Lowland Malt at end of tour.

Blairquhan Castle
Straiton, Maybole. Walled garden, pinetum and 3 mile private drive. Tearoom in Castle. Opening times: 15 July-12 Aug, Tues-Sun 13.30–16.15. Parking facilities. Tel: Straiton (065 57) 239.
Blairquhan was a castle built in 1820–24 for Sir David Hunter Blair, 3rd Baronet, replacing an earlier one which dated from the 14th century, part of which is included in the new castle. It was designed by the well known Scottish architect, William Burn.

Blowplain Open Farm
Balmaclellan, Castle Douglas. Easter-end Oct, 14.00 every day except Sat. Tour at 14.00 daily or by appointment (Mrs. Mary Blyth). Parking facilities. Tel: New Galloway (06442) 206.
Guided tour showing day-to-day life on a small hill-farm, and in particular the different types of animals and their uses. Winner of the 1987 Best Scottish Farm Tour Award; also Dumfries & Galloway Tourist Board Good Service Award.

Boswell Museum and Mausoleum
In Auchinleck. A76, 17m E of Ayr. Seen from outside at all times. For entry and guided tour, contact Mr. A. Wilson, 86 Main Street, Auchinleck; prior notice appreciated. Free: donations welcome. (Auchinleck Boswell Society). Tel: Cumnock (0290) 20757.
The ancient Parish Church, formerly a Celtic well, was enlarged by Walter fitz Alan in 1145–65, and again by David Boswell in 1641–43. It is now a museum of the Boswell family, and also contains a memorial to William Murdoch (1745–1839), a pioneer of lighting and heating by gas. The Boswell Mausoleum, attached, built by Alexander Boswell (Lord Auchinleck) in 1754, is the burial place of five known generations, including James Boswell, Dr Johnson's famous biographer. (Tour 1¹/₂ hrs). Small car park. 2 miles away at Lugar a walking tour on Murdoch, including his birthplace at Belo Mill, opened in 1984.

Bothwell Castle
At Uddingston on A74, 7m SE of Glasgow. Opening standard, except OctMar closed. Thu afternoon and Fri. (HS). Tel: 031–244 3101.
Once the largest and finest stone castle in Scotland, dating from the 13th century and reconstructed by the Douglases in the 15th century. In a picturesque setting above the Clyde Valley.

Broughton House
In Kirkcudbright centre, follow signs. Easter-mid Oct, Wed-Mon 11.00–13.00 and 14.00–17.00; Sun 14.00–17.00. Tel: (0557) 30437.

Home of the artist E.A. Hornel. House, gallery and beautiful gardens.

Bruce's Stone

6m W of New Galloway by A712. All reasonable times. Free. (NTS). Tel: 041–552 8391.
This granite boulder on Moss Raploch records a victory by Robert the Bruce over the English in March 1307, during the fight for Scotland's independence.

Bruce's Stone

N side of Loch Trool, unclassified road off A714, 13m N of Newton Stewart. All times. Free. Tel: Newton Stewart (0671) 2431.
A massive granite memorial to Robert the Bruce's first victory over the English leading to his subsequent success at Bannockburn. Fine views of Loch Trool and the hills of Galloway.

Robert Burns Centre

Mill Road, Dumfries. Apr-Sept, Mon-Sat 10.00–20.00, Sun 14.00–17.00. Oct-Mar, Tues-Sat 10.00–13.00, 14.00–17.00. Audio-visual theatre. Licensed restaurant. Parking available. Tel: Dumfries (0387) 64808.
The Robert Burns Centre is the major feature on the Scottish Tourist Board Burns Heritage Trail which runs through Dumfries and Galloway. The centre is housed in an attractive sand stone mill built on the banks of the River Nith in 1781. The mill now contains a 70 seat luxury theatre used for audio visual presentations, an exhibition on Burns life in Dumfries, a bookshop and a cafe. Also public film theatre in evenings. Induction loop.

Burns Cottage and Museum

B7024, at Alloway, 2m S of Ayr. All year. Jun-Aug 09.00–19.00, Apr, May, Sep, Oct 10.00–17.00 (Sun 14.00–17.00); Nov-Mar 10.00–16.00 (not Sun). (Trustees of Burns Monument). Tel: Ayr (0292) 41215.
In this thatched cottage built by his father, Robert Burns was born, 25 January 1759, and this was his home until 1766. Adjoining the cottage is a leading museum of Burnsiana. This is the start of the Burns Heritage Trail which can be followed to trace the places linked with Scotland's greatest poet. Tearoom, gift shop, museum and gardens. Information available on cassette.

Burns House, Dumfries

Burns Street. All year. Mon-Sat 10.00–13.00, 14.00–17.00, Sun 14.00–17.00. Closed Sun and Mon Oct-Mar. Tel: Dumfries (0387) 55297.
In November 1791 Robert Burns moved to Dumfries as an Exciseman and rented a three-room flat (not open to public) in the Wee Vennel (now Bank Street). In May 1793 he moved to a better house in Mill Vennel (now Burns Street) and here he died on 21 July 1796, though his wife Jean Armour stayed in the house until her death in 1834. The house has been completely refurbished and many relics of the poet are on show.

Burns House Museum, Mauchline

Castle Street, Mauchline, 11m ENE of Ayr. Easter-30 Sept, Mon-Sat 11.00–12.30, 13.30–17.30, Sun 14.00–17.00 (or by arrangement). Tel: Mauchline (0290) 50045.
On the upper floor is the room which Robert Burns took for Jean Armour in 1788: It has been kept intact and is furnished in the style of that period. The remainder of the museum contains Burnsiana and a collection of folk objects. There is a large collection of Mauchline boxware and an exhibition devoted to curling and curling stones which are made in the village. Nearby is Mauchline Kirkyard (scene of the Holy Fair) in which are buried four of Burns' daughters and a number of his friends and contemporaries. Other places of interest nearby are 15th-century Mauchline Castle and Poosie Nansie's Tavern.

Burns Mausoleum

St Michael's Churchyard, Dumfries. All reasonable times. Free. Tel: Dumfries (0387) 53862.
Burns was buried in St Michael's Churchyard near to the house in Mill Vennel where he died in 1796. In 1819 his remains were moved into the present elaborate mausoleum.

Burns Monument, Alloway

B7024 at Alloway, 2m S of Ayr. Open all year. June-Aug 09.00–19.00; Apr, May, Sept, Oct 10.00–17.00 (Sun 14.00–17.00), Nov-Mar 10.00–16.00 (not Sun). (Trustees of Burns Monument). Tel: Ayr (0292) 41321.
Grecian monument (1823) to the poet with relics dating back to the 1820's. Nearby is the attractive River Doon, spanned by the famous Brig o' Doon, a single arch (possibly 13th century), central to Burns' poem Tam o' Shanter. Museum, gift shop, gardens.

Burns Monument and Museum, Kilmarnock

Kay Park. Closed till further notice. View from outside only. Tel: Kilmarnock (0563) 26401.
The Monument is a statue by W G Stevenson, offering fine views over the surrounding countryside. The Kay Park Museum houses displays on the life and works of Burns, and has an extensive Burns Library.

Caerlaverock Castle.

Off B725, 9m S of Dumfries. Opening standard. (HS). Tel: 031–244 3101.

This seat of the Maxwell family dates back to 1270. In 1330, Edward I laid siege to it and in 1638 it capitulated to the Covenanters after a siege lasting 13 weeks. The castle is triangular with round towers. The heavy machicolation is 15th century and over the gateway between two splendid towers can be seen the Maxwell crest and motto. The interior was reconstructed in the 17th century as a Renaissance mansion, with fine carving.

Caerlaverock National Nature Reserve

B725, S of Dumfries by Caerlaverock Castle. All year. Free. (NCC). Tel: Glencaple (038 777) 275.

13,594 acres of salt marsh and intertidal mud and sand flats between the River Nith and the Lochar Water. A noted winter haunt of wildfowl, including barnacle geese. Access unrestricted, except in sanctuary area (600 acres), but intending visitors should contact the warden for advice on safety. Care must be taken relating to tides and quicksand.

Calderglen Country Park

Strathaven Road, East Kilbride. Park: all times; Children's Zoo: daily, 10.00-dusk; Visitor Centre (summer): Mon-Fri 12.00–15.00, Sat & Sun 12.00–16.00; (winter): Sat & Sun 12.00–16.00. Free. (East Kilbride District Council). Tel: East Kilbride (03552) 36644.

Park consists of over 300 acres of wooded gorge and parkland 5km in length. Extensive path system, nature trails, picnic sites, woodland and river with large waterfalls. Visitor Centre gives history of the landscape in the area and includes 'hidden worlds' natural history display. Ornamental garden, children's zoo and adventure playground. Ranger service.

Cameronians (Scottish Rifles) Regimental Museum

Mote Hill, off Muir Street, Hamilton. All year. Mon-Sat 10.00–13.00, 14.00–17.00, closed all day Thursday. Free. Tel: Hamilton (0698) 428 688.

Display of uniforms, medals, banners, silver and documents, relating to the regiment and also to Covenanting times.

Cardoness Castle

On A75, 1m Sw of Gatehouse of Fleet. Opening standard. Parking available. (HS). Tel: 031–244 3101.

This 15th-century tower house was long the home of the McCullochs of Galloway. It is four storeys high, with a vaulted basement. Features include the original stairway, stone benches and elaborate fireplaces.

Carfin Grotto

Carfin Village, 2m N of Motherwell. Daily. Outdoor devotions only on Sun (May-Oct) at 15.00. Free. Tel: Motherwell (0698) 63308.

Grotto of Our Lady of Lourdes and a place of pilgrimage. Hall open for teas during the summer (Sunday only).

Carlyle's Birthplace

A74 at Ecclefechan, 5$1/2$m SE of Lockerbie. 1 Apr-28 Oct, daily 12.00–17.00 (last tour 16.30). (NTS). (Mrs. Nancy Walter). Tel: Ecclefechan (05763) 666.

Thomas Carlyle (1795–1881) was born in this little house built by his father and uncle, both master masons, and itself of considerable architectural interest.

Carrick Castle

On W bank of Loch Goil, 5m S of Lochgoilhead. Can be viewed but not entered, privately owned. Free.

Built in the 14th century and first recorded in 1511, the walls of this great rectangular keep are entire though roofless. The Argylls kept their writs and charters here, and used it as a prison. Fortified in 1651 in expectation of a siege by Commonwealth forces, it was burned by the Earl of Atholl's troops in 1685.

Cartland Bridge

On A73 W of Lanark. All times. Free. Tel: (0555) 25444.

An impressive bridge built by Telford in 1822 over a gorge, carrying the Mouse Water. It is one of the highest road bridges in Scotland.

Castle Campbell

In Dollar Glen, 1m N of Dollar. Opening standard, except Oct-Mar closed Thurs afternoon and Fri. (HS). Tel: 031–244 3101.

On a steep mound with extensive views to the plains of the Forth, this castle was built towards the end of the 15th century by the first Earl of Argyll, and it was at one time known as Castle Gloom. It was burned by Cromwell's troops in the 1650's. The courtyard, great hall, and the great barrel roof of the third floor are well worth seeing. The 60 acres of woodland of Dollar Glen (NTS) make an attractive walk to the castle. The glen has a variety of steep paths and bridges through spectacular woodland scenery.

Castle Kennedy Gardens

N of A75, 3m E of Stranraer. Apr-Sep, daily 10.00–17.00. Tel: Stranraer (0776) 2024.
The Earl and Countess of Stair live at the adjoining Castle. These are nationally famous gardens particularly well known for their rhododendrons, azaleas, magnolias and embothriums. The notable pinetum was the first in Scotland. Tearoom and plant centre.

Castle of St. John

In Stranraer town centre, Castle Street. Apr-Sept, Mon-Sat 10.00–13.00, 14.00–17.00. Free. (Wigtown District Council). Tel: Stranraer (0776) 5088.
16th-century towerhouse later used as the town jail. Now open as a visitor centre with displays on Stranraer and Wigtown District. Shop. Information point.

Castle Semple Country Park

Off Largs Road, Lochwinnoch, 9m SW of Paisley. 09.00-dusk; closed for Christmas and New Year holidays. Free, but charges (various) for use of loch. (Strathclyde Regional Council). Tel: Lochwinnoch (0505) 842882 or Bridge of Weir (0505) 614791.
Country park based on Castle Semple Loch; about 200 acres. Bring your own boat or hire (no motor boats or keel boats). Bank angling. Next to RSPB visitor centre. Picnic areas and information centre.

Castle Sween

On E shore of Loch Sween, 15m SW of Lochgilphead. All reasonable times. Free. (HS). Tel: 031244 3101.
This is probably the oldest stone castle on the Scottish mainland, built in the mid-12th century. It was destroyed by Sir Alexander MacDonald in 1647.

Cathcartston Visitor Centre

Centre of Dalmellington. Easter-October, daily 10.00–15.00. Donations to Dalmellington & District Conservation Trust gratefully received. Tel: (0292) 550633/550339/531144.
Interpretation centre containing tableau of weaving period, exhibition area and audio visual presentation.

Chatelherault

At Ferniegair, 1m S of Hamilton off A72. Visitor Centre: 1 Apr-30 Sept 10.30–18.00; 1 Oct-31 Mar 10.30–17.00 daily. Last admission ¹/₂ hour before closing. House: All year, daily 11.00–16.00 (last admission 15.45) closed for functions – check.
Restored 18th century gardens, terraces and paterre. Parking available. Tel: (0698) 426213.
Magnificent hunting lodge and kennels built in 1732 by William Adam for the Duke of Hamilton. The buildings have been restored and there are extensive country walks and a fascinating visitor centre giving a vivid portrayal of the 18th century characters who helped to build it.

The Church of the Holy Rude

St. John's Street, Stirling. May-Sept, weekdays 10.00–17.00. Free. Sundays 11.00 (worship). Tel: (0786) 74154.
The only church in Scotland still in use which has witnessed a coronation, when in 1567, the infant James VI, aged 13 months, was crowned. John Knox preached the sermon. The church dates from 1414, and Mary, Queen of Scots worshipped there. Notable pipe-organ; extensive restoration currently in progress.

Coats Observatory

Coats Observatory, Oakshaw Street, Paisley. Mon, Tues & Thur 14.00–20.00, Wed, Fri and Sat 10.00–17.00. Free. Groups by prior arrangement. (Renfrew District Council). Tel: 041–889 2013.
There has been a continuous tradition of astronomical observation and meteorological recording since the observatory was built in 1882. The recent updating of seismic equipment and the installation of a satellite weather picture receiver has made it one of the best equipped observatories in the country.

Colzium House and Grounds

Turn left 1m E of Kilsyth on A803. Opening times may vary throughout the various parts of house and grounds. Free. Parking available. Tel: (0236) 823281.
18th to 19th century mansion house with museum, function suites, courtyard, walled garden, fountain, children's zoo. Grounds with picnic areas, curling pond, loch, woodland walks and historic remains. Tearoom at curling pond (seasonal).

Comlongon Castle

Situated in Clarencefield, midway between Dumfries and Annan on B724. Mar-Nov, daily 10.00–16.00. Closed all day Thurs. Sun 12.00–16.00. No dogs allowed on site except guide dogs. Parking available. Tel: Clarencefield (038787) 283.
Exceptionally well-preserved 15th century Border castle now being restored. It contains many original features including dungeons, kitchen, great hall, Heraldic devices, bed chambers with 'privies'.

Picnic area, nature trail, woodland walks, peacocks etc. Bed and Breakfast available.

Craignethan Castle
2¹/₂m W of A72 at Crossford, 5m NW of Lanark. Opening standard. Parking available. (HS). Tel: 031–244 3101.
This extensive and well-preserved ruin, chief stronghold of the Hamiltons who were supporters of Mary, Queen of Scots, was repeatedly assailed by the Protestant party and partly dismantled by them in 1579. The oldest, central portion is a large tower house of unusual and ornate design. Recent excavations have revealed possibly the earliest example in Britain of a caponier, a covered gun-looped passageway across a defensive ditch.

Crarae Glen Garden
A83, 10m SW of Inveraray. All year, daily 09.00–18.00. (Crarae Garden Charitable Trust). Tel: Minard (0546) 86614/86607.
Among the lovliest open to the public in Scotland, these gardens of Crarae Lodge, beside Loch Fyne and set in a Highland Glen, are note for rhododendrons, azaleas, conifers and ornamental shrubs.

Creetown Gem Rock Museum & Gallery
Approach by A75 to Creetown, turn up opposite clock tower. Daily, Easter-Sept 09.30–18.00, Oct-Easter 09.30–17.00. Unlicensed restaurant. Parking available. Tel: Creetown (0671 82) 554.
A beautiful collection of gems and minerals from around the world. This large worldwide collection has taken over 50 years to gather together and is recognised as being one of the most comprehensive collection of its type, and shows the many fascinating mineral forms created by nature. Tearoom, gift shop and custom gemstone cutting workshop.

Crichton Royal Museum
Off B725 Glencaple road, 1m S of Dumfries centre in hospital grounds. Square building with clock face behind church. All year, Thurs, Fri 13.30–16.30, Easter-Oct Thurs, Fri, Sat 13.30–16.30. Outwith these times, open for parties by appointment. Free. Parking available. Tel: (0387) 55301, ext.2360.
Museum highlights, in a spacious setting, developments in one of Britain's leading hospitals. Special features include operating theatre, patients' art 1839–61; library and reading room. Beautiful grounds with splendid rock garden and arboretum; garden shop and tearoom.

Crossraguel Abbey
A77, 2m SW of Maybole. Opening standard, except Oct-Mar Thu and Fri. (HS). Tel: 031244 3101.
A Cluniac monastery built in 1244 by the Earl of Carrick during the reign of Alexander II. The Abbey was inhabited by Benedictine monks from 1244 until the end of the 16th century, and the extensive remains are of high architectural distinction. The gatehouse and dovecot are specially illuminating.

Culzean Castle and Country Park
A719, 12m SSW of Ayr. Castle, Restaurant and Shop: 1 Apr-28 Oct, daily 10.30–17.30. Country park: daily all year 09.30-sunset. Best seen Apr-Sept. Tel: Kirkoswald (065 56) 269. Ranger service. Environmental Education service. Interpretative programme and special events. (NTS; Strathclyde Regional Council; Kyle and Carrick, Cumnock and Doon Valley District Councils). Tel: Kirkoswald (065 56) 274.
The splendid castle, one of Robert Adam's most notable creations, although built around an ancient tower of the Kennedy's dates mainly from 1777. Special features are the Round Drawing Room, the fine plaster ceilings and magnificent oval staircase. The Eisenhower Presentation explains the General's associaion with Culzean.
In 1970 Culzean became the first country park in Scotland; in 1973 a Reception and Interpretation Centre with exhibition etc was opened in the farm buildings designed by Robert Adam. The 565-acre grounds include a walled garden established in 1783, aviary, swan pond, camelia house and orangery. Ranger naturalist service with guided walks, talks and films in summer. Licensed self-service restaurant.

Dalgarven Mill – The Ayrshire Museum of Countryside and Costume
On A737, Dalry Road, Kilwinning. Mon-Sat 10.00–17.00, Sun 12.30–17.00. Tel: Kilwinning (0294) 52448.
The museum is within a restored working water mill. There are extensive displays of agricultural and rural life including machinery, hand tools, furnishings and photographs. The costume collection has been gathered locally and there are three display changes per year. The mill has been in the same family since 1883 and was in existence prior to 1602. There is a bakehouse which supplies wholemeal bread and rolls and home baking for the coffee room.

Darvel

Under 10m E of Kilmarnock on A71.
Birth place of Sir Alexander Fleming, discoverer of penicillin; a garden commemorates him and his work.

Dean Castle and Country Park

Dean Road, off Glasgow Road, Kilmarnock. Daily 12.00–17.00. All year (Closed Dec. 25,26; Jan 1,2). Country park: all year, free. Parking available. Tel: Kilmarnock (0563) 22702/26401.
14th-century fortified keep with dungeon and battlements and 15th-century palace, the ancestral home of the Boyd family. It contains an outstanding collection of medieval arms, armour, tapestries and musical instruments. Display of Burns manuscripts. The country park has 200 acres of woodland with rivers, nature trail, children's corner, fawns, picnic areas. Tearoom and riding centre.

Denny Ship Model Experiment Tank

Building adjacent to Safeway supermarket, access by Castle Street 200yds E of Dumbarton town centre. Daily, Mon-Sat 10.00–16.00. Parking available. Tel: (0389) 63444 (09.00–16.00 hrs).
The world's oldest surviving ship model experiment tank. Visitors can witness the process of making wax hull forms, unchanged since 1883.

Dick Institute

Elmbank Avenue, off London Road, Kilmarnock. Apr-Sept, Mon, Tues, Thurs, Fri 10.00–20.00; Wed & Sat 10.00–17.00; Oct-Mar, Mon-Sat 10.00–17.00. Free. Parking available. Tel: Kilmarnock (0563) 26401/22702.
The museum has an important collection of geological specimens, local archaeology, Scottish broadswords, firearms and natural history. The Art Gallery has frequently changing exhibitions.

Doune Castle

Off A84 at Doune, 8m NW of Stirling. Opening standard except Oct-Mar closed, Fri and alternate Sat. (HS). Tel: 031244 3101.
Splendid ruins of one of the best preserved mediaeval castles in Scotland, built late 14th or early 15th century by the Regent Albany. After his execution in 1424 it came into the hands of the Stuarts of Doune, Earls of Moray, in the 16th century, and the 'Bonnie Earl of Moray' lived here before his murder in 1592. The bridge in the village was built in 1535 by Robert Spittal, James IV's tailor, to spite the ferryman who had refused him a passage.

Doune Motor Museum

At Doune on A84, 8m NW of Stirling. Apr-Oct, daily 10.00–17.00. (Earl of Moray). Tel: Doune (0786) 841 203.
The Earl of Moray's collection of vintage and post-vintage cars, including examples of Hispano Suiza, Bentley, Jaguar, Aston Martin, Lagonda and the second oldest Rolls Royce in the world. Cafeteria.

Drumlanrig Castle

Off A76, 3m N of Thornhill, Dumfriesshire and 16m off A74 by A702. Grounds open: 28 Apr-30 Sept; Castle 5 May-19 Aug. Weekdays 11.00–17.00 (check for closure day during week), Sun 14.00–18.00. Tel: Thornhill (0848) 30248.
Unique example of late 17th century Renaissance architecture in pink sandstone, built on the site of earlier Douglas strongholds. Set in parkland ringed by the wild Dumfriesshire hills. Louis XIV furniture, and paintings by Rembrandt, Holbein, Murillo, Ruysdael. Adventure woodland play area, nature trail, gift shop and tearoom. Guide dogs by prior arrangement. Lift available but unaccompanied.

Drumpellier Country Park

From Glasgow leave M8 at junction 8 to A89 to traffic lights, filter left to B8752 and proceed 1¹/₄m to 'T' junction. Turn right and proceed for 700yds for entrance to park. Apr-Oct, Mon-Sun, daily 09.00–20.00; Nov-Mar, Wed-Sun 12.00–17.00. Free. Parking available. Tel: (0236) 22257.
Modern pursuit centre, site of crannog plus walks round loch and Monkland Canal. Orienteering course with maps. Ranger-guided walks, play areas; exhibitions. Peace garden, butterfly house, glass house complex.

Dumfries Museum

The Observatory, Dumfries. All year, Mon-Sat 10.00–13.00, 14.00–17.00, Sun 14.00–17.00, closed Sun and Mon Oct-Mar. Museum and gardens free. Tel: Dumfries (0387) 53374.
This regional museum for the Solway area has recently been refurbished and contains a wide variety of interesting exhibits. It is based on an 18th century windmill and has a camera obscura.

Dunblane Cathedral

In Dunblane, A9, 6m N of Stirling. Opening standard, except summer when 14.00–17.00 on Sunday. Free. (HS). Tel: 031–244 3101.
The existing building dates mainly from the 13th century but incorporates a 12th-century tower. The nave was unroofed after the Reformation but the whole building was restored in 1829–95.

Dundonald Castle
4¹/₂m SW of Kilmarnock.
Both Robert II and Robert III of Scotland died here.
On isolated hill, most of the tower survives.

Dundrennan Abbey
A711, 7m SE of Kirkcudbright. Opening standard. Parking available. (HS). Tel: 031–244 3101.
A Cistercian house founded in 1142 whose ruins include much late Norman and transitional work. Here it is believed Mary, Queen of Scots spent her last night in Scotland, 15 May, 1568.

Dunmore Pineapple
N of Airth, 7m E of Stirling off A905, then B9124. Not open to public, viewed from the outside only. Parking nearby. (NTS, leased to the Landmark Trust). Tel: (0738) 31296.
This curious structure, built as a 'garden retreat' and shaped like a pineapple, stands in the grounds of Dunmore Park, and bears the date 1761. It is the focal point of the garden and is available for holiday and other short lets by phoning the Landmark Trust (062882) 5925.

Eglinton Country Park
2m N of Irvine. Ranger service 08.45–16.45. Visitors centre 10.00–16.30. Park open daily 09.00–17.00. Tel: Irvine (0294) 51776.
This is a major country park built around the former Eglinton Montgomery Estate. Displays in the visitor centre explain the natural history and the history of the area, including material on the Eglinton tournament of 1839.

Electric Brae
A719 9m S of Ayr (also known as Croy Brae). All times. Free.
An optical illusion is created so that a car appears to be going down the hill when it is in fact going up.

Ellisland Farm
Off A76, 6¹/₂m NNW of Dumfries. All reasonable times, but intending visitors are advised to phone in advance. Free. (Ellisland Trust). Tel: Dumfries (0387) 74 426.
Robert Burns took over this farm in June 1788, built the farmhouse, and tried to introduce new farming methods. Unsuccessful, he became an Exciseman in September 1789; in August 1791 the stock was auctioned, and he moved to Dumfries in November 1791. Some of the poet's most famous works were written at Ellisland, including Tam o'Shanter and Auld Lang Syne. The Granary houses a display showing Burns as a farmer.

Farmhouse with museum room; granary building with Burns display; riverside walk.

Finlarig Castle
S point of Loch Tay near Killin.
One time seat of the Breadalbanes these ruins have a beheading pit thought to be the only one left in Scotland.

Finlaystone
By A8 W of Langbank, 17m W of Glasgow. Gardens open daily 10.30–17.00. (House) Apr–Aug, Sun afternoon, or by arrangement. (Mr. George MacMillian). Tel: Langbank (047 554) 285 (12.30–13.00 or evenings) or (047 554) 505.
Country estate with woodland walks, nursery gardens, formal gardens, adventure playgrounds and pony trekking. Countryside Ranger Service. The house has some fine rooms, Victorian relics, flower prints and an international collection of dolls shown in the billiard room. Historical connections with John Knox and Robert Burns. Afternoon teas (Apr-Sep).

Galloway Deer Museum
On A712, by Clatteringshaws Loch, 6m W of New Galloway. Easter-Mid Oct, daily 10.00–17.00. Free. (FC). Tel: New Galloway (064 42) 285/(0556) 3626.
The museum, in a converted farm steading, has a live trout exhibit as well as many features on deer and other aspects of Galloway wildlife, Geology and history. Bruce's Stone on Raploch Moss is a short walk away.

Galloway Farm Museum
From New Galloway take A712 W for 1m. Car park on left beside A712. Easter-end June, Sun only. July-end Sept open 6 days (closed Sat). Conducted tour 14.00. Parking available. Tel: (06443) 317.
Comprehensive display of horse implements dating from early 19th century. Demonstrations of farm horses at work with interesting talks on each implement showing how oats, hay, turnips and potatoes are produced. Cart horse/sleigh rides.

Galloway Forest Park
Off A714, 10m NW of Newton Stewart. Free. (FC). Tel: Newton Stewart (0671) 2420.
250 square miles of magnificent countryside in Central Galloway, including Merrick (2,765 feet) the highest hill in southern Scotland. The land is owned by the Forestry Commission and there is a wide variety of leisure facilities including forest trails, fishing, a red deer range, a wild goat park, a forest drive and a deer museum. Murray's

monument dominates a hillside off the A712. It was erected to commemorate the son of a local shepherd who became a professor at Edinburgh University.

Galloway House Gardens
At Garlieston, 8m S of Wigtown. All year, daily, all reasonable times. Admission by collection box, in aid of Scotland's Garden Scheme and Sorbie Church Organ Fund. Tel: Garlieston (098 86) 225.
Galloway House was built in 1740 by Lord Garlies, eldest son of the 7th Earl of Galloway, and later enlarged by Burn, and the hall decorated by Lorimer. Not open to the public.
The grounds cover some 30 acres and go down to the sea and sandy beach. There are fine old trees, and as a speciality in May/June there is a well-grown handkerchief tree. In season there are many snowdrops, pretty old-fashioned daffodils and a good collection of rhododendrons and azaleas. Also a walled garden with greenhouses and a camellia house. Home-baked teas are available in Garlieston village.

Gartmorm Dam Country Park and Nature Reserve
By Sauchie, 2m NE of Alloa off A908. (Park) all year at all times. (Visitor centre) Apr-Sept, daily 08.30–17.30; Oct-Mar, Sat & Sun 14.00–16.00. Free. (Clackmannan District Council). Tel: Alloa (0259) 214319.
The oldest dam in Scotland, with reservoir. The park is an important winter roost for migratory duck, there are pleasant walks and fishing is available. Visitor Centre has exhibits, information and slide shows. Talks and escorted walks can be arranged through the ranger service.

MV 'Gipsy Princess'
B802, 1m S of Kilsyth. May-Sept, Sun afternoons: 1 hour round trips from Auchinstarry Bridge at 14.00 and 15.00; also from Craigmarloch Bridge (1½m to the E) at 14.30. Tel: (0236) 721856 or (0236) 822437.
The Gipsy Princess is a new (1990) custom-built, 36-seater passenger boat with open air and covered accommodation, designed and operated by the Forth & Clyde Canal Society. She follows the route of the former 'Gypsy Queen' which cruised in the early part of the century beneath the wooded slopes of Craigmarloch Hill through the historic Kelvin Valley.

Girvan
23m S of Ayr on A77.
Small fishing port from which boat trips to the 114 foot high Ailsa Craig take place. Also the location of Grant's Whisky distillery.

Glenkiln
10m W of Dumfries in immediate vicinity of Shawhead (signposted from the A75).
Around the reservoir stand sculptures by Henry Moore, Epstein, Rodin and others.

Glenluce Abbey
Off A75, 2m N of Glenluce. Opening standard. (HS). Tel: 031244 3101.
Founded in 1192 by Roland, Earl of Galloway, for the Cistercian order. A fine vaulted chapter house is of architectural interest.

Glenluce Motor Museum
½m N of centre of Glenluce. Daily, 1 Mar-31 Oct 10.00–19.00; 1 Nov-28 Feb 11.00–16.00; closed Mon and Tues. Parking available. Tel: (05813) 534.
Farm buildings containing a collection of vintage and classic motor cars and bikes. Restoration work is also on display. Tearoom (seating 24).

Grangemouth Museum
Victoria Library, Bo'ness Road, Grangemouth. All year Mon-Sat 14.00–17.00. Free. Parking available. (Falkirk District Council). Tel: Grangemouth (0324) 483291/24911, ext. 2472.
Display relating to growth of Grangemouth from sea-lock to a Victorian town. Exhibits on canals, shipping and shipbuilding. The world's first practical steamship, the Charlotte Dundas and local industries. Museum Shop.

Greenhill Covenanter's House
In Biggar on A702, 26m from Edinburgh, A74 (South) 12m. Easter, then mid May-mid Oct, daily 14.00–17.00. (Biggar Museum Trust). Tel: Biggar (0899) 21050.
Burn Braes Farmhouse, rescued in ruinous condition and rebuilt at Biggar, ten miles from the original site. Exhibits include relics of local Covenanters, Donald Cargill's bed (1681), 17th century furnishings, costume dolls rare breeds of animals and poultry. Reduced price for joint admission to Gladstone Court Street Museum. Audio-visual programme.

Guildhall
St. John's Street, Stirling. May-Sept, Mon-Fri 09.30–17.30; Oct-Apr, Mon-Fri 09.30–16.30. Free. Tel: Stirling (0786) 62373/79000.
The Guildhall, or Cowane's Hospital, was built between 1634 and 1649 as an almshouse for elderly

members of the Guild of Merchants. It contains portraits of former Deans of Guild, and weights and measures.

Hamilton District Museum

¹/₂m SW of M74 at A723 interchange. All year, Mon-Sat 10.00–17.00. Closed 12.00–13.00 on Wed and Sat. Parking available. Free. Tel: Hamilton (0698) 283981.

Local history museum housed in a 17th-century coaching inn complete with original stable and 18th-century Assembly room. Displays include costume, art, archaeology, natural history, transport and a reconstructed Victorian kitchen. Also regular temporary exhibition programme. Museum shop with a wide range of publications and souvenirs.

Heatherbank Museum and Library of Social Work Trust

163 Mugdock Road, Milngavie, 8m NW of Glasgow. All year. Open every afternoon. 14.00–17.00 except Sat or by arrangement. Tea by arrangement. Free. (Donations welcome). Tel: 041–956 2687.

The only museum of social work in Europe. There is an extensive reference library and archive collection, picture library and exhibition room.

Highland Mary's Monument

At Failford, on B743 3m W of Mauchline. All times. Free. Tel: (0292) 282109.

The monument commemorates the place where, it is said, Robert Burns parted from his 'Highland Mary', Mary Campbell. They exchanged vows, but she died the following autumn.

Highland Mary's Statue

Dunoon, near pier. All times. Free. Parking available.

The statue of Burns' Highland Mary at the foot of the Castle Hill. Mary Campbell was born on a farm in Dunoon, and consented to become Burns' wife before he married Jean Armour.

The Hill House

Upper Colquhoun Street, Helensburgh. All year (except 25/26 Dec and 1/2 Jan), 13.00–17.00. (NTS). Tel: Helensburgh (0436) 73900.

Overlooking the estuary of the River Clyde, this house is considered to be the finest example of the domestic architecture of Charles Rennie Mackintosh. Gardens are being restored. Special display about Mackintosh. Tearoom.

Hunterston Power Station

By the A78, 5m S of Largs. Early May-end Sept.

Guided tours, Mon-Sat 10.00, 11.30, 14.00, 15.30; Sun 14.00, 15.30. Free. Parking available. Refreshments available. To book Tel: (0800) 838557 (freephone), or (0294) 822311.

Nuclear Power Station, video plus displays. This plant, operated by Scottish Nuclear Ltd., produces a quarter of all electricity consumed in Scotland.

Kelburn Country Park

Off A78 between Largs and Fairlie. Easter-mid Oct, daily 10.00–18.00. (Earl of Glasgow). Tel: Fairlie (0475) 568685.

The historic estate of the Earls of Glasgow, famous for rare trees and the Kelburn Glen. Also waterfalls, gardens, nature trails, exhibitions, adventure course, Marine Assault Course, children's stockade, pets' corner and pony-trekking. The central, 18th-century farm buildings have been converted to form a village square with craft shop, workshops, display rooms and licensed cafe. Ranger Service. Car park. Picnic tables and Commando Assault Course.

M.V. 'Kenilworth' Cruises

Car and coach park at pier in Helensburgh. May-Sept, Mon-Sat, cruises from 10.40. Parking available. Tel: (0475) 21281.

Attractive 1930's vintage well-maintained passenger vessel. Other sailings to Dunoon, Rothesay, Millport, etc. Light refreshments available.

Kilberry Sculptured Stones

Off B8024, 20m SSW of Lochgilphead. All reasonable times. Free. (HS). Tel: 031–244 3101.

A fine collection of late mediaeval sculptured stones.

Kilmarnock

13m N of Ayr on A77.

The first collection of poems by Robert Burns was published here in 1786; a copy and other original mss are held at the Burns museum. Dean Castle has outstanding collection of mediaeval musical instruments and is within the Dean Castle Country Park. The Johnnie Walker distillery is open for visitor's tours.

Kilmun Arboretum

By Forest Office on A880, 1m E of junction with A815. 5m N of Dunoon. All year. Daily, all day. Free. Parking available. (FC). Tel: (03964) 666.

A fascinating collection of tree species on a hillside to the northeast of Holy Loch within the Argyll Forest Park.

Kilsyth's Heritage Museum

Turn right off A803 (Kirkintilloch-Falkirk) into Station Road, Kilsyth. Follow road into Burngreen in library building. All year, Mon, Wed, Fri 09.30–13.00 & 14.30–19.00; Tues 09.30–13.00 & 14.00–17.00; Thurs 09.30–13.00; Sat 09.00–12.00. Free. Parking available. Tel: (0236) 823147.
Museum illustrating the history of the Kilsyth area.

Kirkoswald

15m S of Ayr on A77.
Souter Johnnie's cottage a thatched 18th century house, was once the home of John Davidson, the souter or cobbler of Burn's Tam o'Shanter.

Lagoon Leisure Centre

Paisley, off Mill Street. Tel: 041–889 4000.
Modern swimming pool complex with bar and cafeteria. Sauna, steam room and jacuzzi.

Land O'Burns Centre

Opposite Alloway Kirk, 2m S of Ayr. All year, daily, spring and autumn 10.00–17.30, Jun 10.00–17.30, Jul-Aug 10.00–18.00, winter 10.00–17.00. Admission free, small charge for audio-visual display (Kyle and Carrick District Council). Tel: Ayr (0292) 43700.
This visitor centre has an exhibition area and an audio-visual display on the life and times of Robert Burns. Landscaped gardens.

Largs Museum

Manse Court, Largs. June-Sept, Mon-Sat 14.00–17.00. Open at other times by arrangement. Donation box. (Largs & District Historical Society). Tel: Largs (0475) 687081 (Kirkgate House).
The museum holds a small collection of local bygones, with a library of local history books and numerous photographs.

Lauder Memorials

Off A815, 3m SE of Strachur. All reasonable times. Free.
Sir Harry Lauder at one time resided at nearby Glenbranter House (now demolished) and during his stay his only son, John, was killed in World War I. Sir Harry erected an obelisk in his memory on a knoll a short distance N of Loch Eck. In the same enclosure is a Celtic Cross, a memorial to Lady Lauder who died in 1927.

Lillie Art Gallery

Milngavie, off A81, 8m N of Glasgow. All year, Tue-Fri 11.00–17.00, 19.00–21.00, Sat & Sun 14.00–17.00. Free. Parking available. Tel: 041–956 2351, ext. 226.
A modern purpose-built art gallery with a permanent collection of 20th-century Scottish paintings, sculpture and ceramics, and temporary exhibitions of contemporary art. Alternative entrance with ramp.

"Little Wheels"

Portpatrick. Easter-Oct. Core times 11.00–16.00, extended during July and Aug. Phone for latest times (Ansaphone service). Limited parking available. Tel: (077 681) 536.
Model Railway (over 100 metres of track), Toy and Transport Exhibition. Children can usually 'drive' some of the trains. Special new displays each year. Hot and cold drinks, collectors' items and gifts for sale.

Livingstone National Memorial

At Blantyre, A724, 3m NW of Hamilton. All year, daily 10.00–18.00, Sun 14.00–18.00. Tel: Blantyre (0698) 823140.
Shuttle Row is an 18th-century block of mill tenements where David Livingstone, the famous explorer/missionary was born in 1813, went to school and worked while studying to become a doctor. The National Memorial, containing very many interesting relics of the Industrial Revolution and of Africa, is in this building, now surrounded by parkland. The Africa Pavilion illustrates modern Africa and a Social History museum deals with agriculture, cotton spinning and mining in Blantyre and district. Tearoom, gardens, picnic area, play equipment and paddling pool.

Loch Doon Castle

From A713, 10m S of Dalmellington, take road to Loch Doon. All reasonable times. Free. (HS). Tel: 031–244 3101.
This mid 14th-century castle was devised to fit the island on which it was originally built. When the waters of the loch were raised in connection with a hydro-electric scheme the castle was dismantled and re-erected on the shores of the loch. The walls of this massive building, once known as Castle Balliol, vary from 7–9 feet thick and stand about 26 feet high.

Lochmaben Castle

Off B7020 on S shore of Castle Loch, by Lochmaben, 9m ENE of Dumfries. All reasonable times. Free. Tel: Dumfries (0387) 53862.
This castle was captured and recaptured twelve times and also withstood six attacks and sieges. James IV was a frequent visitor, and Mary, Queen

of Scots, was here in 1565. Now a ruin, this early 14th-century castle is on the site of a castle of the de Brus family, ancestors of Robert the Bruce who is said to have been born here.

Lochore Meadows Country Park
Between Lochgelly and Ballingry on B920. (Country Park) At all times. (Park Centre) Summer 08.00–20.00, winter 09.00–17.00. (Fishery) 15 Mar-6 Oct. (Country Park facilities: rates on application). Tel: Ballingry (0592) 860086.
Green, pleasant countryside around large loch reclaimed from coal mining waste in the 1960s. Reclamation makes fascinating story told in slide show, displays and ranger guided walks. Plenty of scope for birdwatching, wildlife study, walks, picnics. Many ancient historical remains. Cafe and information in park centre. Activities include boat and bank fishing, sailing, windsurfing, canoeing, golf, horse riding, trim trail, wayfaring, self-guided trails, picnic areas and cafeteria. Wide range of provisions for visitors with special needs. Groups welcome.

Lochwinnoch Community Museum
Main Street, Lochwinnoch. Mon, Wed & Fri 10.00–13.00, 14.00–17.00 & 18.00–20.00; Tues & Sat 10.00–13.00 & 14.00–17.00. Closed Thurs & Sun. Free. (Renfrew District Council Museums and Art Galleries Service). Tel: 041–889 3151 or Lochwinnoch (0505) 842615.
Lochwinnoch Community Museum features a series of changing exhibitions reflecting the historic background of local agriculture, industry and village life. There are occasional special exhibitions.

Lochwinnoch Nature Reserve
Largs Road, Lochwinnoch, 9m SW of Paisley. All year, daily 10.00–17.15. Closed all day Thurs. School parties by arrangement. (RSPB). Tel: Lochwinnoch (0505) 842663/031–557 3136.
Purpose built Nature Centre with observation tower, displays and shop. Two observation hides overlooking marsh reached by walk through woods. Third hide overlooking Barr Loch. Shop.

Logan Botanic Gardens
Off B7065, 14m S of Stranraer. Daily 15 Mar-31 Oct 10.00–18.00. Tel: Stranraer (077 686) 231.
Here a profusion of plants from the warm and temperate regions of the world flourish in some of the mildest conditions in Scotland. There are cabbage palms, tree ferns and many other Southern Hemisphere species. Salad bar, meals served all day.

Logan Fish Pond
Off B7065, 14m S of Stranraer. Easter-Sept, daily 12.00–20.00. (Sir Ninian Buchan-Hepburn, Bt). Tel: Ayr (0292) 268181.
This tidal pool in the rocks, 30 feet deep and 53 feet round, was completed in 1800 as a fresh-fish larder for Logan House. Damaged by a mine in 1942, it was reopened in 1955. It holds some 30 fish, mainly cod, so tame that they come to be fed by hand.

Loudoun Hall
Boat Vennel, off Cross in Ayr town centre. Jul-end Aug, Mon-Sat 11.00–16.00 or by arrangement. Free, but donation box available. Group visits if booked can have guided walk of Ayr (approx 1 hour) with light refreshments. Parking available. (Loudoun Hall Trustees). Tel: Ayr (0292) 282109/611290.
A late 15th-century/early 16th-century town house built for a rich merchant, one of the oldest surviving examples of burgh architecture to remain in Scotland. For a period it was the town house of the Campbells, Earls of Loudoun, and the Moore family; both families played prominent parts in the life of Ayr. Local history publications for sale.

MacLaurin Gallery & Rozelle House
1 1/2m S of Ayr, off road to Burns Cottage at Alloway. Mon-Sat 10.00–17.00; Sun (Apr-Oct) 14.00–17.00. Free. Parking available. (Trustees of the late Mrs. Mary Ellen Maclaurin with Kyle and Carrick District Libraries and Museums). Tel: Ayr (0292) 45447.
Set in extensive parkland, the gallery was formerly stables and servants' quarters attached to the mansion house. A programme of temporary exhibitions operates throughout the year covering Fine Art, Sculpture, Photography and Crafts. The gallery shows many major Arts Council exhibitions. Rozelle House operates a programme of temporary exhibitions and also houses the Maclaurin Contemporary Art Collection and the District Collection's Henry Moore sculpture in the gallery courtyard. Rozelle House Pantry offers meals and refreshments throughout the day. Open during gallery hours.

McLean Museum and Art Gallery
Greenock. All year, Mon-Sat 10.00–12.00, 13.00–17.00. Free. (Inverclyde District Council). Tel: Greenock (0475) 23741.
A local museum with art collection, natural history, shipping exhibits, ethnographic material and items relating to James Watt, who was born in Greenock. Small shop. Wheelchair access at rear of building.

MacLellan's Castle

Off High Street, Kirkcudbright. Opening standard except Oct-Mar closed Mon-Fri. (HS). Tel: 031-244 3101.

A handsome castellated mansion overlooking the harbour, dating from 1577. Elaborately planned with fine architectural details, it has been a ruin since 1752. In Kirkcudbright also see the 16th/17th-century Tolbooth, the Mercat Cross of 1610 and the Stewartry Museum.

MacRobert Arts Centre

University of Stirling. Parking available. Tel: Stirling (0786) 61081 or 73171, ext. 2543.

A five-hundred seat theatre, art gallery and studio, providing all year theatre, opera, dance, films, concerts, conferences and exhibitions. Theatre bar. For details of events, contact the box office. Induction loop system.

Magnum Leisure Centre

From Glasgow take the A736 to Irvine and follows signs for Harbourside (Magnum). All year, daily 09.00-22.00. Parking available. Tel: (0294) 78381.

Leisure Centre attractions include new state-of-the art indoor water park, indoor bowling, sports hall, ice rink, theatre/cinema, soft play area, kiddies superbounce area, squash courts, sauna, fitness salon. Two licensed bars, fast food area and restaurant.

Mariner Leisure Centre

On A803 1m W of Falkirk's High Street and 24m from Glasgow and Edinburgh. All year, Mon 09.00-17.00; Tues-Sun 09.00-21.00 (swimming); Mon-Sun 09.00-22.00 (sports facilities). Parking available. Tel: (0324) 22083.

Lagoon-shaped pool with wave machine, games hall, squash courts, sauna and solarium, fitness room, creche or general purpose room. Cafeteria and licensed lounge bar offering hot and cold snacks overlooking the pool below.

Mar's Wark

At the top of Castle Wynd, Stirling. All times. Free. (HS). Tel: 031-244 3101.

Mar's Wark is one of a number of fine old buildings on the approach to Stirling Castle. Built c 1570 by the first Earl of Mar, Regent of Scotland, it was a residence of the Earls of Mar until the 6th Earl had to flee the country after leading the 1715 Jacobite Rebellion.

Maxwelton House

13m NW of Dumfries on B729, near Moniaive. Gardens, Chapel and Museum: May-Sept 14.00-17.00. House: July-Aug (other times by arrangement). Chapel: Admission charge. (Mr. M.R.L. Stenhouse). Tel: Moniaive (084 82) 385.

The house dates back to the 14th/15th centuries. Originally it was a stronghold of the Earls of Glencairn and later the birthplace of Annie Laurie, to whom William Douglas of Fingland wrote the famous poem. Museum of early kitchen, dairy and small farming implements.

Maybole

10m S of Ayr on A77.

Stronghold of the Earls of Cassilis, the chiefs of the Kennedy's. A 17th century mansion used by them has been restored.

Morton Castle

A702, 17m NNW of Dumfries. Closed to the public but may be viewed from the outside (HS). Tel: 031-244 3101.

Beside a small loch, this castle was occupied by Randolph, first Earl of Moray, as Regent for David II. It afterwards passed to the Douglases and is now a well-preserved ruin.

Muirshiel Country Park

Off B786, N of Lochwinnoch, 9m SW of Paisley. Free. (Strathclyde Regional Council). Tel: Lochwinnoch (0505) 842803.

Attractive countryside featuring trails and walks in a high valley above moorland, with picnic sites and an information centre.

Museum of the Scottish Lead Mining Industry

Goldscaur Road, Wanlockhead, on B797, 8m ENE of Sanquhar. Easter-Oct, daily 11.00-16.00. (Wanlockhead Museum Trust). Tel: Wanlockhead (065974) 387.

Indoor museum with mining and social relics. Visitor lead mine. Open air museum with beam engines, mines, smelt mill, but-and-ben cottages. Miners' Reading Society Library, founded 1756. Local gold, silver and minerals collection. Situated near Scotland's highest village.

The National Burns Memorial Tower

Lies on A76 Dumfries-Kilmarnock Road in Mauchline. All year, daily 09.00-17.00. Free. Roadside parking. Tel: (0290) 51916.

Opened in 1896 as a memorial to Robert Burns. Tourist Information Office on ground floor. There is an interpretation centre on the first and second floors and viewing area at the top of the tower.

New Lanark

1m S of Lanark. Visitor Centre open 11.00-17.00

daily all year. Parking available. Tel: (0555) 61345.

The best example in Scotland of an industrial village, the product of the Industrial Revolution in the late 18th and early 19th centuries, now the subject of a major conservation programme. Founded in 1785 by David Dale and Richard Arkwright, it was the scene of early experiments in the paternalistic management and care for the workers, particularly by Robert Owen (1771–1858), Dale's son-in-law. Imaginative new Visitor Centre with exhibitions, working machinery, coffee and gift shop.

Newark Castle, Port Glasgow
Off A8, through shipyard at E side of Port Glasgow. Opening standard, closed Oct-Mar. Parking available (HS). Tel: 031–244 3101.

A large, fine-turreted mansion house of the Maxwells, overlooking the River Clyde, still almost entire and in a remarkably good state of preservation, with a 15th-century tower, a courtyard and hall, the latter dated 1597.

North Ayrshire Museum
Manse Street, Saltcoats, past railway station. 1 June-30 Sept, May, Tues-Thurs, Sat 10.00–13.00 and 14.00–17.00; 1 Oct-31 May, Tues, Thurs-Sat 10.00–13.00 and 14.00–17.00. Free. Tel: Saltcoats (0294) 64174/75059.

A fine museum in a classic mid-18th century Scottish church. Exhibits include local and national items and a varied programme of temporary exhibitions.

North Glen Gallery
Palnackie, 5m SE of Castle Douglas. Daily 10.00–18.00 by arrangement. Parking available. Tel: Palnackie (055 660) 200.

Studio demonstrating the blowing of glass, assembly of sculpture, welding and cutting of steel.

Old Bridge House
Mill Road, Dumfries at Devorgilla's Bridge. Apr-Sept, Mon-Sat 10.00–13.00, 14.00–17.00; Sun 14.00–17.00. Free. Parking available. Tel: Dumfries (0387) 53374/56904.

The house, built in 1660, now has rooms furnished in period style to illustrate life in Dumfries over the centuries. Devorgilla's Bridge was originally built in the mid-15th century by Lady Devorgilla Balliol, who endowed-Baliol College, Oxford. The present stone bridge dates from 1431.

Orchardton Tower
Off A711, 6m SE of Castle Douglas. Opening

standard. Free. Apply custodian at nearby cottage. *(HS). Tel: 031–244 3101.*

An example, unique in Scotland, of a circular tower house, built by John Cairns about the middle of the 15th century.

Paisley Abbey
In Paisley, 7m W of Glasgow. Outwith the hours of divine worship, open all year, Mon-Sat 10.00–15.30. Closed 12.30–13.30. Free. Group visits by arrangement. Tel: 041–889 7654 (0930–1230).

A fine Cluniac Abbey Church founded in 1163. Almost completely destroyed by order of Edward I of England in 1307. Rebuilt and restored after Bannockburn and in the century following. In 1553 the tower collapsed, wrecking N-transept, crossing the choir; they lay open to the sky for 350 years while the nave alone was the parish church; but they were rebuilt and rejoined to the nave this century (1898–1907 and 1922–28). The choir contains a fine stone-vaulted roof, stained glass and the tombs of Princess Marjory Bruce and King Robert III. See the St. Mirin Chapel with St. Mirin carvings (1499). Note outside the Norman doorway, cloisters and Place of Paisley. The Barochan Cross, a weathered Celtic cross, 11 feet high and attributed to the 10th century, is also in the Abbey.

Paisley Museum & Art Gallery
High Street, Paisley. All year, Mon-Sat 10.00–17.00. Free. Closed public holidays. Tel: 041–889 3151.

The late 19th-century museum and art galleries house the world-famous collection of Paisley shawls. Displays trace the history of the Paisley pattern; the development of weaving techniques is explained and the social aspects of what was a tight-knit weaving community are explored. There are also fine collections of local history, natural history, ceramics and Scottish painting.

Palacerigg Country Park
Unclassified road, 2¹/₂m SE of Cumbernauld. All year. (Park) dawn to dusk. (Visitor Centre) winter 10.00–16.30, summer 10.00–18.00 (closed Tues). No dogs. Free. Booking required for parties over 6. Tearoom. Parking available. (Cumbernauld and Kilsyth District Council). Tel: Cumbernauld (0236) 720047.

Wildlife includes roe deer, badger, fox and stoat. Bison, wolves, lynx and chamois in paddocks. Deer park, 18-hole golf course and pony-trekking. Children's farm and rare breeds. Coffee shop from 11.00 daily in season (except Tues) and weekends in winter. Picnic sites and barbecues; ranger service.

Palgowan Open Farm
By Glentrool, Newton Stewart. From 14.00 each day. Parties any time by arrangement. Easter week, then mid-May, June, Sept, Oct, Tues, Wed & Thurs. Jul-Aug Mon-Fri. Tel: 0671 84 227.
Highland and Galloway cattle, sheep, sheep dogs. Demonstrations in stane dyking, stick making, skin curing. Special career opportunity demonstrations and talk for schools. Picnic areas. Information on cassette.

Queen Elizabeth Forest Park
Between the E shore of Loch Lomond and the Trossachs. (FC).
In this 45,000 acres of forest, moor and mountainside there are many walks. On A821 is the David Marshall Lodge, a picnic pavilion and information centre. 'Duke's Road' from Aberfoyle to the Trossachs has fine views.

Raiders Road
From A712 near Clatteringshaws Dam, or A762 at Bennan near Mossdale. Jun-Sep daily 09.00–21.00. (FC).
A 10-mile forest drive through the fine scenery of the Galloway Forest Park.

Rob Roy's Grave
Balquhidder Churchyard, off A84, 14m NNW of Callander. All reasonable times. Free.
Three flat gravestones enclosed by railings are the graves of Rob Roy, his wife and two of his sons. The church itself contains St Angus' Stone (8th century), a 17th century bell from the old church and old Gaelic Bibles.

Rob Roy and Trossachs Visitor Centre
In Ancaster Square in Callander town centre. Mar-May and Oct-Nov, daily 10.00–17.00; June & Sept, daily 10.00–18.00; July & Aug, daily 09.30–19.30; Dec-Feb, Sat & Sun 10.00–16.30 (last admission 30 mins before closing). Parking available. Tel: (0877) 30342.
Exciting new visitor attraction using modern technology to take the visitor back three centuries to rediscover the daring adventures of Scotland's most colourful folk hero, Rob Roy Macgregor, in the heart of his wildly beautiful homelands – the Trossachs. Themed souvenir shop. Full-scale tourist information centre. Refreshments nearby.

Roman Bath House
Roman Road, Bearsden, 5m NW of Glasgow. All times. Free. (HS). Tel: 031–244 3101.
A Roman bath house built in the 140s AD for the use of the soldiers stationed in the adjacent Antonine Wall fort. The best surviving visible Roman building in Scotland.

Sanquhar Post Office
Main Street, Sanquhar. Parking available. Free access during business hours. Tel: Sanquhar (0659) 50201.
Britain's oldest post office, functioning in 1763, 20 years before the introduction of the mail coach service, and still in use today.

Savings Banks Museum
In Ruthwell, 6$\frac{1}{2}$m W of Annan. All year (except Sun and Mon in Winter) 10.00–13.00, 14.00–17.00. Free (pre-booking for large parties). (TSB Bank Scotland plc). Tel: Clarencefield (038 787) 640.
The first Savings Bank, founded by Rev. Dr. Henry Duncan in 1810. This room is a mine of information on the early days of the Savings Bank movement and the restoration of the Ruthwell Cross.

Scotland's Safari Park
At Blair Drummond on A84 between Stirling and Doune (exit 10 off M9). 4 Apr-5 Oct (approx), daily from 10.00. Admission charge for car and per head; includes several attractions; alternatively, safari bus available for visitors without own transport. Admission charge includes attractions inside. Last admission 16.30. Group rates. For details of times and charges Tel: Doune (0786) 841456.
The collection includes lions, zebras, camels, a monkey jungle, elephants, tigers, antelopes, bison, Ankole cattle and Pere David deer. There is a Pets Corner, sea lion show, Boat Safari round chimp island and an adventure playground. Self-service restaurant and bar, ice cream kiosks. Drive through wild animal reserves. Giant astraglide, amusements, picnic and barbecue areas, shops. Kennels for dogs and special arrangements for groups of disabled visitors.

Scottish Industrial Railway Centre
At Minnivey Colliery, Dalmellington, take the A713 S from Ayr, turn left to Burnton just before Dalmellington Village, left again at 'T' junction, follow road right up to the Centre. Every Sat beginning of June to end of Sept. Steam Open Days: last Sun of May and Sept; last Sat and Sun June, July and Aug. 11.00–16.00. Parking available. Tel: (0292) 313579.
8 steam locomotives (including one fireless), 12

diesels and a large collection of rolling stock. Museum, loco shed, brake van rides. Tearoom seating 24.

Scottish Maritime Museum
Harbourside, Irvine. Apr-Oct. Tel: (0294) 78283.
Boatshed Special Exhibition. Historic vessels at pontoon moorings. Vessels include a Scottish puffer, lifeboat and tug. Wharf and harbour. Ferry. Restored Edwardian shipyard worker's flat. Shop and exhibition. Boatshed suitable for disabled.

Shambellie House Museum of Costume
New Abbey, 6m S of Dumfries on A710. May-Sept, Thurs-Sat, Mon 10.00–17.30, Sun 12.00–17.30. Free. (National Museums of Scotland). Tel: 031–225 7534.
A mid-Victorian small country house designed by David Bryce. Each year there is a new display of material from the National Costume Collection.

SS "Sir Walter Scott"
From Trossachs Pier, E end of Loch Katrine, 9m W of Callander. Early May-late Sept, Mon-Fri 11.00, 13.45 and 15.15; Sat and Sun 14.00, 15.30. Parking available. (Strathclyde Regional Council Water Dept). Tel: 041–355 5333.
Regular sailings in summer from the pier to Stronachlachar in this fine old steamer. Winner of Steam Heritage's Premium Prize for 1989. Views include Ben Lomond. Cafeteria, shop, Visitor Centre.

Skelmorlie Aisle
Bellman's Close, off main street, Largs. Opening standard, closed in winter. (HS). Tel: 031–244 3101.
A splendid mausoleum of 1636, with painted roof, interesting tombs and monuments.

Smith Art Gallery and Museum
Dumbarton Road, Stirling. Open all year. Free. Cafe. Tel: (0786) 71917 for programme details and opening hours. Parking available.
A lively award-winning museum and art gallery near the King's Park, below the dramatic skyline of Stirling Castle and old town. There is a wide-ranging programme of exhibitions and events offering opportunities for seeing, joining in and finding out about art, history, craft and design. Small shop stocks local interest books, postcards and souvenirs.

Souter Johnnie's Cottage
At Kirkoswald, on A77, 4m W of Maybole. April-28 Oct, daily 12.00–17.00, or by arrangement. (NTS). Tel: Kirkoswald (065 56) 603 or 274.

This thatched cottage was the home of the village cobbler (Souter) John Davidson at the end of the 18th century. Davidson and his friend Douglas Graham of Shanter Farm, known to Robert Burns in his youth in Kirkoswald, were later immortalised in Tam o' Shanter. The cottage contains Burnsiana and contemporary tools of the cobbler's craft.

Stewartry Museum
St. Mary Street, Kirkcudbright. Easter-Oct, Mon-Sat 11.00–16.00: Jul-Aug, 11.00–17.00. (Stewartry Museum Association). Tel: Kirkcudbright (0557) 31643.
A museum depicting the life of the area with prehistoric articles, relics of domestic life and crafts of earlier days. Works of local artists are featured, especially Jessie M. King (1875–1949). John Paul Jones, a founder of the American Navy who was born in the Stewartry and had varied associations with Kirkcudbright, is also the subject of a special display.

Stirling Bridge
By A9 off Stirling town centre. All times. Free.
The Old Bridge built c 1400, was for centuries of great strategic importance as the 'gateway to the north' and the lowest bridging point of the River Forth.

Stirling Castle
In central Stirling. Apr-Sep, Mon-Sat 09.30–17.15, Sun 10.30–16.45; Oct-Mar, Mon-Sat 09.30–16.20, Sun 12.30–15.35, (HS). Tel: 031–244 3101.
Stirling Castle on its 250-feet great rock has dominated much of Scotland's vivid history. Wallace recaptured it from the English in 1297; Edward I retook it in 1304, until Bruce won at nearby Bannockburn in 1314. Later it was a favourite Royal residence: James II was born here in 1430 and Mary, Queen of Scots and James VI both spent some years here. Long used as a barracks, and frequently rebuilt, the old towers built by James IV remain, as do the fine 16th-century hall, the splendid Renaissance palace of James V, the Chapel Royal of 1594 and other buildings. On castle hill there is a visitor centre (same hours as castle; NTS) which has an audio-visual display as an introduction to the castle.

Stranraer Museum
Old Town Hall, George Street, Stranraer. All year. Mon-Fri 10.00–17.00, Sat 10.00–13.00, 14.00–17.00. Free. (Wigtown District Council). Tel: Stranraer (0776) 5088.
A local history museum with changing exhibitions. Free town trail leaflets available. Shop. Information on town trail which can be followed by wheelchair

users. Exhibitions on the Town Hall, archaeology, farming and polar explorers. Shop, information point.

Strathclyde Country Park

On both sides of M74 between Hamilton and Bothwell interchanges (A723 and A725). All year. Tours start: Easter-Sept, daily at 15.00, also Sat & Sun at 19.00 during July & Aug; winter Sat & Sun at 14.00 (groups by arrangement, Tel: Motherwell (0698) 66155). Free (charges for facilities). Tel: Motherwell (0698) 66155.

A countryside park with man-made loch, nature reserve (permit only), sandy beach and a wide variety of sporting facilities. Within the park is Hamilton Mausoleum, created in the 1840's by the 10th Duke of Hamilton, which has a remarkable echo and huge bronze doors. Tours start: Summer daily at 15.00, also Sat and Sun at 19.00; winter Sat and Sun at 14.00 (groups by arrangement, tel: Motherwell (0698) 66155).

Summerlee Heritage Trust

West Canal Street, Coatbridge. All year (closed for 2 weeks at Christmas). Admission free. Parking available. Tel: (0236) 31261.

Museum of industrial and social history featuring machine exhibition hall with working historic machinery, reconstructed historic buildings, award winning archaeological excavations of 1835 ironworks, working electric tramway and restored canal. Shop, tearoom and picnic area.

Sweetheart Abbey

At New Abbey, A710, 7¹/₂m S of Dumfries. Opening standard. (HS). Tel: 031-244 3101.

Founded in 1273 by Devorgilla in memory of her husband, John Balliol (she also founded Balliol College, Oxford), this beautiful ruin has a precinct wall built of enormous boulders.

Threave Castle

N of A75, 3m W of Castle Douglas. Opening standard. Admission free. (HS). Tel: 031-244 3101.

Early stronghold of the Black Douglases, on an island in the Dee. The four-storeyed tower was bult between 1639 and 1690 by Archibald the Grim, Lord of Galloway. In 1455 it was the last Douglas stronghold to surrender to James II.

Threave House Gardens and Wildfowl Refuge

S of A75, 1m W of Castle Douglas. Gardens: all year, daily 09.00-sunset. Walled garden and glasshouses all year 09.00-17.00. Visitor Centre: 1 Apr-28 Oct. Wildfowl refuge: access Nov-Mar. Tel: (0556) 2575.

The gardens of this Victorian mansion display acres of naturalised daffodils in April and May. There are peat, rock and water gardens and a visitor centre. The garden is of 60 acres and is at its best in June to August with good autumn colours in November. Threave Wildfowl refuge nearby is a roosting and feeding place for many species of wild geese and ducks on and near the River Dee, access during November to March, to selected points only to avoid disturbance. Tearoom.

Torhouse Stone Circle

Off B733, 4m W of Wigtown. All reasonable times. Free. (HS). Tel: 031-244 3101.

A circle of 19 boulders standing on the edge of a low mound. Probably Bronze Age.

Wallace Memorial

On A737, 2m W of Paisley at Elderslie. All times. Free.

The town is the traditional birthplace of William Wallace. A modern memorial has been erected near an old house, perhaps on the site of the patriot's former home.

Wallace Monument

Off A997 (Hillfoots Road), 1¹/₂m NNE of Stirling. Feb, Mar, Oct, 10.00-16.30, closed Wed & Thu; Apr, May, Sept daily 10.00-17.00. June, July & Aug daily 10.00-18.00. (Stirling District Council). Tel: Stirling (0786) 72140.

Commemorates William Wallace, who defeated the English at the Battle of Stirling Bridge in 1297. Built in 1870, with a statue of Wallace on the side of the tower. There are two audio-visual displays, a cafe, woodland walks and the Wallace Sword.

Wanlockhead Beam Engine

Wanlockhead Village, Dumfries and Galloway. At all times. Free. Tel: (0659) 74387.

An early 19th-century wooden water-balance pump for lead mining with the track of a horse engine beside it. Nearby is the Museum of Scottish Lead Mines.

P.S. 'Waverley'

Rates and full details of departure points and times from Waverley Excursions Ltd., Anderston Quay, Glasow G3 8HA. Parking available. Tel: 041-221 8152.

Historically one of the most interesting vessels still in operation in the British Isles, the Waverley is the last paddle steamer to be built for service on the Clyde, and now the last sea-going paddle steamer in the world. A variety of cruises from Glasgow and Ayr along the Clyde Coast, with meals, bar and light refreshments available.

Weaver's Cottage

At Kilbarchan, off A737, 5m W of Paisley. 3 Apr-31 May, 1 Sept-end Oct, Tue, Thu, Sat and Sun 14.00–17.00; 2 Jun-31 Aug, daily 14.00–17.00, last admission 16.30. (NTS). Tel: Kilbarchan (050 57) 5588.

In the 18th century Kilbarchan was a thriving centre of handloom weaving. The cottage is preserved as a typical weaver's home of the period, with looms, weaving equipment and domestic utensils. Attractive cottage garden.

The Whithorn Dig and Visitor Centre

45–47 George Street, Whithorn. Easter to end-Oct, daily 10.30–17.00, Sun 13.00–17.00. Tel: (09885) 508.

See the archaeologist at work at the site of Scotland's first recorded Christian community. Visitors can view work on medieval burials, the remains of a Norse settlement and early Christian buildings dating as far back as the 5th century AD. Explore the new Visitor Centre and exhibitions. See "The Light Shineth in the Darkness" – a new picture show, telling of St. Ninian, Dark Age settlers and medieval pilgrims. Go on an informal guided tour of the dig; see a re-created Hiberno-Norse building, the ruins of Whithorn Priory and the superb early Christian crosses in the Priory Museum. Other attractions include a herb garden, outdoor picnic area and craft shop.

Whithorn Priory and Museum

Main Street, Whithorn, 10m S of Wigtown. Opening standard except Oct-Mar closed, Mon-Fri. (HS). Tel: 031–244 3101.

Here St Ninian founded the first Christian Church in Scotland in 397. The present priory ruins date from the 12th century. Early Christian crosses, some carved in the rock, others now displayed in the museum attached to the priory are notable.

Wigtown Museum

County Buildings, Wigtown. Summer months, Mon-Fri 14.00–16.00. Free. Tel: Stranraer (0776) 5088.

Town Museum telling the story of Wigtown martyrs. New signposts to points of interest in Wigtown. Shop. Information on town trail which can be followed by wheelchair users.

Wood of Cree Nature Reserve

On minor road from Minigaff, 4m NW of Newton Stewart. Can be viewed at any time from road or paths through the wood. Car park. (RSPB). Tel: Newton Stewart (0671) 2861.

One of the finest areas of remaining native oak and birch woodland in Scotland with woodland birds and flowers.

Younger Botanic Garden, Benmore

A815, 7m NNW of Dunoon. 15 mar-31 Oct, daily 10.00–18.00. Parking available. Tel: Dunoon (0369) 6261.

Extensive woodland gardens featuring conifers, rhododendrons, azaleas, many other shrubs and a magnificent avenue of Sierra redwoods. Part of the Royal Botanic Garden, Edinburgh. Tearoom.

GLASGOW

Art Gallery and Museum

In Kelvingrove Park. All year, weekdays 10.00–17.00, Sat 10.00–22.00, Sun 12.00–18.00. Free. (Glasgow Museums and Art Galleries). Tel: 041–357 3929.

This fine municipal art collection has outstanding Flemish, Dutch and Italian canvases, including magnificent works by Giorgione and Rembrandt, as well as a wide range of French Impressionist and British pictures. Other areas include sculpture, furniture designed by Charles Rennie Mackintosh and his contemporaries, silver, pottery, glass and porcelain, an important collection of European arms and armour and displays of archaeological, historical and ethnographic material.

The natural history displays illustrate geology, with minerals, dinosaurs and other fossils. There is a comprehensive collection of British birds. The natural history of Scotland is treated in depth in a developing new gallery. Alternative entrance for wheelchairs.

The Art Lover's House

Exit M8 at Junction 23 westbound, turn sharp left onto Dumbreck Road then right into Bellahouston Park after 400 yds. Eastbound: exit at Junction 24 turn right at top of slip road, then left at next traffic lights onto Paisley Road West. Proceed to traffic lights, turning right, back over the M8 through further traffic lights then first right into Bellahouston Park after about 400 yds. For times and prices Tel: 041–427 6884.

Charles Rennie Mackintosh's largest and greatest domestic design brought to life in 1990. The house was originally designed for a competition in Darmstadt in 1900. It contains four of his finest interiors. These have been created using the skills of craftspeople from all over Scotland. Featured art works include: stonecarving, stained glass, gesso panels, embroidery. Apart from exhibitions covering the construction of the house, the lower ground floor holds a series of temporary art exhibitions from Britain and abroad. There is a shop selling replicas of many of the works of art produced for the Mackintosh rooms. The house stands in open parkland surrounded by lawns and mature shrubs and trees. It is adjacent to a beautiful walled garden maintained by Glasgow's Parks Department.

The Barras
1/4m E of Glasgow Cross. All year, Sat and Sun 09.00–17.00. Free. Tel: 041–552 7258 (Wed-Sun 10.00–16.00).
Glasgow's world famous weekend market, with an amazing variety of stalls and shops. Founded one hundred years ago, the Barras is now home to over 800 traders each weekend. Look out for the Barras archways, children's creche and buskers. Numerous licensed premises and cafes. All markets are covered.

Botanic Gardens
Entrance from Great Western Road (A82). Gardens 07.00–dusk; Kibble Palace 10.00–16.45; Main Range 13.00 (Sun 12.00)-16.45. Closes 16.15 Oct-Mar. Free. Tel: 041–334 2422.
The glasshouses contain a wide range of tropical plants including an internationally recognised collection of orchids and the 'National Collection' of begonias. The Kibble Palace, an outstanding Victorian glasshouse, has a unique collection of tree ferns and other plants from temperate areas of the world. Outside features include a Systematic Garden, a Herb Garden and a Chronological Border.

The Burrell Collection
Pollok Country Park. All year, Weekdays 10.00–17.00, Wed 10.00–22.00, Sun 12.00–18.00. Free. (Glasgow Museums and Art Galleries). Tel: 041–649 7151.
Housed in a building opened in 1983, a world famous collection of textiles, furniture, ceramics, stained glass, art objects and pictures (especially 19th century French) gifted to Glasgow by Sir William and Lady Burrell. Restaurant and bar, parking and facilities for handicapped.

Cathcart Castle
In Linn Park. All reasonable times. Free. Tel: 041–637 1147.
Sparse ruins of a 15th century castle now in a city park. Nearby is the Court Knowe, associated with Mary, Queen of Scots.

Glasgow Cathedral
At E end of Cathedral Street. Opening standard. Free. (HS). Tel: 031–244 3101.
The Cathedral, dedicated to St. Mungo, is the most complete survivor of the great Gothic churches of south Scotland. A fragment dates from the late 12th century, though several periods (mainly 13th century) are represented in its architecture. The splendid crypt of the mid-13th century is the chief glory of the cathedral, which is now the Parish Church of Glasgow.

Citizens' Theatre
Gorbals. Sep-May. Concessions for OAPs, unemployed and students. Tel: 041–429 0022 (10.00–20.00, box office); 041–429 5561 (admin).
Opened in 1878 originally as a Music Hall and now a listed building. Stalls, upper and dress circle bars, confectionary and coffee available during performances. Alternative wheelchair entrance.

City Chambers
George Square, Mon-Fri, guided tours at 10.30 and 14.30 or by arrangement. Sometimes restricted owing to Council functions. Free. Tel: 041–227 4017/8 (08.30–17.00).
Built in Italian Renaissance style, and opened in 1888 by Queen Victoria. The interiors, particularly the function suites and the staircases, reflect all the opulence of Victorian Glasgow.

Collins Gallery
University of Strathclyde, Richmond Street, off George Street. Open during exhibitions, Mon-Fri 10.00–17.00, Sat 12.00–16.00. Free. Sales Desk. Refreshments. Tel: 041–552 4400, ext. 2682/4145.
Modern Gallery which presents a lively programme of contemporary exhibitions throughout the year, ranging from contemporary painting and sculpture, crafts and photography to local history and architecture. Most exhibitions include demonstrations, talks, workshops or films with special events for children.

Crookston Castle
4m SW of city centre. Opening keykeeper monument. All year. (HS) Tel: 031–244 3101.
On the site of a castle built by Robert Croc in the mid-12th century, the present tower house dates from the early 15th century. Darnley and Mary, Queen of Scots stayed here after their marriage in 1565.

Custom House Quay
N shore of the Clyde, between Glasgow Bridge and Victoria Bridge. Tel: 041–649 0331.
The Quay is part of the Clyde Walkway, an ambitious project to give new life to the riverside. By Victoria Bridge is moored the Carrick (1864) and there is a fine view of Carlton Place on the opposite bank.

George Square

Glasgow city centre. Tel: 041–649 0331.
The heart of Glasgow with the City Chambers and statues of Sir Walter Scott, Queen Victoria, Prince Albert, Robert Burns, Sir John Moore, Lord Clyde, Thomas Campbell, Dr Thomas Graham, James Oswald, James Watt, William Gladstone and Sir Robert Peel.

Greenbank Garden

Flenders Road, Clarkston, Glasgow (6m S of city centre), off Mearns Road (B761) off A726. All year, daily 09.30-sunset. No access to house. (NTS) Tel: 041–639 3281.
Two and a half acres of walled garden and 13 acres of policies surround an elegant Georgian house (not open to the public). Dogs on leash. Disabled visitors' facilities including special garden, greenhouse and also regular walks and events programme available on request. Shop and refreshments in season.

Haggs Castle

100 St. Andrew's Drive. All year, Mon-Sat 10.00–17.00, Sun 12.00–18.00. Free. (Glasgow Museums and Art Galleries). Tel: 041–427 2725.
Built in 1585 by John Maxwell of Pollok, the castle was acquired by the city in 1972, and, after restoration, was developed as a museum of history for children. As well as the exhibitions, there are workshops where every Saturday, there are museum-based activities for children. The gardens have been landscaped and include herb and vegetable plots and a knot garden. Shop and workshop.

Hunterian Art Gallery

Glasgow University, Hillhead Street, 2m NW of city centre. All year (closed Glasgow Public Holidays) Mon-Sat 09.30–17.00, Sun 14.00–17.00. Free. Tel: 041–330 5431.
Unrivalled collections of work by Charles Rennie Mackintosh, including reconstructed interiors of the architect's house, and by J M Whistler. Works by Rembrandt, Chardin, Stubbs, Reynolds, Pissarro, Sisley, Rodin, plus Scottish painting from the 18th century to the present. Sculpture Courtyard. Varied programme of temporary exhibitions from 16th century to present. Sales point, university refectory nearby. Alternative wheelchair entrance.

Hunterian Museum

Glasgow University, 2m NW of city centre. All year, Mon-Fri 09.30–17.00, Sat 09.30–13.00. May-Oct, Sat open until 17.00; Sun 14.00–17.00. Free. Tel: 041–330 4221.
Glasgow's oldest museum, opened in 1807. Exhibits include geological, archaeological and ethnological material; new coin gallery and exhibition on history of Glasgow University. Scottish Museum of the Year Award 1983 and 1984. Temporary exhibitions of scientific instruments are exhibited in the Natural Philosophy Building. The anatomical and zoological collections, and manuscripts and early printed books, can be seen on application. Bookstall and small coffee house in 18th-century style. Alternative wheelchair entrance (via lift), please telephone.

Hutchesons' Hall

158 Ingram Street, near SE corner of George Square. All year, Mon-Fri 09.00–17.00, Sat 10.00–16.00. Subject to functions in hall. Shop: Mon-Sat 10.00–16.00. Free. (NTS). Tel: 041–552 8391.
Described as one of the most elegant buildings in Glasgow's city centre, Hutchesons' Hall was built in 1802–5 to a design by David Hamilton and includes a handsome meeting hall introduced by James Baird II in 1876. It incorporates on its frontage the statues of the founders, George and Thomas Hutcheson, from an earlier building. It is now used as a visitor centre, gift shop and the Trust's regional offices.

King's Theatre

Bath Street, Glasgow. Parking available. Tel: 041–227 5511.
This 1,785 seat theatre dates back to 1904 and preserves the style and elegance of the Edwardian period. Now carefully modernised, it has become one of the best equipped civic theatres in Scotland.

Charles Rennie Mackintosh Society

Queens Cross, 870 Garscube Road (enter by Springbank Street). All year, Tue, Thu, Fri 12.00–17.30, Sun 14.30–17.00, and by arrangement. Free. Tel: 041–946 6600/(0360) 50595.
Queens Cross, a MacKintosh church, and now the international headquarters of the Charles Rennie MacKintosh Society. Reference library and small exhibition area, bookstall and tearoom.

McLellan Galleries

Sauchiehall Street. Mon-Sat 10.00–17.00, Thurs 10.00–22.00, Sun 12.00–18.00. Admission: details of charges on request. Closed between exhibitions. Tel: 041–331 1854.
The purpose-built 1854 exhibition galleries, completely refurbished in time for Glasgow's

celebrations as Cultural Capital of Europe, now provide Glasgow Museums with a major exhibition venue for large exhibitions.

Merchants' House
W side of George Square. May-Sep, Mon-Fri 14.00–16.00. Free. The hall and ante-rooms may be seen by arrangement. (The Merchants' House of Glasgow). Tel: 041–221 8272.

This handsome building occupies one of the best sites in the city. Built in 1874 by John Burnet, it contains the Glasgow Chamber of Commerce, the oldest in Britain, the fine Merchants' Hall with ancient relics and good stained-glass windows, and the House's own offices. Tour and commentary on history of Merchants' House.

The Mitchell Library
North Street. Mon-Fri 09.30–21.00. Sat 09.30–17.00. Free. (Glasgow District Council). Tel: 041–221 7030.

Founded in 1874, this is the largest public reference library in Scotland, with stock of over one million volumes. Its many collections include probably the largest on Robert Burns in the world. Coffee room (10.30–16.30).

SCOTLAND'S ISLANDS

ARRAN

Brodick Castle Garden and Country Park
1¹/₂m N of Brodick pier, Isle of Arran. Castle: 13 Apr-30 Sept daily 13.00–17.00; 1–20 Oct, Mon, Wed and Sat 13.00–17.00 (last admission 16.40). Goatfell Park and Gardens: all year, daily 09.30-sunset. Restaurant (dates as Castle). Mon-Sat 10.00–17.00, Sun 12.00–17.00. Last admission 20 mins before closing. (NTS). Tel: Brodick (0770) 2202.

This ancient seat of the Dukes of Hamilton dates in part from the 13th century, with extensions of 1652 and 1844. The contents include silver, porcelain and fine paintings, sporting pictures and trophies. There are two gardens: the woodland garden (1923) is now one of the finest rhododendron gardens in Britain; the formal garden dates from 1710. In 1980 the gardens became a country park, supported by the Countryside Commission for Scotland, with a ranger service. Nature trail specially designed for wheelchair users. Tearoom, shop, nature trail and adventure playground.

Goatfell
3¹/₂m NNW of Brodick, Arran.

At 2,866 feet this is the highest peak on Arran. NTS property includes Glen Rosa and Cir Mhor, with grand walking and climbing. The golden eagle may occasionally be seen, along with hawks, harriers, etc.

Isle of Arran Heritage Museum
Rosaburn, Brodick, Isle of Arran. Early May to end Sep, Mon-Sat 10.00–13.00 and 14.00–17.00. Tel: Brodick (0770) 2636.

A group of old buildings which were originally an 18th-century croft farm on the edge of the village. Smithy, cottage furnished in late 19th-century style, stable block with displays of local history, archaeology and geology. Demonstrations of spinning and other hand crafts arranged periodically. Picnic area and tearoom.

Kilmory Cairns
At S end of Arran, off A841. All times. Free.

Cairn Baan, 3¹/₂m NE of Kilmory village, is a notable Neolithic long cairn. ¹/₂m SW of A841 at the Lagg Hotel is Torrylin Cairn, a Neolithic chambered cairn. There are many other cairns in this area.

King's Cave
On shore; 2m N of Blackwaterfoot on the west coast of Arran. All times. Free.

A two-mile walk along the shore from the golf course at Blackwaterfoot leads to a series of caves, the largest being the King's Cave. Said to have been occupied by Finn MacCoul and later by Robert the Bruce, this is one of the possible settings for the 'Bruce and the spider' legend. Carvings of figures are on the walls.

Lochranza Castle
On N coast of Isle of Arran. Opening standard. Free. Apply custodian. (HS). Tel: 031–244 3101.

A picturesque ruin of a castle erected in the 13th-14th centuries and enlarged in the 16th. Robert the Bruce is said to have landed here on his return in 1307 from Rathlin in Ireland at the start of his campaign for Scottish Independence.

Machrie Moor Standing Stones
1¹/₂m E of A841, along Moss Farm Road, S of Machrie on W coast of Arran. All reasonable times. Free. (HS). Tel: 031–244 3101.

These 15-feet high standing stones are the impressive remains of six Bronze Age stone circles. Some have now fallen.

MULL

Carsaig Arches
On shore 3m W of Carsaig, South Mull. All times. Free. Tel: Tobermory (0688) 2182.
A 3-mile walk from Carsaig leads to these remarkable tunnels formed by the sea in the basaltic rock. Reached only at low tide. On the way is the Nun's Cave, with curious carvings; it is said that nuns driven out of Iona at the time of the Reformation sheltered here. Tearoom facilities available at Bunessan.

Duart Castle
Off A849, on E point of Mull. May-Sept, daily 10.30–18.00. Tel: Craignure (068 02) 309.
The keep, dominating the Sound of Mull, was built in the 13th century. A royal charter of 1390 confirmed the lands, including Duart, to the Macleans. The clans supported the Stuarts and the castle, extended in 1633, was taken and ruined by the Duke of Argyll in 1691. During the 1745 Rising, Sir Hector Maclean of Duart was imprisoned in the Tower of London and his estate forfeited, not to be recovered until 1911 when Sir Fitzroy Maclean restored it. Tearoom.

House of Treshnish
On the B8073, 14m from Tobermory on Isle of Mull. Apr-end Oct, daily 08.00–21.00. Small admission charge. Parking available.
On a hillside near Calgary which gave its name to Calgary, Alberta, through the Canadian city's founder, Colonel J.F. MacLeod. Extensive footpaths through rare and beautiful shrubs, with magnificent views over Calgary Bay.

Mull & Iona Museum
Tobermory, Isle of Mull. May-Sept, Mon-Fri 10.30–16.30. Parking available.
Local history museum situated on Main Street.

Mull Little Theatre
Dervaig, Isle of Mull. Open Spring-Autumn. Tel: Dervaig (06884) 267/245.
Officially the smallest professional theatre in the country, according to the Guinness Book of Records, providing a variety of performances in summer.

Mull and West Highland Narrow Gauge Railway.
Easter, then 5 May-13 Oct. Mon-Sat. Sunday operates only when Caledonian-MacBrayne are running a Sunday service. Trains can be chartered by prior arrangement and group booking and charters must be made direct with the company.
(Mull & West Highland Narrow Gauge Railway Co Ltd). Tel: Craignure (06802) 494 (out of season) or (0680) 300 389.
10¼ gauge railway operating a scheduled service to Torosay Castle and Gardens from Craignure (Old Pier) Station. Steam and diesel-hauled trains, superb sea and mountain panorama and woodland journey. Distance 1¼ miles, journey time 20 minutes. Souvenir shop at booking office at Craignure. Tearoom at Torosay Castle. Disabled must be able to get in and out of wheelchairs.

The Old Byre
Dervaig, Isle of Mull, 1m along Torloisk road. Easter-Oct, daily, 10.30–18.30. Tel: Dervaig (06884) 229.
An audio-visual museum and visitor centre with displays of the bird and animal life of Mull, supported by audio-visual shows at ½-hourly intervals. Licensed tearoom and craft/gift shop.

Torosay Castle
A849, 1½m SSE of Craignure, Isle of Mull. Mid Apr-mid Oct, daily 10.30–17.00. Gardens open all year sunrise to sunset. Tel: Craignure (06802) 421.
The gardens and much of the house are open to the public. The Victorian castle is of Scottish Baronial architecture in a magnificent setting; its features include reception rooms and a variety of exhibition rooms. The 11 acres of Italian terraced gardens by Lorimer contain a statue walk and water garden. Served by a 10¼-inch gauge steam railway from Craignure Old Pier. Tearoom.

SKYE

Clan Donald Centre and Armadale Gardens
At Armadale on A851, ½m N of Armadale Pier. Apr-Oct, every day 09.30–17.30. Gardens open at all times. Tel: Ardvasar (047 14) 227/305.
Skye's Award-winning Visitor Centre, located in a rebuilt section of Armadale Castle, once home of Lord Macdonald. The Museum of the Isles has an audio-visual display telling the history of the great Gaelic Kingdom of the Lords of the Isles. The Stables houses a licensed Restaurant serving fresh local produce, particularly fish and home-baking. Shop well stocked with gifts and books. There are 46 acres of Sheltered Woodland Gardens and several miles of Nature Trails. A Countryside Ranger Service offers guided walks and talks. Also a Children's Skyelark Scheme and evening Theatre and Music events. Quality self-catering cottages available. Toilets. Car-park, suitable for disabled. Contact the Visitor Services Manager.

Colbost Folk Museum
3m W of Dunvegan, Isle of Skye Daily 10.00–18.00. Parking available.Tel: (047022) 296.
Thatched traditional 'black house', typical of living conditions in the 19th century.

Dunvegan Castle
Dunvegan, Isle of Skye. Mar–end Oct 10.00–17.30. Castle closed Sundays. (J MacLeod of MacLeod). Tel: Dunvegan (047 022) 206.
Historic stronghold of the Clan MacLeod, set on the sea loch of Dunvegan, still the home after 700 years of the chiefs of MacLeod. Possessions on view, books, pictures, arms and treasured relics, trace the history of the family and clan from the days of their Norse ancestry through thirty generations to the present day. Boat trips from the castle jetty to the seal colony. Restaurant and shops.

Kilmuir
N of Uig, A855
Burial place of Flora MacDonald.

Kilt Rock
OffA855, 17m N of Portree, Skye. Seen from the road. Care should be taken not to go too near the edge of the cliff.
The top rock is composed of columnar basalt, the lower portion of horizontal beds, giving the impression of the pleats in a kilt. There is also a waterfall nearby.

Knock Castle
Off A851, 12m S of Broadford, Isle of Skye. All reasonable times. Free.
A ruined stronghold of the MacDonalds

Old Skye Crofter's House
Luib, 7m NW of Broadford, Isle of Skye. Daily 10.00-18.00. Parking available. Tel (047022) 296.
Thatched traditional dwelling house furnished in keeping with the early 20th century, including agricultural implements.

The Piping Centre, Borreraig
Dunvegan, Isle of Skye. Easter-mid Oct. Mon–Sat 10.00–18.00, Sun 14.00–18.00. Parking available. Tel: (047 081) 213/295.
Old school and schoolhouse now museum of the Highland Bagpipe and the family MacCrimmon, pipers to the chiefs of the clan MacLeod from circa 1500 to 1800. Famous pipers, teachers and composers of piobaireachd.

Quraing
Off A855 at Digg, 19m N of Portree, Isle of Skye. Parking available.
An extraordinary mass of towers and pinnacles into which cattle were driven during forays. A rough track zigzags up to The Needle, an imposing obelisk 120 feet high, beyond which, in a large amphitheatre, stands The Table, a huge grass-covered rock-mass. Impressive views.

Skye Museum & Island Life
Off A855, 20m NNW of Portree, Skye. Apr-Oct, Mon-Sat 09.00–17.30. Tel: (047 052) 279.
Seven thatched cottages. Exhibits include a wall bed, farming and domestic implements, hand loom and a collection of old photographs and historical papers.

SEE COLOUR ROAD MAPS
ON
PAGES 1 - 6

THE TASTE OF SCOTLAND

It was Robert Louis Stevenson, I believe, who said "it is better to travel hopefully than to arrive". That may have been true in the 19th century but it is not a sentiment to which I would subscribe.

Most of us travel to reach a specific place and the planned destination is surely a very important element in any journey. Certainly there may well be a degree of unease until we have seen where we are going to stay overnight and been satisfied that it measures up to expectation.

But if you can travel hopefully with pleasurable anticipation of good food and good accommodation at the end of the journey then there are no niggling worries to detract from the enjoyment of the scenery or the places of interest you may be visiting on the way.

Our eating habits have changed to a marked degree in recent years, to the point where some commentators describe us as 'grazing' during the day. The formal three course lunch between 1 & 2pm is now in little demand, although the business community still clings to it either for entertainment purposes or because a leisurely relaxed lunch is conducive to the conclusion of the 'deals' that seem to be so much a part of the fraternity – and sorority I hasten to add!

The great majority of people nowadays prefer a light snack around the conventional lunch time and consequently look forward even more eagerly to the enjoyment of a good evening meal in relaxing, comfortable surroundings and a pleasing ambience.

The Taste of Scotland Scheme, which was set up initially by the Scottish Tourist Board, but is now an independent non-profit making company, has done a great deal over recent years to raise standards in food preparation, presentation and service.

Establishments which are selected for membership of the Scheme undertake to use the best of fresh local produce and wherever practicable to include occasionally in their menus speciality regional dishes. All are subject to regular inspection, and membership is terminated if they fail to maintain the standards and meet the objectives of the Scheme.

Membership of Taste of Scotland, therefore identifies the establishment of having standards well above average and whatever its classification – be it hotel, country house, guest house, farmhouse or restaurant – you may expect to be welcomed with courtesy, to have comfortable accommodation and to enjoy really good food.

Jack MacMillan
Chief Executive
Taste of Scotland Scheme

THE TASTE OF SCOTLAND

AYRSHIRE

Malin Court Hotel,

Turnberry,

Girvan KA26 9PB.

Tel: (0655) 31457/8.
On A719 south of Maidens.

Situated between Ayr and Girvan, on the west coast of Scotland and ideal for touring the `Burns Trail'. Central to a lot of major golf courses, including the famous Turnberry. All bedrooms have full amenities, including colour and Satellite television and full central heating. Table d'hote or full a la carte menus are available in the splendid restaurant with an excellent view of Arran and the hills beyond. Fully refurbished.
Open all year.
Rooms: 17 with private facilities.
Bar Lunch 12.30–2.30pm
Dining Room/Restaurant Lunch 12.30–2.30 pm
Afternoon Tea 2–5pm
Dinner 7.30–9.30 pm
Bed & Breakfast £35.00–£48.00
Dinner B & B £39.50–£52.50
Hotel enjoys more or less all year round availability of fresh local beef, lamb and pork, salmon and fresh sea produce.
STB 4 Crown Commended
Credit Cards:
Access/Mastercard/Eurocard/American Express/Visa/Diners Club/Mastercharge

CAITHNESS

SinclairBay Hotel,

Keiss, by Wick.

Tel: (0955 83) 233.
Just 7 miles south of John O'Groats and 8 miles north of Wick on the A9.

Our hotel is fully licensed and is well appointed and pleasingly decorated throughout. All 7 bedrooms (1 single, 3 twin, 2 double and 1 family) have washbasins, hot water, tea/coffee making facilities and television; 1 with private facilities. Golf, sea angling and loch fishing can be arranged through the hotel. Free golf for residents.

Open all year round.

■

Breakfast: 7.30am-9am (last orders)
Lunch: 12.30pm-2pm (last orders)
Dinner: 6.30pm-8.30pm (last orders)

■

We pride ourselves on our wide and varied menus to suit all tastes.

■

Credit Cards:
Access/Visa/Mastercard/Eurocard

INVERNESS-SHIRE

The Priory Hotel,
The Square, Beauly.

Tel: (0463) 782309.
12 miles from Inverness on the A9.

Family run hotel–excellent accommodation with all facilities–particularly good food and pleasant helpful staff. The hotel has been completely refurbished and features welcoming log fires and relaxed atmosphere. Well located for touring, fishing, trekking, hill walking or simply relaxing.

■

Open all year.

■

Rooms: 22 all with full facilities.
Passenger lift.

■

A wide range of food available
all day. Bed and
Breakfast from £23.75.

■

AA/RAC 3 Star

STB 4 Crown Commended

INVERNESS-SHIRE

The Moorings Hotel,
Banavie,
Fort William PH33 7LY.

Tel: 0397 772 797.

3 miles from Fort William, just off the A830 at Banavie.

Beautifully situated alongside the Caledonian Canal with magnificent views of Ben Nevis and Aonach Mor. Jacobean styled restaurant featuring

Gourmet dining served in elegant surroundings with an informal and welcoming atmosphere. Alternatively our cellar bar–Mariners–offers full meals to simple bar snacks and both have their own extensive wine selection.

Open all year, except Christmas.
Rooms: 24 with private facilities.
Breakfast 7.30–9.15am
Bar Lunch 12.30–2.00pm
Dinner 7.00–9.30pm
Table d'hote & a la carte (Sundays 8.30pm T d'H only)
Rates on application
Rainbow trout, locally smoked salmon, Loch Linnhe prawns, prime Aberdeen Angus sirloin or fillet, Scottish lamb, Highland venison, vegetarian selection, home-made sweets.

STB 4 Crown Commended
RAC 3 Star
AA 3 Star
All major credit cards accepted.

KINCARDINESHIRE

Horse Mill Restaurant

(National Trust for Scotland)

Crathes Castle,

Banchory

AB31 3QJ.

Tel: (033044) 634.
(Out of season: (033044) 525)
Fax: (033044) 797.

Royal Deeside A93, 3 miles east of Banchory.

An attractive and colourful restaurant with helpful staff and a friendly atmosphere. Situated in a converted horse mill it is in the grounds of the picturesque 16th century Crathes Castle famous for its painted ceilings, fine furniture and interesting decorations. The walled garden (33/4 acres) is considered to be among the finest in Britain: it includes a notable collection of unusual plants and has its own plant sales centre. A visitor centre contains permanent exhibitions and a gift shop. The grounds extend to 600 acres, with 15 miles of well marked woodland trails. Frequent events add to the attraction of this charming property.

Open Easter/1st Apr to late Oct.
Snacks 10.30am–6pm
Food service 12–5.30pm
Dinner–booked parties only–menu and price negotiable
Private room available
Facilities for disabled
No smoking in restaurant
Coffee or tea with home-baked scones and cakes. Lunch from an a la carte menu includes home-made soup, traditional dishes and sweets, or freshly made sandwiches and salads– all home-made.
Credit Cards:
Access/Mastercard/Eurocard/Visa

PERTHSHIRE

Bridgend House Hotel

Bridgend,

Callander FK17 8AH.

Tel: 0877 30130.
Fax: 0877 31512.

On A81–200 yards from Callander main road.

Bridgend House Hotel, family run, 17th century house hotel, which prides itself in providing personal, friendly service in a warm and relaxed atmosphere. En suite rooms with teamakers and televisions, two bars and restaurant, offering bar lunches, bar suppers and a la carte dinners, special children's menu. Pets welcome.

Open all year
Rooms: 6, 5 with private facilities
Breakfast 8–9.30am
Bar Lunch 12–2.00pm
Dinner 7–9pm
High Teas–parties only at 5pm by arrangement.
Bed & Breakfast £14.50-£39.50
Dinner B & B from £32.00
A wide range of food from traditional home made Scottish soup, prime roast beef and lamb to local salmon and game when in season.
AA 2 Star
STB 3 Crowns Commended
Credit cards:
Access/Mastercard/Eurocard/
American Express/Visa
Proprietors: Sandy & Maria Park

ROSS-SHIRE

An Shebeen,
Curin, Strathconon,
By Muir of Ord IV6 7QG.

Tel: 09976 227.

28 miles north of Inverness. From A9
(Tore roundabout) take A835
(Ullapool) then Marybank/Strathconon
road. Restaurant 7 miles along single
track road.
`An Shebeen' nestles in the rugged
hills overlooking Loch Meig, along the
secluded unspoilt glen of Strathconon,
28 miles from Inverness   capital of the
Highlands. It is an old 18th century
croft which was locally renowned as
an illicit drinking house and has now
been restored with great care to
preserve the stone walls and beamed
ceilings which gave the original
`Shebeen' so much of its character. In
this traditional atmosphere, good Scots
fare is featured in the Phoit Dhubh
dining room or in the Bothan Bar.
Open early Apr to late Oct: Nov to
Mar open weekends only, unless by
prior arrangement.
Bar lunch 12 2.30pm
Bar supper 6 8.30pm
Dinner 7.30 9.30pm
Facilities for disabled.
Kiste of prawns. Mushrooms in
oatmeal batter served with home-made
rowan jelly. Supreme of chicken
served with a silver birch and cream
sauce. Marinade of venison. Wild
fruits in Scottish mead. Cranachan.
No credit cards.
Proprietors: Nairn & Sheila MacEwan.

ROXBURGHSHIRE

Mansfield House Hotel,
Weensland Road,
Hawick TD9 8LB.

Tel: (0450) 73988
Fax: (0450) 72007

On A698 approximately 1 mile from
centre of Hawick.
The MacKinnon family own and run
this Victorian country house hotel in
10 acres of grounds.
Large public rooms with high ornately
plastered ceilings, magnificent
fireplaces of Italian marble and elegant
brass chandeliers. Bedrooms en suite
with TV and tea/coffee making
facilities.

Open all year.

Rooms: 10 with private facilities.
Bar Lunch 12 2pm
Dining room/restaurant Lunch 12
2pm, except Suns.
Dinner 7 9.15pm
No smoking area in restaurant
Bed & Breakfast from £30.00
Dinner B & B from £45.00

All meals individually prepared by
prize winning chef using the best local
produce. Home-made desserts a
speciality. Extensive range of Scottish
cheeses, malt whiskies and liqueurs.

Credit Cards:
Access/Mastercard/Eurocard/
American Express/Visa/Diners.
Proprietors: Sheila & Ian MacKinnon

STIRLINGSHIRE

Inchyra Grange Hotel,
Grange Road, Polmont,
Falkirk FK2 0YB.

Tel: 0324 711911.
Fax: 0324 716134.
Telex: 777693.

Junction 4 or 5 M9 motorway.

Situated on border of
Polmont/Grangemouth.
A fine example of a Scottish country
house set in 8 acres of private grounds
and offering every modern amenity. In
the restaurant you can choose from the
varied a la carte or table d'hote menus,
carefully prepared dishes featuring
local favourites.

Open all year.

Rooms: 43 with private facilities
Bar Lunch 12–2pm: 12.30–2pm (Sun)
Diningroom/Restaurant Lunch
12.30–2pm except Sat
Bar supper 6–10pm
Dinner 7–9.30pm
Dinner Sat–a la carte only

Bed & Breakfast from £30pp
Dinner, B. & B. from £45pp

STB 4 Crown Commended

Credit Cards:
Access/Mastercard/Eurocard/
American Express/Visa/Diners
Proprietor: Mr. Burgess.

WIGTOWNSHIRE

Corsemalzie House Hotel
Corsemalzie, Port William,
Newton Stewart DG8 9RL.
Tel: 098 886 254.

Off A714 Newton Stewart to Port
William, take B7005 Wigtown to
Glenluce Road.

Sporting country house hotel set in 40
acres of woodland and gardens.
Extensive game, fishing and shooting
rights. Dogs accepted (small charge).
Open Mar to mid Jan.
Rooms: 15, 14 with private facilities.
Breakfast 8.30–10am
Lunch 12.30–2pm
Dinner 7.30–9pm
Bed & Breakfast from £31.50
Dinner B & B rates on application
Fresh and smoked Bladnoch salmon
and trout. Game in season, steaks and
roasts a speciality; home-grown
vegetables. Scottish sweet table and
cheese board with oatcakes (Friday
and Saturday evenings).

STB 4 Crown Commended
AA 3 Star
RAC 3 Star

Credit Cards:
Access/Mastercard/Eurocard/
American Express/Visa/Mastercharge.
Proprietor: Peter McDougall.

ISLE OF MULL

ISLE OF SKYE

Tiroran House,

Tiroran,

Isle of Mull PA69 6ES.

Tel: 06815 232.

From Craignure, A849 towards
Iona, turn right onto B8035 at head
of Loch Scridain until signposted to
Tiroran.

A remote and enchanting country
house hotel, beautifully situated on
Loch Scridain, offering the highest
standards of comfort for those seeking
to explore the lovely islands of Mull,
Iona and Staffa. Set in over 50 acres of
grounds, the lovely gardens include
lawns, shrubberies and woodlands
which slope down to the loch. Dinners
are elegantly served by candlelight in
the diningroom overlooking gardens
and sea loch.

Open end May to early Oct.
Rooms: 9 with private facilities.
Lunch as required–residents only.
Dinner from 7.45pm
No smoking in diningroom.
Dinner, B. & B. from £85.00

Fresh seafood, including scallops and
crab, Hebridean smoked trout and own
gravadlax are regular starters. Main
courses using lamb and beef from the
estate and island venison, with fresh
vegetables.
No credit cards.
Proprietors: Robin & Susan Blockey.

Loch Bay Seafood Restaurant,

1/2 Macleod's Terrace,

Stein, Waternish IV55 8GA.

Tel: 047083 235.

Situated 5 miles down the
Waternish Peninsula, in Stein
Village. Last house in the village.

Situated in the old fishing village of
Stein and located just 30 yards from
the jetty and shore with some lovely
unspoilt views of the loch and the
Outer Isles. It has been converted from
two cottages which were built in 1740
and is now a speciality seafood
restaurant with accommodation. There
is a lot of atmosphere about this
friendly little restaurant where you
will be made welcome whether
formally or informally dressed.

Open Easter to late Oct.
Rooms: 3
Diningroom/restaurant Lunch 12–3pm
Dinner 6–8.30pm
Restaurant closed Sat
Bed & Breakfast from £16.00

Starters of squat, lobster, princess
scallops, oysters, mussels etc. Seafood
platter, lobster, king prawns, scallop,
various selection of fresh fish. Clootie
dumpling etc.

No credit cards.
Proprietors: Peter & Margaret
Greenhalgh.

SCOTLAND FOR THE MOTORIST
A Pastime Publication

I/We have seen your advertisement and wish to know if you have the following vacancy:

Name..

Address ....

....

Dates from pm..

Please give date and day of week in each case ....

To am ....

Number in Party ....

Details of Children ....

(Please remember to include a stamped addressed envelope with your enquiry.)

SCOTLAND FOR THE MOTORIST
A Pastime Publication

I/We have seen your advertisement and wish to know if you have the following vacancy:

Name..

Address ....

....

Dates from pm..

Please give date and day of week in each case ....

To am ....

Number in Party ....

Details of Children ....

(Please remember to include a stamped addressed envelope with your enquiry.)

HOLIDAY NOTES